THE
POVERTY
OF
CORRUPT NATIONS

"Roy Cullen through his work with the Global Organization of Parliamentarians Against Corruption is performing an invaluable service for the world's poor. The facts are irrefutable. Corruption is leaving millions in shameful poverty."

RT. HON. PAUL MARTIN, P.C., M.P., *former Prime Minister of Canada*

"Government ministers and parliamentarians around the world know Roy Cullen as a tireless fighter in the battle against corruption. I have had the privilege of working with him in the Organization for Security and Cooperation in the Europe Parliamentary Assembly to combat corruption and money laundering. Publication of *The Poverty of Corrupt Nations* is sure to be a valuable resource for policymakers and practitioners."

BENJAMIN L. CARDIN, *United States Senator for Maryland*

"Roy Cullen has been a tireless worker in the fight against corruption, and in the anti money laundering agenda. Through his work the poor can hopefully look forward to some prosperity while the corrupt leaders, having stolen so much from their citizens who have so little, can anticipate greater scrutiny and accountability. *The Poverty of Corrupt Nations* is a 'must read' for everyone with a conscience."

JOHN G. WILLIAMS, F.C.G.A., *Member of Parliament, Canada; Chair, Global Organization of Parliamentarians Against Corruption*

"The significant negative impact of corruption on the lives of citizens is well documented in *The Poverty of Corrupt Nations*. Roy Cullen's commitment to the Global Organization of Parliamentarians Against Corruption (GOPAC), and to the fight against corruption and money laundering is legendary. The solutions he proposes to attack this problem will be of great interest to policymakers in developing countries, and to citizens of the world."

MRS. FATIMA BELMOUDEN, *Member, Moroccan Parliament; Vice-Chair, Arab Region Parliamentarians Against Corruption*

"Roy Cullen's pioneering work goes straight to the heart of the corruption phenomenon. He shows us not only its true nature and extent but also its links with many other ills befalling the world community. *The Poverty of Corrupt Nations* should be obligatory reading for policymakers, businesspeople, and concerned citizens."

RT. HON. TERRY DAVIS, *Secretary General, Council of Europe*

"Nobody combines compassion for the poor with a clear-eyed resolve to eliminating corruption the way Roy Cullen does. He is not only high-minded in believing we can live in a better world, but he has a down-to-earth pragmatic 20-point plan for eradicating corruption as a major step to eliminating poverty and getting us there."

PATRICK BOYER, *author of* Ethical Conduct in the Public Sector

THE
POVERTY
OF
CORRUPT NATIONS

ROY CULLEN

Blue Butterfly Books
THINK FREE, BE FREE

Blue Butterfly Book Publishing Inc.
2583 Lakeshore Boulevard West, Toronto, Ontario, Canada M8V 1G3
Tel 416-255-3930   Fax 416-252-8291   www.bluebutterflybooks.ca

Ordering Blue Butterfly titles: see information on the next to last page of this book.

LIBRARY AND ARCHIVES CANADA CATALOGUING IN PUBLICATION

Cullen, Roy, 1944–
    The poverty of corrupt nations / Roy Cullen.

Includes bibliographical references and index.
ISBN 978-0-9781600-9-8

    1. Bureaucracy—Corrupt practices—Developing countries. 2. Administrative agencies—Corrupt practices—Developing countries. 3. Political corruption—Developing countries. I. Title.

JF1525.C66C85 2008   364.1'323091724   C2008-902215-7

Design and typesetting by Fox Meadow Creations
Text set in Minion and Myriad
Front cover photo © Stockbyte Photography
Printed in Canada by Transcontinental-Gagné

The paper in this book, Rolland Envrio 100, contains 100 per cent post-consumer fibre, is processed chlorine-free, and is manufactured with biogas energy.

No government grants were sought nor any public subsidies received for publication of this book. Blue Butterfly Books thanks book buyers for their support in the marketplace.

To my wife, Ethne

Source of constant love and support

Contents

Introduction: Why Bother about Poverty and Corruption? 1

1. THE POVERTY OF DEVELOPING NATIONS 8
   Global Poverty 8
   New Paradigm Needed 10

2. CORRUPTION AND POVERTY 14
   The Relationship between Poverty and Corruption 16

3. CONSEQUENCES OF CORRUPTION FOR DEVELOPING NATIONS 35
   Political Corruption 37
   The Problem of Investment 45
   The Problem of Partnerships 49
   Bureaucratic Corruption 51
   Business Corruption 54
   Corruption and Society 59

4. CONSEQUENCES OF CORRUPTION FOR DEVELOPED NATIONS 61
   Exporting Corporate Corruption 61
   Economic Migration 65
   Crime and Terrorism 70

5. TRANSNATIONAL CORPORATIONS AND CORRUPTION 74
    Corruption: Supply and Demand 77
    Dealing with Those Who Offer Bribes 78

6. MONEY LAUNDERING 87
    Politically Exposed Persons 91
    Anti-Money-Laundering Initiatives 94
    AMLI and Anti-Terrorism Initiatives 98

7. AID, DEVELOPMENT AND CORRUPTION 110
    Official Development Assistance (ODA) Trends 111
    Problems with Aid 117

8. DEVELOPMENT AND THE MARKET 125
    The Environment, Labour Standards and Trade Barriers ... 126
    International Financial Markets and their Impact on the Poor 138

9. GOVERNANCE, DEVELOPMENT AND CORRUPTION 145
    The Relevance of Good Governance 146
    The Role of Education, Communication and Collaboration 147

10. SOME SOLUTIONS TO THE PROBLEM 157

11. CONCLUSION 182

    Appendix: The Index of Public Governance 186

    Notes 198

    Sources 208

    Index 213

    Credits 222

    Author Interview 225

Nations where corruption is rampant also tend to have a large proportion of the population living in poverty—such as the people in this shanty town—while the countries' leaders may be diverting millions from national wealth to Swiss bank accounts for their own personal benefit.

Why Bother About Poverty and Corruption?

In March 2006, Nigeria's then mining minister, Oby Ezekwesili, was in Toronto attending the annual Prospectors and Developers Association of Canada global mining conference. Nicknamed "Madame Due Process" for her interest in cleaning up public administration, Ezekwesili came to the conference to convince those in attendance that Nigeria was open for business—especially for mining. The country's leadership, she asserted, was cleaning up the corruption that has suffocated Nigeria for so many years. She argued that just cleaning up the government's procurement processes had resulted in savings of about US $13 billion during the previous two and a half years. This amount would apparently have left the country in the form of inflated contracts benefiting senior government officials. And this was only the beginning, she said.

This robbing of the public purse would be bad enough in any country; however, Nigeria's poverty makes such acts of public larceny even worse. Nigeria is one of the poorest countries in the world, ranked 199th out of 208 countries according to the *2003 World Bank Atlas* report. In addition, according to Transparency International, an independent think-tank, Nigeria was ranked as one of the most corrupt nations in the world in 2005—154th out of 159 countries on the Corruption Perceptions Index (where country 159 is the most corrupt). Canada ranked fourteenth on this same list (i.e., Canada was the fourteenth least-corrupt country).

Nigeria's anti-corruption commission recently reported that the country's past rulers stole or misused $500 billion (equal to all the Western aid to Africa in four decades), so Ms. Ezekwesili had some convincing to do. The country's leadership also has a great deal of work to do in cleaning up corruption in its natural resource sector, an important part of Nigeria's economy. Indeed, oil and gas production contributes about 20 per cent of Nigeria's gross national product (GNP),[1] and nearly all of its foreign exchange earnings. Nigeria is not alone in suffering from this problem, however; it has been noted that the natural resource sectors in developing economies are particularly prone to corruption. (This is a subject I will discuss later in the book.) If Nigeria is serious about cleaning up its act, its government will need a great deal of good fortune. More importantly, though, the current government and future ones will need to maintain and build upon the improvements made in public affairs initiated by Ms. Ezekwesili.

Bribery and corruption are pervasive throughout the world—probably at their worst in Africa, Asia, South and Central America, and Eastern Europe. In Africa, by way of example, from estimates derived by the African Union itself, some US $148 billion a year is lost every year to corruption. Africa is also the continent with the greatest number of people living in poverty. By contrast, Africa is also a continent rich in natural resources, owning 50 per cent of the world's gold, 98 per cent of its chromium, 90 per cent of its cobalt, 64 per cent of its manganese and 33 per cent of its uranium.

Something is wrong with this picture! We know that there is a high degree of correlation between poverty and corruption. A country that is poor is likely to be corrupt also; and likewise, a country that is corrupt is also likely to be poor. What we don't know is which is the cause and which is the effect. Did the country become poor because it was corrupt or did corruption take hold because of abject poverty? We may never know the answers to these questions, but it seems obvious that if we could eliminate, or at least reduce, corruption, we could make a positive impact on poverty.

A recent World Bank survey on Africa claims, "The amount stolen and now held in foreign banks is equivalent to more than half of the continent's external debt."[2] While the rest of the world looks for ways to relieve African nations of their debt burdens, which in many cases is prohibitive, these misappropriated funds would be more useful in paying down some of these debts.

In the late 1990s, world leaders committed themselves to alleviating poverty in Africa, but there has been very little progress in meeting this objective. In fact, Africa has slipped deeper into poverty during this period.

To fight the war against poverty in Africa, affluent countries must not only ensure that Africans get aid, donor countries must also get to the root of the problem by arming Africans with information and support to battle corruption. Nigeria, which is rich in oil resources, has had most of its wealth confiscated by a series of military dictators. Transparency International estimates that the late dictator Sani Abacha embezzled $5 billion of public funds, leaving people of the Niger Delta, where most of the oil comes from, in abject poverty.[3] The same is true for other African nations. The Congo, which is rich in copper, cobalt, gold, and diamonds, suffers extreme poverty while the late Congolese dictator Mobutu Sese Seko is alleged to have removed for personal use $5 billion from government funds. Had these countries been given a chance to operate without corruption, money that was misdirected could have provided a better standard of living for all the people of these nations.

The World Bank has indicated that it will strive for more transparent accounting from governments who receive their funds. Canada and the rest of the world could be doing more. Canada can help these impoverished nations by empowering African citizens with information to prevent and monitor corruption. Having Canadian companies that operate in the developing world ensure that all transactions are completely transparent, indicating how much money they pay to a particular government, can do this. Such is the purpose of Publish What You Pay, an international coalition of 300 non-governmental organizations, which is attempting to ensure that resource-rich countries are not robbed of their profits. It should be mandatory for all investing companies to be a part of coalitions like these. If Africans are not aware of the facts on corruption, they cannot hold their governments accountable. By providing this information to Africans, we can empower them to move away from corruption and one step closer to eliminating poverty.

While Africa has been receiving much of the attention of the world in its struggle with poverty and corruption, it certainly is not alone. Many other countries are poor and corrupt. It is estimated, for example, that in China, corruption accounts for 15 per cent of the country's GDP. More than 846,000 Communist Party members were punished for corruption from 1998 to 2002 alone, and 58,000 officials have been punished in recent years at the state-owned banks in China.[4]

Why do we keep beating our heads against the wall and not coming to grips with the underlying problem? What I will attempt to demonstrate in this book is that while bribery and corruption may have cultural connotations and roots, they are morally and economically indefensible. This book places its focus on the relationship between corruption and poverty. It has two major themes.

First, there is the need for world leaders to address the growing disparities between the rich and poor nations. How big is this gap and what are the trends? As David Landes highlights in *The Wealth and Poverty of Nations*, "The difference in income per head between the richest industrial nation, say Switzerland, and the poorest non-industrial country, Mozambique, is about 400 to 1. Two hundred and fifty years ago, this gap between richest and poorest was perhaps 5 to 1."[5] These developments are significant and not inconsequential. Without effective intervention the problem is likely to worsen, as most of the projected population increase in coming years will be in the poorest countries. It is estimated that in today's world, 20,000 people perish every day from extreme poverty (some argue that the figure is 50,000 daily deaths from poverty-related causes).

Second, there is a need to deal with bribery and corruption, a growing activity that is getting completely out of hand, and one of the key factors that is slowing growth and reducing economic opportunities in the developing world.

I then argue that conventional approaches to battling poverty and corruption have not worked and need to be examined. We need to begin thinking and acting creatively to develop a new paradigm. Executing corrupt officials (25 officials have met this fate in China in the past four years) is not the answer for progressive nations with a respect for human rights and the rule of law.

The two themes mentioned above are closely interconnected. The poverty of the world's poor nations is significantly exacerbated through bribery and corruption. Later on I will describe the high degree of correlation between poverty and corruption. Not only do the problems of income distribution amongst the political elites, the working poor, and the poverty-stricken become more exaggerated, but it saps hope. Corruption also leads to political instability, donor fatigue, and the disappearance of much needed investment capital in the affected countries.

My work in Latin America, China, and Russia has convinced me that the unequal distribution of income amongst citizens in various parts of the world is becoming a very significant political problem—and it is concentrated in areas where corruption is rampant. In China and Russia, for example, a very few in the coastal areas and big cities are witnessing significant improvements in their standard of living; others are being left behind. As a consequence, societies become unstable and migration patterns change as people leave their country of birth to destinations afar as economic refugees.

We know that disparities between the rich and poor nations are not a function of poverty alone. In fact, corruption is not an unknown phenomenon in the so-called developed world. We know also that there is a strong correlation between poverty and geography. As John Kenneth Galbraith put it when he was an agricultural economist, "[If] one marks off a belt a couple of thousand miles in width encircling the earth at the equator one finds within it no developed countries…Everywhere the standard of living is low and the span of human life is short."[6] This generalization may not be as relevant today, given some of the recent economic growth in Asia and South America, but the observation is valid nonetheless. Tropical diseases take their toll, the lack of rainfall and water in the tropical areas can be very challenging, and cold is easier to tolerate than heat. There are many underlying reasons for the wealth and income disparities. Some of these factors are not controllable, whereas corruption, with political will, can be controlled.

This book on poverty and corruption is written by a general practitioner, someone who has worked in the public and private sectors; an individual who has worked and lived in various locations around the world, and is currently an elected member of Parliament in Canada's House of Commons. The perspective offered in the book is based on human experience, with a pragmatic approach to suggested prescriptions and public policy responses to the challenges of poverty and corruption.

My experience in government in Canada has given me first-hand knowledge of the fact that so-called rich countries are not immune from corruption either. As my former boss and renowned forest economist Mike Apsey rightly points out in his book, *What's All This Got to do with the Price of 2 × 4s?*,[7] we in the developed economies shouldn't feel holier than thou because we are not immune from corruption ourselves. After the uncovering of the sponsorship scandal in Canada, we slipped in the worldwide ranking to 12th place (the 12th least-corrupt country) on a list of 146 countries. The Government of Canada appointed Mr. Justice John Gomery in 2004 to enquire into the operation of the government's sponsorship program—a program that was abused by bureaucrats, with possibly some political interference, in the attempt to raise the profile of the federal government in Quebec.

Transparent and accountable political systems, like those we have in Canada, flushed out the workings and abuse of the sponsorship program and held the responsible officials accountable. Institutional safeguards like the auditor general of Canada, together with a free and independent media and significant levels of parliamentary oversight, produced the intended result—a result I respected notwithstanding the negative consequences for the political party I support.

These independent mechanisms of oversight and accountability, however, are not in existence in many countries throughout the world—in particular in the developing and emerging economies. As a result, corruption and money-laundering activities are often hidden from public view or tolerated and accepted because of the cynicism that is associated with political systems that lack transparency and accountability. It is this tragically damaging phenomenon that we will now turn our attention to.

CHAPTER 1

The Poverty of Developing Nations

Global Poverty

We know that poor nations are usually corrupt, and that corrupt nations are usually poor, but we also know that the factors driving global poverty are diverse and complex. In some countries poverty can be explained by mere geography: a poor land base can limit opportunities for agricultural and natural resource development, while an isolated location, one situated outside conventional trade routes, can stunt opportunities for trade. Weather patterns and drought conditions can seriously inhibit economic growth in many instances. Ethnic and tribal conflict can exact a very heavy toll on economic performance. In a recent report by Oxfam and two other non-governmental organizations (NGOs), the economic impact of conflict in Africa, for example, was estimated to be in the range of US $284 billion between 1990 and 2005. This is a staggering amount, and begs the question how this amount of money could have been used to reduce poverty in Africa over the same 15-year period.

The impact of colonialism can still be felt around the world, and its legacy is often one of poverty. Colonies were often stripped of their wealth and resources, leaving very little for the original inhabitants and few opportunities to share in the economic activity. Likewise, paternalistic attitudes by colonizers, which may have inculcated feelings of dependence, could have limited the growth of entrepreneurial and independent economic activities by those colonized. In countries like Zimbabwe, a desire to correct the wrongs of its colonial past has resulted in the current excesses of a people and a government lacking the experience and grounded institutions to bring in appropriate reforms in a measured way. Zimbabwe's President Robert Mugabe stripped productive agricultural land away from white farmers and gave it to his friends and cronies in a feeble attempt to redistribute land. While land reform was needed to redress the inequities of the Rhodesian regime of Ian Smith, Robert Mugabe went about it the wrong way, with disastrous consequences. His approach to the problem was more oriented to political vote buying rather than a commitment to policy reform. The result: a country now mired in poverty, unemployment, corruption, hugely diminished economic output, and runaway inflation. The chaos in Zimbabwe is a result of the corruption and mismanagement in that country under the leadership (or lack thereof) of Robert Mugabe. In addition to crop failures and shortages in a country that was once the "breadbasket" of Africa, it was reported more recently that "more than half of the residents in Zimbabwe's capital are either chronically short of water or without any, just days before the start of the hottest month of the year. Hardest hit are the poorest residents, many of whom now also have to endure raw sewage running past their homes in what was once one of Africa's most orderly cities."[8]

Even an abundance of natural resources does not guarantee the absence of poverty in countries around the world. This is because the wealth generated from the development of these national assets is frequently not shared equally by all of its citizens. Local governments and officials, typically far removed and remote from their nations' capitals, exploit the resources largely for their own benefit. The result is often huge income disparities amongst citizens of those countries. Asia and Latin America are good cases in point, where the rich are growing richer much more quickly than the poor. In

Russia, the average citizen is not benefiting from the resurgence in the economy of the former member state of the USSR in the same way as the few in the larger centres like Moscow and St. Petersburg are prospering—especially those individuals who were part of the former KGB and the so-called Russian mafia. Data from Russia supports this. According to a 2004 report from the Russian Economic Development and Trade Ministry, the level of incomes between the well-off Russians are 15 times greater than the worst-off Russians, and this gap is deepening. In the first quarter of 2004, 10 per cent of the most well-to-do Russians accounted for 30 per cent of the population's monetary incomes, while 10 per cent of the worst-off for only two per cent.

With respect to Latin America, the evidence suggests that income distribution in that region is not very equitable, especially when we examine Gini coefficients—measures of statistical dispersion most often used as a measure of inequality of income distribution, or inequality, of wealth distribution. A low Gini coefficient indicates more equal income or wealth distribution, while a high Gini coefficient indicates more unequal distribution. Most developed European countries have Gini coefficients in the range of 0.24 to 0.36. In 2004, according to US Aid, Argentina had a Gini coefficient of 0.51, Brazil 0.57, the Dominican Republic 0.52, Jamaica 0.46, and Mexico 0.46.

New Paradigm Needed

The increasing disparities between rich and poor nations as well as the growing pace of globalization, are calling out for a new paradigm in international relations. Thomas Homer-Dixon, in his book *The Ingenuity Gap*, makes the point that "in our political systems, we need great ingenuity to set up institutions that successfully manage struggles over wealth and power."[9] He goes on to say, "As ingenuity gaps widen the gulfs of wealth and power among us, we need imagination, metaphor and empathy more than ever, to help us remember each other's essential humanity."

Since 1960, the ratio of the income of the wealthiest 20 per cent of nations to the poorest 20 per cent has increased from 30:1 to 74:1. In Africa, 340 million people, or half the population, live on less than US $1 per day. Fifty-two per cent of the people in sub-Sahara Africa live on less than US $1 per day.[10] The mortality rate of children under five years of age is 140 per 1000, and life expectancy at birth is only 54 years. Only 58 per cent of the population has access to safe water. The rate of illiteracy for people over 15 is 41 per cent. There are only 18 mainline telephones per 1000 people in Africa, compared with 146 for the world as a whole and 567 for high-income countries.[11] It has been said that there are more telephones in Manhattan than in the entire continent of Africa, and more foreign direct investment in any one year in Singapore than there is in Africa.

It is true that poverty levels were significantly reduced in counties like China and India in the 1990s and early 2000s, but many countries continue to be left behind—especially in Africa.

Why should those of us in the developed world be concerned? First of all, our sense of what is right and wrong should start ringing a few bells. The huge disparities between the rich and the poor should cause us to reflect on whether or not this is fair and just.

There are more pragmatic reasons as well. If we don't help the poor to help themselves, this disparity will foster discontent and instability in the world. Those who are impoverished, and believe that they are oppressed, will eventually take by force what they feel is their fair share.

As Lieutenant-General Roméo Dallaire so aptly put it in his book, *Shake Hands With the Devil*, following his experience in Rwanda:

If September 11 taught us that we have to fight and win the "war on terrorism," it should also have taught us that if we do not immediately address the underlying (even if misguided) causes of those young terrorists' rage, we will not win the war. For every al-Qaeda bomber that we kill there will be a thousand more volunteers from all over the earth to take his place...

Human beings who have no rights, no security, no future, no hope and no means to survive are a desperate group who will do desperate things to take what they believe they need and deserve.[12]

Today we are witnessing increasing levels of emigration—people taking extraordinary risks to leave the country of their birth in the hopes of achieving economic salvation. They become refugees, or more accurately economic refugees—not refugees from tyranny in the true sense. They take their lives in their hands when they board a "rust bucket" vessel and head off to a Promised Land. If economic prospects were better in the country of their birth, they would be inclined to stay there and avoid the upheaval of settlement and integration in a foreign land.

There are other reasons why the developed world should help poor countries to help themselves. For example, increasing the spending power in poorer countries creates markets for the products and services produced by the more developed economies. A case in point is the economic growth in countries like India and China—growth that is fuelling a significant increase in their demand for commodity products like oil, gas, minerals, and metals. This in turn is positive for countries like Canada that produce and export these products. Generally the argument is made that improved economic performance in a country results in improved environmental performance in that jurisdiction, but there is likely a phase-in period for this to take hold. Reducing poverty in developing countries also results in the growth of a middle class which typically enhances political stability and leads to a growth in democratic institutions. More and more people are convinced that this assistance should emphasize providing developing nations with the tools they need to help themselves (i.e. provide them with fishing rods, not fish). Thomas Homer-Dixon suggests that "cropland and water scarcities are unquestionably limiting food output in many parts of Asia, Africa and Latin America."[13] He goes on to develop the point that a great deal more social and technical creativity in these countries would reduce many of these scarcities. Research also suggests that where per capita GDP grows, the incomes of the poor also grow—in fact typically on a one-for-one basis.

As former US Secretary of State Colin Powell stated, "We have to go after poverty. We have to go after despair. We have to go after hopelessness."[14] But hopelessness cannot be tackled without first addressing the large-scale corruption in poverty-stricken nations.

CHAPTER 2

Corruption and Poverty

In his novel *The In-Between World of Vikram Lall*, M.G. Vassanji
describes the role Mr. Lall plays as a go-between for bribes directed
to the corrupt Kenyan president, Jomo Kenyatta (the "Old Man"),
and his ministers in the mid-1960s following the Mau Mau guerrilla
war. Although the book is fiction, it undoubtedly reflects the way
that the government conducted business at that time (and to this
day—notwithstanding the departure of President Moi in 2002). In
the book, Mr. Lall works directly for one of Kenyatta's ministers, Paul
Nderi. Lall describes the experience this way:

> I was doing well in my job with Paul Nderi; the salary was
> modest, in accordance with government schedules, but the
> Christmas bonuses from Paul, in thick flabby envelopes, were
> hugely generous, and I could hardly refuse the car and house
> allowance he gave me. One day in my absence the two Ameri-
> cans Jim and Gerald left a thick manila envelope full of hard
> currency at my home as a present for Shobha's birthday and I
> let her convince me to put the sum aside for a rainy day, just
> in case. Perhaps I was influenced by my boss Paul Nderi's cold
> calculations. Once he had uttered an aphorism: If you don't
> take it, someone else will; but if you take it, my friend, at least

you could do someone some good. How right that sounds.
Total corruption, I've been told, occurs in inches and proceeds
through veils of ambiguity.[15]

He goes on to say:

> The mouse blows kisses as it nibbles away, was the Javeris'
> *modus operandi.* You ate and let others eat, was the more
> widely quoted adage of the day, to which all our city's business
> leaders subscribed. Bribes were extorted, offered, paid until
> they became casual as handshakes. My brother-in-law Chand
> explained the situation this way, with his businessman's cyni-
> cal humour and folksy wisdom: Bribes were a form of taxa-
> tion; before the Europeans arrived, the Africans collected a tax
> called hongo which you paid if you passed through their area.
> Missionaries and explorers had all paid hongo in the past, hav-
> ing learned from the Swahili, *Ukiwa na udhia, penyeza rupia:*
> when in trouble, offer a dollar. A bribe today was simply hongo
> tax, payment for services rendered, or for permission to pass
> on unobstructed to the next stage of your enterprise. Since the
> government paid so little to its employees, they simply col-
> lected their own hongo, calling it "tea money." In most of the
> countries of the world, he claimed, people were used to pay-
> ing this surcharge. I had been appointed the Javeris' facilita-
> tor; I could open doors for them that would otherwise remain
> shut. My influence reached far, for I had been chosen: I had
> recourse to the fount of all power in the country. I had the ears
> of the Old Man...[16]

These excerpts from the novel say it all about how corruption can
creep in and eventually take over, and how it gets rationalized and
accepted as the norm.

The Relationship between Poverty and Corruption

We know from empirical evidence that there is a very strong correlation between poverty and corruption. What we don't know is
whether poverty attracts people to corrupt practices or vice versa—
whether corruption leads to poverty in countries around the world.
If we reduce the incidence of corruption in developing countries,
will we succeed in reducing poverty in those same countries? No
one really knows the answer to this but my instincts tell me that
reducing corruption would have a positive affect on poverty reduction. Here we need to distinguish between grand or big ticket corruption and petty bribery. In many countries, government officials
are frequently paid a wage or salary that is not sufficient to live on,
and they are expected to demand and receive bribes so that they can
support themselves and their families. This type of bribery, which
is problematical, needs to be distinguished from the grand larceny
perpetrated by various world leaders (like those listed in Table 3,
page 37). Imagine how many hospitals and schools could have been
built, or how many doses of HIV/AIDS vaccines administered, or
the countless other ways the US $32–$58 billion described in Table
3 could have been spent to reduce poverty and improve the lives of
citizens in Indonesia, the Philippines, Zaire (Democratic Republic of
the Congo), or indeed in many other countries.

Why do certain government leaders divert such massive amounts
of public funds to their own private use? Greed and the lust for
power come to mind. In countries like Bangladesh, India, China,
and Nigeria, regrettably, bribery and corruption are the norm, not
the exception. In some instances large-scale corruption is considered culturally acceptable because of history and precedent. But
what about the poor people—do they get a vote on this?

Kenya is a good example of tribalism intersecting with corruption. I was told on good authority on a visit to Nairobi, Kenya,
some years ago that the former Kenyan president Daniel arap Moi,

and Kenyan leaders before and after him, view their role as president as parallel to that of tribal chief. As a tribal chief he would be expected to have the most livestock, wives, etc. When Mwai Kibaki of the Kikuyu tribe was elected president of Kenya in 2002, nothing much changed, according to Simon Roughneen, a journalist who has worked in Kenya and for the development organization GOAL. Writing about the flawed 2006 election in Kenya and the resulting violence, Roughneen noted:

> In fact, the underlying cause of the violence is endemic political corruption and flawed governance by Kenya's political elite. Upon coming to power in a clean election in 2002, Kibaki dismantled his National Alliance Rainbow Coalition and concentrated power—and access to wealth and patronage—in a cabal of cronies drawn down from the foothills of the Kikuyu dominated region just north of Nairobi. Odinga was a key member of Kibaki's 2002 team but lost out in the post-election power shake-up, leaving the two men bitter rivals.[17]

Roughneen goes on to say:

> All too often in Africa, politics is played as a zero-sum game. The state is often seen as a cash cow to be captured and retained at all costs. Power-grabs by particular ethnic groups are nothing new. But when combined with institutional graft and cronyism, it can be explosive. Kenya has not bucked the trend, and the post-election violence is not the surprise some observers would have us believe. Luo, Luhya and Kalenjin ethnic groups saw the elections as a means to take their turn to eat from the lavish table of power at the expense of deposed rivals, perpetuating the dynamic that saw party and candidate votes coalesce on ethnic lines. Rewards for one's colleagues and allies must be doled out—whether this transpires after an election victory or triumph in a civil war.[18]

Corruption can take many forms, including bribery and kick-backs, "grease payments" (euphemistically referred to as "facilitation fees"), nepotism, patronage, theft of state assets, manipulation of laws and market regulations, evasion of taxes, diversion of revenues, and electoral fraud. Whatever form it takes, however, corruption results in a massive misallocation of the resources of states. According to the United Nations Office of Drugs and Crime (UNODC), US $100 million could be used to fund full immunizations for four million children and at the same time these monies could also provide water connections for some 250,000 households. Unfortunately, this same $100 million is often used by leaders to line their own pockets or reward their friends.

Another country where corruption is a large problem is Russia. Hopes were high in the West when the USSR was dismantled and Russia and the other countries within the former Soviet Union committed themselves to democratic institutions and market economies. Many years later, after some progress, the expectations, which may have been unreasonably high, have largely not been met.

The Soviet Union and Eastern Europe chose the "big bang" approach to reform following the demise of communism. The big bang theory emphasized the need for simultaneous changes to the economy, political institutions, and the system of law and contracts. This contrasts with China's strategy of piecemeal and carefully sequenced reforms. In terms of industrial strategy,

> Mikhail Gorbachev's early programs emphasized massive equipment imports, building more machines, intensified use of machine tools, organization of industry under super ministries, improvement of the of the petroleum industry, and reorganization of the automobile and high-technology sectors. All of these are capital-intensive industries ... but these failed policies also owe much to a premature emphasis on privatizing giant state enterprises which was encouraged by West European and (especially) American professors.[19]

In a 1998 speech delivered at the Parliamentary Assembly of the Council of Europe in Strasbourg, on the topic of economic crimes, in my closing remarks, I stated:

> In Canada, more can and will be done, but we are moving in the right direction. Unfortunately, many Eastern Europeans are witnessing the very worst side of a market-based economy. Wealth oligarchies have been created very fast and in many cases have been coupled with coercive elements. The results have often been disastrous. Average citizens feel victimized and unable to participate in the emerging market economy— they feel left out. For the original sceptics, that provides support for their argument that the old ways are better.
>
> The real issue is how long those who feel victimized and excluded will wait before their patience runs out. The goal of a market economy coupled with democratic principles is to create a more inclusive society, not the other way around. To be sure, a perfect world is not possible under any system, but we must develop and put in place the governance models that will achieve the needed results.
>
> In my view, the challenge in Eastern Europe is to limit as quickly as possible the growth of mafia-like activities so as to allow all citizens the opportunity to improve their economic prospects. In our role as parliamentarians, I am confident that we can work together constructively and effectively to make that change.

Since I made those remarks much has changed, but much, regrettably, has remained the same. I believe the challenges I described in Strasbourg still exist.

I raised the topic of Russia's move to a market economy once with Russia's ambassador to Canada at a dinner in Ottawa a few years ago, and he strenuously disagreed with me that Westerners had influenced their country's choice of the big-bang approach. I suppose national pride was getting in the way; however, the alternative might be less attractive, i.e. that the Russians made the wrong choices on their own.

Despite some of the recent retrograde centralizing actions of President Putin, the Russians have been working very hard to learn how to build their democratic institutions. Their Accounts Chamber, Russia's equivalent to Canada's auditor general, is rapidly gaining an ability to hold the executive branch of the government to account. When I asked visiting members of the Accounts Chamber, however, on one of their visits to Canada, if they would ever conduct an audit of a privatization transaction to assess whether or not the process had been fair, transparent, and whether or not the government received fair value in the circumstances, I could never get a straight answer. I was curious about privatizations, because in the 1990s many of these transactions in Russia were renowned for the way in which privatizations were steered towards friends of the government at very low prices. I had to conclude that the auditors weren't quite ready for such an adventure yet. Better governance is developing slowly but surely, but it will take time to evolve. After all, it was only in 1991, less than 20 years ago, that the USSR ceased to exist as a legal entity, and the move to democratic institutions and a market economy began in that part of the world.

Russia still has some way to go in its governance models. Rewarding corrupt and criminal individuals is not a recommended strategy for enhancing governance, but election to the Russian State Duma may do just that because of an anomaly in the way the State Duma representation is structured. Legislators with shady pasts who face the possibility of criminal or civil charges being brought against them, can, upon their election to the State Duma, receive the protection of this institution and escape prosecution—at least while they are elected. This type of circumstance does not bode well for attracting people of integrity—those committed to good governance and fighting corruption.

The pre-eminent non-governmental organization in the fight

against corruption is Transparency International (TI), founded in 1993. Its stated mission is to create change towards a world free of corruption. One of the great challenges involved in achieving this objective is to measure what countries are corrupt and what progress, if any, is being made in reducing corruption in various jurisdictions.

The Transparency International Corruption Perceptions Index ranks 133 countries by the degree to which corruption is perceived to exist among public officials and politicians. It is a composite index, drawing on 17 different polls and surveys from 13 independent institutions carried out among business people and country analysts, including surveys of residents, both local and expatriate.

It is most useful to examine corruption in relative terms because there is no known way to measure it in absolute terms. A British member of Parliament, at an anti-corruption conference organized by the World Bank in Nairobi in 2001, argued that there is corruption in every nation throughout the world. He offered that in the United Kingdom corruption was perhaps more subtle than the type of corruption that might occur in Kenya, for example, but that it did occur. For a moment, elected MPs in the conference room—those from the most corrupt countries—appeared to breathe a sigh of relief. After all, if corruption was universal, why worry about it? This was the wrong message to take away from the meeting and I attempted to correct this by pointing out that one could not reasonably compare the level of corruption in countries like Bangladesh with that in countries like Great Britain. They are in a different league altogether; but no one should be complacent.

The Transparency International's Corruption Perceptions Index for 2003, and presented on the next pages, points to high levels of corruption in many rich countries as well as poorer ones. Seventy per cent of countries score less than 5 out of a clean score of 10 in the TI CPI 2003, which reflects perceived levels of corruption among politicians and public officials in 133 countries. Fifty per cent of developing countries score less than 3 out of 10, indicating a high level of corruption.

TABLE 1: Transparency International Corruption Perceptions Index (CPI) 2003

Rank	Country	CPI[1]	Surveys[2]	S.D.[3]	Range[4]
1	Finland	9.7	8	0.3	9.2–10.0
2	Iceland	9.6	7	0.3	9.2–10.0
3	Denmark	9.5	9	0.4	8.8–9.9
	New Zealand	9.5	8	0.2	9.2–9.6
5	Singapore	9.4	12	0.1	9.2–9.5
6	Sweden	9.3	11	0.2	8.8–9.6
7	Netherlands	8.9	9	0.3	8.5–9.3
8	Australia	8.8	12	0.9	6.7–9.5
	Norway	8.8	8	0.5	8.0–9.3
	Switzerland	8.8	9	0.8	6.9–9.4
11	Canada	8.7	12	0.9	6.5–9.4
	Luxembourg	8.7	6	0.4	8.0–9.2
	United Kingdom	8.7	13	0.5	7.8–9.2
14	Austria	8.0	9	0.7	7.3–9.3
	Hong Kong	8.0	11	1.1	5.6–9.3
16	Germany	7.7	11	1.2	4.9–9.2
17	Belgium	7.6	9	0.9	6.6–9.2
18	Ireland	7.5	9	0.7	6.5–8.8
	USA	7.5	13	1.2	4.9–9.2
20	Chile	7.4	12	0.9	5.6–8.8
21	Israel	7.0	10	1.2	4.7–8.1
	Japan	7.0	13	1.1	5.5–8.8
23	France	6.9	12	1.1	4.8–9.0
	Spain	6.9	11	0.8	5.2–7.8
25	Portugal	6.6	9	1.2	4.9–8.1
26	Oman	6.3	4	0.9	5.5–7.3
27	Bahrain	6.1	3	1.1	5.5–7.4
	Cyprus	6.1	3	1.6	4.7–7.8
29	Slovenia	5.9	12	1.2	4.7–8.8
30	Botswana	5.7	6	0.9	4.7–7.3
	Taiwan	5.7	13	1.0	3.6–7.8
32	Qatar	5.6	3	0.1	5.5–5.7
33	Estonia	5.5	12	0.6	4.7–6.6
	Uruguay	5.5	7	1.1	4.1–7.4

Rank	Country	CPI	Surveys	S.D.	Range
35	Italy	5.3	11	1.1	3.3–7.3
	Kuwait	5.3	4	1.7	3.3–7.4
37	Malaysia	5.2	13	1.1	3.6–8.0
	United Arab Emirates	5.2	3	0.5	4.6–5.6
39	Tunisia	4.9	6	0.7	3.6–5.6
40	Hungary	4.8	13	0.6	4.0–5.6
41	Lithuania	4.7	10	1.6	3.0–7.7
	Namibia	4.7	6	1.3	3.6–6.6
43	Cuba	4.6	3	1.0	3.6–5.5
	Jordan	4.6	7	1.1	3.6–6.5
	Trinidad and Tobago	4.6	6	1.3	3.4–6.9
46	Belize	4.5	3	0.9	3.6–5.5
	Saudi Arabia	4.5	4	2.0	2.8–7.4
48	Mauritius	4.4	5	0.7	3.6–5.5
	South Africa	4.4	12	0.6	3.6–5.5
50	Costa Rica	4.3	8	0.7	3.5–5.5
	Greece	4.3	9	0.8	3.7–5.6
	South Korea	4.3	12	1.0	2.0–5.6
53	Belarus	4.2	5	1.8	2.0–5.8
54	Brazil	3.9	12	0.5	3.3–4.7
	Bulgaria	3.9	10	0.9	2.8–5.7
	Czech Republic	3.9	12	0.9	2.6–5.6
57	Jamaica	3.8	5	0.4	3.3–4.3
	Latvia	3.8	7	0.4	3.4–4.7
59	Colombia	3.7	11	0.5	2.7–4.4
	Croatia	3.7	8	0.6	2.6–4.7
	El Salvador	3.7	7	1.5	2.0–6.3
	Peru	3.7	9	0.6	2.7–4.9
	Slovakia	3.7	11	0.7	2.9–4.7
64	Mexico	3.6	12	0.6	2.4–4.9
	Poland	3.6	14	1.1	2.4–5.6
66	China	3.4	13	1.0	2.0–5.5
	Panama	3.4	7	0.8	2.7–5.0
	Sri Lanka	3.4	7	0.7	2.4–4.4
	Syria	3.4	4	1.3	2.0–5.0
70	Bosnia & Herzegovina	3.3	6	0.7	2.2–3.9
	Dominican Republic	3.3	6	0.4	2.7–3.8

Rank	Country	CPI	Surveys	S.D.	Range
	Egypt	3.3	9	1.3	1.8–5.3
	Ghana	3.3	6	0.9	2.7–5.0
	Morocco	3.3	5	1.3	2.4–5.5
	Thailand	3.3	13	0.9	1.4–4.4
76	Senegal	3.2	6	1.2	2.2–5.5
77	Turkey	3.1	14	0.9	1.8–5.4
78	Armenia	3.0	5	0.8	2.2–4.1
	Iran	3.0	4	1.0	1.5–3.6
	Lebanon	3.0	4	0.8	2.1–3.6
	Mali	3.0	3	1.8	1.4–5.0
	Palestine	3.0	3	1.2	2.0–4.3
83	India	2.8	14	0.4	2.1–3.6
	Malawi	2.8	4	1.2	2.0–4.4
	Romania	2.8	12	1.0	1.6–5.0
86	Mozambique	2.7	5	0.7	2.0–3.6
	Russia	2.7	16	0.8	1.4–4.9
88	Algeria	2.6	4	0.5	2.0–3.0
	Madagascar	2.6	3	1.8	1.2–4.7
	Nicaragua	2.6	7	0.5	2.0–3.3
	Yemen	2.6	4	0.7	2.0–3.4
92	Albania	2.5	5	0.6	1.9–3.2
	Argentina	2.5	12	0.5	1.6–3.2
	Ethiopia	2.5	5	0.8	1.5–3.6
	Gambia	2.5	4	0.9	1.5–3.6
	Pakistan	2.5	7	0.9	1.5–3.9
	Philippines	2.5	12	0.5	1.6–3.6
	Tanzania	2.5	6	0.6	2.0–3.3
	Zambia	2.5	5	0.6	2.0–3.3
100	Guatemala	2.4	8	0.6	1.5–3.4
	Kazakhstan	2.4	7	0.9	1.6–3.8
	Moldova	2.4	5	0.8	1.6–3.6
	Uzbekistan	2.4	6	0.5	2.0–3.3
	Venezuela	2.4	12	0.5	1.4–3.1
	Vietnam	2.4	8	0.8	1.4–3.6
106	Bolivia	2.3	6	0.4	1.9–2.9
	Honduras	2.3	7	0.6	1.4–3.3
	Macedonia	2.3	5	0.3	2.0–2.7

Rank	Country	CPI	Surveys	S.D.	Range
	Serbia & Montenegro	2.3	5	0.5	2.0–3.2
	Sudan	2.3	4	0.3	2.0–2.7
	Ukraine	2.3	10	0.6	1.6–3.8
	Zimbabwe	2.3	7	0.3	2.0–2.7
113	Congo, Republic of the	2.2	3	0.5	2.0–2.8
	Ecuador	2.2	8	0.3	1.8–2.6
	Iraq	2.2	3	1.1	1.2–3.4
	Sierra Leone	2.2	3	0.5	2.0–2.8
	Uganda	2.2	6	0.7	1.8–3.5
118	Cote d'Ivoire	2.1	5	0.5	1.5–2.7
	Kyrgyzstan	2.1	5	0.4	1.6–2.7
	Libya	2.1	3	0.5	1.7–2.7
	Papua New Guinea	2.1	3	0.6	1.5–2.7
122	Indonesia	1.9	13	0.5	0.7–2.9
	Kenya	1.9	7	0.3	1.5–2.4
124	Angola	1.8	3	0.3	1.4–2.0
	Azerbaijan	1.8	7	0.3	1.4–2.3
	Cameroon	1.8	5	0.2	1.4–2.0
	Georgia	1.8	6	0.7	0.9–2.8
	Tajikistan	1.8	3	0.3	1.5–2.0
129	Myanmar	1.6	3	0.3	1.4–2.0
	Paraguay	1.6	6	0.3	1.2–2.0
131	Haiti	1.5	5	0.6	0.7–2.3
132	Nigeria	1.4	9	0.4	0.9–2.0
133	Bangladesh	1.3	8	0.7	0.3–2.2

Source: Transparency International

1. CPI 2003 Score—perceptions of the degree of corruption as seen by business people, academics, and risk analysts; range 10 (highly clean) to 0 (highly corrupt).

2. Surveys Used—number of surveys that assessed a country's performance. A total of 17 surveys were used from 13 independent institutions; at least three were required for a country to be included in the CPI.

3. S.D. (Standard Deviation)—magnitude of differences in the values of sources: the greater the standard deviation, the greater the differences of perceptions of a country among the sources.

4. High-Low Range—highest and lowest values of the different sources.

The CPI focuses on corruption in the public sector and defines corruption as the abuse of public office for private gain. The surveys used in compiling the CPI tend to ask questions in line with the misuse of public power for private benefit, with a focus, for example, on bribe-taking by public officials in public procurement. The sources do not distinguish between administrative and political corruption.

Corruption is perceived to be pervasive in Bangladesh, Nigeria, Haiti, Paraguay, Myanmar, Tajikistan, Georgia, Cameroon, Azerbaijan, Angola, Kenya, and Indonesia, countries with a score of less than two in the index. Countries with a score of higher than nine, with very low levels of perceived corruption, are rich countries, namely Finland, Iceland, Denmark, New Zealand, Singapore, and Sweden. Some changes can be identified in the CPI. On the basis of data from sources that have been consistently used for the index, improvements can be observed for Austria, Belgium, Colombia, France, Germany, Ireland, Malaysia, Norway, and Tunisia. Noteworthy examples of a worsening situation are Argentina, Belarus, Chile, Canada, Israel, Luxembourg, Poland, USA, and Zimbabwe. Ninety per cent of developing countries score less than 5 against a clean score of 10 in the TI CPI 2003.[20]

Stable and sound government institutions are more important than good economic policy or geography, according to a recent paper released by the Centre for Global Development.[21] The institutions of government to which they refer include political stability, property rights, legal systems, patterns of land tenure, and general good governance. In fact, policy and geography don't even come close to the impact of institutions on the rate of growth in poor countries.

In Uganda, it has been estimated that bribes increase a company's costs by eight per cent.[22] This estimate was also recently mentioned in the context of Kenya by Britain's high commissioner to Kenya as the cost of corruption in that country as well. This rough estimate of the economic loss that corruption ravages on a domestic economy, therefore, seems to have some credibility and agreement. This estimate takes into account institutionalized bribery and corruption but largely omits big-ticket corruption, such as that perpetrated by the country's elites, who skim off the "economic cream" and move it into offshore bank accounts. Given that fact, it would seem to me that eight per cent is a minimum, depending on the country and the leadership at any point in time.

Quite clearly, corruption is a disease that affects every functioning aspect of governments. To better understand the correlation between corruption and good governance, researcher Tony Hahn created an Index of Public Governance (IPG).[23] Hahn uses three levels of measurement to compute the index, drawing on data from the Freedom House's 2004 indices of political rights and civil liberties, Transparency International's 2004 Corruptions Perceptions Index, and the Economic Freedom of the World's 2004 annual report. Each set of data represents a democratic and capitalist perspective of government based on the fundamentals that good governance ensures the ability of citizens to vote, encourages free enterprise, improves quality of life, and allows citizens to exercise their civil liberties.

Hahn's Index ranks 114 countries, revealing New Zealand at the top of the list with the highest model of good governance with a ranking of 9.45 out of 10. Following closely behind are Finland, Switzerland, Iceland, and Denmark. Also included in the top 10 are the United Kingdom, with a ranking of 9.2, and Australia and Canada, each of which have a perfect score in the areas of political rights and civil liberties. Surprisingly the United States missed the top 10 by one, ranking 11th with a score of only 8.2 on economic freedom.

Most importantly, however, are the results for Africa. The first of the African countries to make the list is Botswana, which ranks 29th with a score of 7.52, with Mauritius and South Africa following closely behind. What is interesting about this, as Hahn points out, is that unemployment in Botswana is over 20 per cent and a third of the population is living with HIV/AIDS. Comparing the Index rankings with indicators of development such as life expectancy and literacy, Botswana is gravely behind South Africa and Mauritius, with a life expectancy at 33.38 years—less than half the expected age of

Mauritians. Another African nation worth noting is war-torn Sierra Leone, which ranks 74th on the Index of Public Governance, ahead of both Russia (91st place) and China (99th place). Yet in comparison to indicators of development, China and Russia also greatly surpass Sierra Leone.

Hahn points to history and culture to explain why a country can have a positive ranking in the Index of Public Governance and a low incidence of development. He argues that if countries that have the foundations of good governance continue with their efforts, development will follow. This means if countries like Sierra Leone stick to the path of comparatively good governance, while countries like Russia do not, then the indicator of development should rise for Sierra Leone in comparison with Russia.

In fact, Hahn's hypothesis on the relationship between corruption and poverty appears to be supported in a correlation analysis between Hahn's IPG and GDP per capita. To undertake this analysis, I conducted a correlation analysis between Hahn's IPG and GDP per capita (2003). The results indicate that there is a correlation between GDP per capita and good governance, and when using the GDP per capita on a Purchasing Power Parity (PPP)[24] basis (2003), an even greater correlation was revealed.

The results of the correlation reveal a positive relationship between GDP per capita and IPG. This means that people in countries with lower GDP per capita are more likely to believe they are not well governed as expressed by factors in Hahn's IPG. Although a correlation analysis does not measure the level of significance, we can conclude from these results that the two variables are highly related.

In fact, results that further support this correlation are the findings of a correlation analysis done between the indices of Hahn's Index of Public Governance and GDP per capita. The indices of Hahn's IPG were analyzed to test their individual correlation with GDP per capita. Of the four indices, corruption, civil liberties, political rights, and economic freedom, the highest correlation is between corruption and GDP per capita and GDP per capita on a PPP basis.

The data also shows that in comparison to political rights, civil liberties and economic freedom, corruption is the most significant indicator of GDP per capita. This is vital for understanding the relationship between economic development and corruption. This evidence of a highly correlated relationship indicates that efforts put into combating corruption will benefit the development of poor countries.

However, good governance is not the only indicator of corruption—poverty plays a role as well. *Governance, Corruption, and Economic Performance*,[25] recently published by the IMF, includes studies on the impact of corruption on economic performance. Amongst the findings are the following:

▶ social indicators (e.g. child mortality rate, school drop-out rates) are worse where corruption is high;
▶ countries with higher corruption tend to have lower per capita income, a higher incidence of poverty and greater income inequality;
▶ tax revenue is lower in more corrupt countries;
▶ transition economies that have made more progress on structural reform tend to be less corrupt; and
▶ decentralization of taxation and spending improves governance.

The World Bank, in its *World Development Report 2002*, states, "Across countries there is evidence that higher levels of corruption are associated with lower growth and lower levels of per capita income."

The economic costs associated with bribery and corruption is very real. Transparency International's *Global Corruption Report* estimates that a one unit increase in bribery or corruption (on a scale of zero to 10) would lower real GDP growth by 0.3 to 1.8 percentage points, or by 1 to 1.3 per cent, depending on the study and/or methodology.[26]

Is there any empirical evidence linking poverty with corruption? If one compares the top 10 most corrupt nations (as measured by the 2003 Corruption Perceptions Index developed by Transparency International) with Gross National Income (GNI) per capita (Purchasing Power Parity method) for the year 2001 (the most recent year available) as disclosed by the World Bank, we find the results listed in Table 2 below.

With the exception perhaps of Paraguay, the 10 most corrupt nations are amongst the poorest nations (all of them in the top quartile of poverty).

Conducting a correlation analysis between the Transparency International Corruption Perceptions Index (CPI 2003) and GDP per capita (2002), the results reveal there is a strong correlation between low GDP per capita and corruption. Corruption is highly correlated with both GDP per capita and GDP per capita on a Purchasing Power Parity basis. Countries with higher GDP per capita

TABLE 2: Gross National Income (GNI) for 10 Most Corrupt Nations

10 most corrupt nations[1] (starting with the worst)	CPI 2003	GNI per capita[2] (USA=$34,280)	GNI world rank (out of 208)[2]
Bangladesh	1.3	$1,600	173
Nigeria	1.4	$790	199
Haiti	1.5	$1,870	166
Paraguay	1.6	$5,180	106
Tajikistan	1.8	$1,140	184
Georgia	1.8	$2,580	148
Cameroon	1.8	$1,580	174
Azerbaijan	1.8	$2,890	141
Angola	1.8	$1,690	171
Kenya	1.9	$970	190

1. *Source:* Transparency International: Corruption Perceptions Index 2003

2. *Source: 2003 World Bank Atlas.* No GNI per capita available for Myanmar, which is in top 10 of most corrupt nations (CPI 1.6)

tend to have a lower perception of the presence of corruption as expressed by the corruption index.

Empirical analysis on corruption is a relatively new domain of research. The research mostly concentrates on cross-country analysis and uses GDP as an indicator or proxy of a country's wealth. Although there is generally a strong correlation between GDP per capita and corruption reported in many studies, there is no general agreement on the existence of a causality link or on the direction of causality between the two variables. The direction of causality between corruption and other economic and social variables can be difficult to measure. Often enough, certain types of government, poor institutions, inequality, lack of competition, and poverty may go along with corruption. However, Lambsdorff (2004) warns, "These indicators and corruption are sometimes two sides of the same coin."[27]

Indeed, it can be useful to examine the correlation between corruption and some economic indicators, such as GDP per capita, but it is necessary to avoid drawing ironclad conclusions with respect to causalities.[28]

For example, while corruption possibly lowers GDP per head, poorer countries lack the resources to fight corruption. This simultaneous relationship is hard to disentangle. In fact, Hall and Jones (1999) maintain that there exist many simultaneity problems associated with corruption correlation analysis. One of them is related to the fact that the indicator of corruption itself is based on perceptions. If countries at an equal stage of development differ in the extent of corruption, perceptions may be informative. But if countries differ widely in their development, perception may be less reliable. A simple regression cannot address this problem. The approach taken by Hall and Jones (1999) and by other researchers in the field is called the instrumental variable technique.[29]

From a literature review on the relationship between poverty and corruption, here is what some of the academics have to say. From Mauro (1998):

Corruption is likely to occur where restrictions and government intervention lead to the presence of excessive profits. Examples include trade restrictions (such as tariffs and import quotas), industrial policies favouring certain sectors (such as subsidies and tax deductions), price controls, multiple exchange rate practices and foreign exchange allocation schemes, and government-controlled provision of credit.

From economic theory, one would expect corruption to reduce economic growth by lowering incentives to invest (for both domestic and foreign entrepreneurs). In cases where entrepreneurs are asked for bribes before enterprises can be started, or corrupt officials later request shares in the proceeds of their investments, corruption acts as a tax, though one of a particularly pernicious nature, given the need for secrecy and the uncertainty as to whether bribe takers will live up to their part of the bargain. Corruption could also be expected to reduce growth by lowering the quality of public infrastructure and services, decreasing tax revenue, causing talented people to engage in rent-seeking rather than productive activities, and distorting the composition of government expenditure. At the same time, there are some theoretical counter arguments. For example, it has been suggested that government employees who are allowed to exact bribes might work harder and that corruption might help entrepreneurs get around bureaucratic impediments.[30]

Lambsdorff (2004) offers a review of empirical efforts that have been made to ascertain the influence of corruption on GDP. His survey shows ambiguous results:

Keefer and Knack (1995) report that a variable of institutional quality, which incorporates corruption among other factors, exerts a significant negative impact on GDP growth. But Brunetti, Kisunko and Weder (1997) produced insignificant results. Mauro (1995) found a slightly significant impact in a bivariate regression. But as soon as the ratio of investment to GDP was included as an explanatory variable, this impact disappeared. Making use of data on corruption provided by the Political Risk Services Group, Mauro (1997) produced significant results at a 95 per cent confidence level. A significant positive impact is also reported by Leite and Weidmann (1999) and Poirson (1998). On the basis of mixed evidence, it is sometimes argued that corruption primarily impacts on the accumulation of capital, which can be derived from the ratio of investment to GDP, but it does not clearly affect the productivity of capital, because otherwise a link between corruption and growth of GDP should be observable.

But the question of whether corruption should affect levels of GDP or its growth may be debated. In line with Paldam (1999), Lambsdorff (1999) argues that lack of corruption is a factor for the production of GDP. If this holds, growth of GDP should not be explained by absolute levels of corruption but by a change in these levels. This is investigated by Lambsdorff (1999) in a cross-section of 53 countries. He uses data by World Economic Forum based on responses to the question of whether corruption has decreased in the past 5 years. This variable is shown to better explain growth of GDP as opposed to absolute levels of corruption.[31]

What does all this mean? For those who are making investments in corrupt countries, the cost of corruption is undoubtedly built into their business case analysis. Returns on investment must take this into account and reflect the often higher risk associated with projects in jurisdictions such as these. The real question is—who benefits from this investment? In some cases, corrupt leaders may offset their corrupt share of the project with reduced rents, royalties, or taxes imposed on the investor. In cases such as this, the tax-paying citizens pay for the bribes in the form or reduced revenues to the state.

The cost of corruption may be buried in the statistics because total output from the project (measured by GDP) may not be impacted. There is an economic cost to corruption, and we should not delude ourselves otherwise.

CHAPTER 3

Consequences of Corruption for Developing Nations

When the topic of corruption is raised, many express the view that bribery and corruption are inevitable and entrenched. They argue that these practices are endemic in many parts of the world and they are with us to stay. It is not surprising that many people hold this view because corruption has been around for some time—it is perhaps an even older vocation than prostitution!

While not being naïve about the challenges of reducing or eliminating corruption, I believe that we, as a society, have become too defeatist in our attitude to the diseases of bribery and corruption. When we witness the world poverty around us, and the way corrupt leaders deprive citizens of their very own resources by appropriating them for their personal use, we should acknowledge that corruption is a very serious issue that deserves our collective attention.

Corruption diverts scarce public resources from very worthwhile projects that would assist in lifting citizens out of poverty. Corruption skews economic decision-making in favour of projects where the opportunities for corruption are greatest. In other words, corruption causes scarce public resources to be misallocated and misused.

Corruption negatively impacts economic growth because it adds to the economic cost of doing business. Corruption reduces the flow of investment, both public and private, into countries where corruption is rife. The economic benefits of foreign direct investment are therefore diminished.

Corruption undermines faith in public institutions and public officials, and encourages people to become cynical about the political process. Citizens disengage from politics and may be disinclined to exercise their democratic rights.

Corruption comes in many forms. Political corruption, bureaucratic corruption, and business corruption are the three primary categories that I will now review. Corruption also impacts society generally in a variety of ways which will be delineated below.

Political corruption is characterized by grand or big-ticket corruption conducted by political elites. Bureaucratic corruption, while it often stems from political corruption, is that corruption practised by state functionaries. It usually involves lower-level, petty corruption—for example, paying $100 to an official to expedite an import permit.

Corruption is not limited to the public sector, however, although public sector corruption has been and continues to be my primary focus. Corruption in government affects the public at large, whereas the impact of business corruption is primarily limited to a smaller and more defined group of stakeholders—shareholders, workers, management, and potentially suppliers and customers.

Corruption also affects society in a number of more general ways, not the least of which is the ability of corrupt leaders to create political instability and social unrest. Income disparities and a loss of confidence and respect for the political system can contribute to this. Corruption and associated money laundering can lead to threats to international security. Corruption can also create health hazards for citizens of the world in a variety of ways. Corrupt states also run the risk of developing their natural resources in ways that are not sustainable. More on all of this follows.

Political Corruption

Some may wonder who would make David Letterman's list of the top 10 most corrupt contemporary world leaders (if he put together such a list). Who are the most infamous leaders, guilty of raping and pillaging their countries' national treasuries for their own personal benefit? In 2004, Transparency International created just such a list, identifying the 10 most corrupt leaders of the past 20 years, together with an estimate of the amounts that they embezzled. Table 3 documents the shameful list.[32]

The Philippines has two corrupt leaders in the top 10—quite a record. And how about Pavlo Lazarenko of the Ukraine, taking just one year to salt away $114 to $200 million! He certainly knew what he was doing. Not a long learning curve for him.

If you total the amounts that were stolen from the citizens of

TABLE 3: Transparency International's Report of the 10 Most Corrupt Leaders

Despot	Country	Embezzled (est.)
President Suharto 1967–98	Indonesia	$15–$35 billion
Ferdinand Marcos 1972–86	Philippines	$5–$10 billion
Mobuto Sese Seko 1965–97	Zaire	$5 billion
Sani Abacha 1993–98	Nigeria	$5 billion
Slobodan Milosevic 1989–2000	Yugoslavia	$1 billion
J.-C. Duvalier 1971–86	Haiti	$300–$800 million
Alberto Fujimori 1990–2000	Peru	$600 million
Pavlo Lazarenko 1996–97	Ukraine	$114–$200 million
Arnoldo Aleman 1997–2002	Nicaragua	$100 million
Joseph Estrada 1998–2001	Philippines	$78–$80 million

Source: Transparency International 2004 Report

these countries (and this list only begins to scratch the surface), one arrives at the grotesque numbers of a low of $32 billion to a high of $58 billion from these 10 criminals alone. Imagine how many hospitals this could build, or how many schools, or how much food could have been purchased to alleviate hunger and starvation around the globe.

For some reason President Daniel arap Moi didn't make this top 10 list, although it is estimated that he and his cronies siphoned off $3–$4 billion. The amount of money stolen by President Moi would be "enough to provide every child in the country with a free education for the next decade."[33]

Although widely known as a corrupt leader, Daniel arap Moi, president of Kenya 1978–2003, often spoke out in public about the need to fight corruption, at the same time as he raped and pillaged the economy of Kenya. According to the 1999 Transparency International Corruption Perceptions Index, Kenya was in the top 10 corrupt countries (or more correctly the bottom 10) as perceived by business people, risk analysts, and the general public. Kenya scored two out of a possible 10 points, with zero being the most corrupt score.[34] The coffee and tea crops in that country, once the country's economic mainstay, remain in a state of disarray and decline—a product of corrupt leaders skimming off the profits. President Moi also argued that Western countries should "back off" and allow Kenyans to deal with corruption in their own way. That would be fine, perhaps, except that the government of Kenya has sought the support of the World Bank and the International Monetary Fund at the same time. Meanwhile, there exists growing poverty in Kenya, and a serious decline in the state of the country's infrastructure.

There is no better example of the squandering of a nation's resources than that of Kenya. "Kenya ... in the 1960s and 1970s enjoyed an annual growth rate of about 6.5 per cent. By the end of the rule of Daniel arap Moi, who was elected on an anti-corruption platform, Kenya's economy had stalled and the country was mired in graft. Unemployment stood at 40 per cent. The election of Mwai Kibaki in December 2002 brought new optimism. Within six months, an anti-corruption act and a public officer ethics act had been passed."[35] Hopefully for the citizens of Kenya, and for other nations around the world who are monitoring this situation, a lasting solution to corruption in Kenya will be found.

Officials in Kenya are trying to retrieve the funds stolen by President Moi and his cronies during his 24-year rule. "The money was stolen by making fictitious payments on the foreign debt and looting the Central Bank, by demanding kickbacks and obtaining phoney contracts. About $2 billion to $3 billion of the money might still be traceable, say officials involved in the investigation. The higher figure equals roughly a third of Kenya's annual economic output, or half its foreign debt…"[36]

After he replaced Daniel arap Moi in the 2002 Kenyan election, running on an anti-graft campaign platform, Mwai Kibaki got off to a good start by firing a large number of judges who were accepting bribes to have charges quashed or dismissed, but then the rot set in again. Mr. Edward Clay, Britain's high commissioner to Kenya, took the unprecedented step of blasting Mwai Kibaki for not tackling corruption and for the "gigantic looting spree" that followed the 2002 election. He went on to say to an audience in Nairobi in July 2004 that "it is outrageous to think that corruption accounts…for about 8 per cent of Kenya's [gross domestic product]. Mr. Clay alleged that since Mr. Kibaki's shaky alliance of opposition parties swept to power, the government has been involved in corrupt deals worth about US $250 million."[37] Interestingly, Mr. Kibaki was re-elected in a very contentious election in December 2007 which has caused serious unrest in Kenya. Most believe the election was rigged and was not free and fair. This has led to a political compromise and the formation of a coalition government.

Like Kenya, many of the countries listed in Table 3 are attempting to locate the funds pilfered by former leaders so that these national assets can be repatriated and used to improve the lives of their citizens. This process of recovering assets is a daunting task because of the ingenious ways corrupt leaders hide the trail of the funds, especially those transfers moving offshore through intermediaries and nominee holdings that often end up in offshore banking centres such as Luxembourg or the Bahamas. Confidentiality agreements are not easily penetrated.

Encouragingly, however, the recent development of a cadre of professionals is increasingly enhancing the expertise and manpower needed to track down these stolen assets and return them to their rightful owners (the citizens). There are private sector experts located in the Channel Islands whose sole mission is to help countries track down and repatriate stolen assets derived from corrupt activities. The Nigerian government has also had some success in recovering stolen assets. As Margaret E. Beare and Stephen Schneider note in their book *Money Laundering in Canada: Chasing Dirty and Dangerous Dollars,* "During the 1980s, Swiss banks were embarrassed by their role in handling funds from the late Ferdinand Marcos of the Philippines... In 2001, British banks were found to have facilitated the looting of Nigeria by the late dictator General Sani Abacha... Citibank was also notorious for handling huge sums of money (over US $87 million) for Raul Salinas."

In order to understand why corruption is such a problem in so many countries in the developing world, it is necessary to examine how their economies work. Since corruption is a particular problem in countries where resource development plays a major role in the economy, the workings of resource-based economies are of particular interest. Many developing countries rely on natural resources to bolster their national treasuries. For example, the average annual hydrocarbon revenues (2000–2003) as a per cent of total fiscal revenues was 77 per cent for Nigeria, 40 per cent for Russia, 31 per cent for Indonesia, 32 per cent for Mexico, 53 per cent for Venezuela, and 81 per cent for Angola. These numbers do not include revenues from mining, forestry, etc.

Unfortunately, the business of natural resource extraction lends itself to political corruption—perhaps more so than other sectors.

Most resource development projects are located in remote locations, far away from the watchful eye of central governments (not that they are often any better!). It is easier in such circumstances for rules to be skirted and bribes to change hands. Often, these projects generate much-desired and needed hard currency (US dollars, Euros, pounds sterling, etc.) from sales into international commodity markets. So, resource development serves as a valuable source of hard currency, something very desirable where the local currency (e.g. the Russian ruble in the early 1990s) is depreciated and lacks value for the purpose of purchasing goods and services outside the country.

Finally, elected and unelected central government officials can participate in corrupt activities associated with natural resource development projects to produce a double bonanza of fraud against the people. Since central and local governments usually have ownership of the country's natural resources, politicians and bureaucrats usually control the issuance of development permits. The result is that foreign and local investments are more frequently directed to natural resource projects in many developing economies. Resources are therefore not allocated based on "highest and best use" but on the ease with which senior government leaders can enrich themselves. Ironically, many international NGOs, such as the Extractive Industries Transparency Initiative, the Publish What You Pay Coalition, and the Revenue Watch Institute, have recognized the corruption that attaches itself to natural resource exploitation, and have labelled it the "resource curse."

This resource curse has the further negative consequence of natural resources being developed in ways that are not sustainable. Examples of this abound—excessive clear-cut logging in Thailand and Sarawak (Indonesia), mining and oil and gas projects in Africa and elsewhere that have left a larger-than-necessary footprint, destruction of rain forests in South America, over-fishing and decimation of species at risk, and so on.

It should be noted that not all non-sustainable natural resource projects are the product of corruption—some are caused by mismanagement. I have argued, for example, that the development of the Canadian oil sands in Alberta is proceeding too quickly, and is not sustainable. These projects are putting enormous pressures on our water resources in the Athabasca River Basin and producing increasingly huge amounts of CO_2 at a time when we should be aggressively reducing greenhouse gas emissions. What we should be doing is accelerating the development and deployment of improved water cycling techniques and carbon capture and sequestration technologies. We should also not be wasting precious natural gas to pump bitumen out of the ground. Until we can deal with these serious environmental problems, in my view oil sands development in Alberta should be slowed down.

A few examples of corruption related to resource extraction serve to illustrate the nature and extent of the problem. Zambia is a case in point.

In the mid-1990s, a large mining company in Canada was anxious to participate in Zambia's copper mine privatization initiative. An agreement-in-principle was negotiated between the company and the Zambian government, and a representative of the company dispatched to Lusaka to cement the deal and finalize the agreement. One year later, this same individual had packed his bags and relocated with the same company to South America to pursue other business opportunities. The problem? Too much graft being demanded by government leaders and officials at every turn and at every opportunity.

Some years later, I recall meeting a parliamentarian from Zambia and I broached the topic of the failed opportunity to attract Canadian investment to Zambia—with the loss in jobs and economic activity. The Zambian MP had coincidentally followed this story quite closely. Upon digesting what I said to him, he paused for a long time, then looked me in the eye and said, "My sense was our minister of mines became too personally involved in this file." He didn't need to spell it out for me. What he said was code for "the minister of mines, and perhaps others, were hoping to extract large sums to top up their

Swiss bank accounts, in exchange for the satisfactory conclusion of the privatization agreement." Another opportunity was squandered because of the greed of a few.

Nigeria provides another example of corruption. Samuel Ladoke Akintola ruled in Nigeria from 1955 to 1959.[38] Ryszard Kapuściński, in his book *The Shadow of the Sun*, describes him this way:

> Akintola was fifty years old, a heavyset man with a wide, baroquely tattooed face. In the past several months he had not left his residence, which was under heavy police guard—he was afraid. Five years ago he had been a middle-class lawyer. After a year of premiership, he already had millions. He simply poured money from the government accounts into his private ones. Wherever you go in Nigeria, you come across his houses—in Lagos, in Ibadan, in Abeokuta. He had twelve limousines, largely unused, but he liked to look at them from his balcony. His ministers also grew rich quickly. We are here in a realm of absolutely fantastical fortunes, all made in politics, or, more precisely, through political gangsterism—by breaking up parties, falsifying election results, killing opponents, firing into angry crowds. One must see this wealth against the background of desperate poverty, in the context of the country over which Akintola ruled—burned, desolate, awash in blood.[39]

Doing business in Indonesia demands a special appreciation of the art of bribery and corruption. Getting deals done in that country often requires that a percentage of revenues or profits find their way into a numbered bank account of an Indonesian general or public official. During the period of President Suharto's rule, I was troubled to learn that a client of mine was obliged to dedicate a portion of the revenues in this way, from the production of crude oil through a joint venture with an Indonesian state-owned corporation, Pertamina, totalling millions of dollars each year.

Authorities in the United States estimate that Saddam Hussein

accumulated as much as $40 billion during his years in power—
funds that he hid in banks in Switzerland, Japan, Germany, and
other countries.

Kim Jong-il, North Korea's ruler, dictator, and "Dear Leader," is
well known for his corrupt practices:

> For years he has been using forced labour to mine gold from
> a mountain in Korea; the gold is deposited directly into his
> Swiss bank accounts. He has quietly salted away more than
> $4 billion in those accounts, according to Chuck Downs, an
> expert on Korea in the Clinton administration. The 'Dear
> Leader' maintains a villa in Geneva (where his son was edu-
> cated) as well as five other villas in Europe, one in Russia and
> one in China.[40]

All of this is occurring as the economy of North Korea has collapsed,
and famine affecting hundreds of thousands is evident. In 1998, Kim
ordered 200 Mercedes Benz and paid US $20 million for them, an
amount equal to one-fifth of the aid promised to North Korea that
year by the United Nations.

Leaders of states without resources have also managed to find illegal ways to enrich themselves. Just before Yasser Arafat's death, the
National Post raised the issue: "With Yasser Arafat reportedly on his
deathbed, many in the Middle East are beginning to pose a delicate
question: Where is the money?"[41] It is estimated that Yasser Arafat "squirreled away" about US $1 billion into various offshore bank
accounts. "Tales of the Palestinian leader's corruption are legendary.
In *Arafat's War*, Efraim Karsh wrote that during the 1982 Israeli invasion of Lebanon, Kuwait donated 10 Mercedes ambulances worth US
$600,000 to the Palestine Liberation Organization. Rather than use
the ambulances to aid casualties, Arafat sold them at half price to the
Syrians, then pocketed the difference."[42]

The stories of corruption are many and varied: Pinochet in Chile,
the Marcos family in the Philippines, whose wealth at its zenith was

estimated by the CIA to be $35 billion. In India, although politicians are paid a modest salary, a great many live a life of opulence. My constituency, which has a large South Asian population, is home to many Indian restaurants and food shops. One day, I ventured into one of them, as I often do, to purchase some samosas and nan bread. The owner of the shop recognized me as the local Member of Parliament. "Aren't you the local MP?" he asked. We shook hands and introduced ourselves. "I am amazed that you would come into my shop," he remarked. "Why so?" I responded—puzzled by his comment. "In India," he said, "a member of parliament would probably not enter such modest premises; but, if they did, it would undoubtedly be with two or three bodyguards!" I guess if you live by graft and corruption, you make friends and enemies and you need protection from the latter.

Political corruption, or grand corruption, is the first problem to be challenged because the amounts stolen are huge and stopping or reducing this type of activity would have the biggest impact. If one can change behaviour and attitudes at the senior levels of governments, changes will follow at the bureaucratic and corporate levels. As the old adage goes, if you wish to kill a snake, you remove its head. And political corruption is the head of the snake, because corrupt political leaders are scaring away both public and private sector investment and starving these developing economies of growth and employment prospects. Donor governments are increasingly hesitant, and rightly so, to spend fifty-cent dollars on international development assistance (fifty cents for the citizens and fifty cents for the corrupt leaders). This does not make any economic sense. It is also a mismanagement of resources.

The Problem of Investment

Investment capital, especially in today's global economy, is highly mobile and it will move to the projects with the best risk/return ratio, that is, where the rate of return and the risk level are optimized. This is especially true for private capital. The public sector comes into play when the market is not responding, or not responding appropriately or adequately. The possible reasons for the private sector not responding are numerous, but an obvious one is that the perceived risk may be too high in relation to the benefit or potential return on investment. Another would be that the development project creates "public goods" (e.g. hospitals, roads, education) where there is no discernable rent to be captured by the private sector (i.e. no private profit). This is where overseas development assistance from governments, and grants and loans from NGOs and institutions like the World Bank and the European Bank for Reconstruction and Development (EBRD) come into play to provide subsidies or bridge financing for "public good" projects or initiatives. But the tolerance of risk for governments, public institutions, and NGOs is not limitless. Risk levels must be manageable—and good governance in the jurisdiction in question plays heavily into this assessment.

James D. Wolfensohn, former president of the World Bank, has indicated that corruption is the "single largest deterrent to private sector investing."[43] Creating a flow of private and public investments to the developing world is one way of increasing economic output, improving productivity, and assisting developing countries in wealth creation. Foreign direct investment, however, will occur when perceived benefits exceed costs and where the risks are acceptable.

Professor Shang-Jin Wei of the Kennedy School of Government at Harvard University stated that "a one-grade increase in the level of corruption (as measured in this case by the International Risk Guide of the Business International Corporation—a subsidiary of the Economist Intelligence Unit) is associated with a 16 per cent reduction in the flow of foreign direct investment—roughly equivalent to the effect of a 3 per cent increase in the marginal tax rate."[44]

According to J. Paul Salembier, "Corruption also decreases the returns that a state derives from a given level of investment. When corruption distorts the approval process for an investment project, the rate of return on investment ceases to be a determining factor in the cost-benefit analysis."[45] According to V. Tanzi and H. Davoodi, "This can also reduce the rate of return a state derives from existing infrastructure."[46]

Investment in developing countries, whether foreign or domestic, will only flow if the rule of law provides investors with protection of their rights and their assets. This implies that recipient states must have committed codes and standards as well as an independent judiciary that is free from corruption.

In a paper developed by the Australian delegation and circulated at the Fifteenth Asia-Pacific Economic Cooperation (APEC) Ministerial Meeting in Bangkok October 17–18, 2003, it is noted that "foreign investors are increasingly looking for good governance practices, sound policies and strong rule of law when making overseas development assistance or foreign direct investment (FDI) decisions. Returns on investment and aid will boost development."

Over the years there has been much speculation on the factors critical for successful economic growth in poor countries. Is good economic policy the most important one? Or are geography and natural resources the key drivers? What about the role that institutions play? How important are factors like political stability, property rights, legal systems, patterns of land tenure, etc? A new paper[47] by William Easterly of the Centre for Global Development and Ross Levine of the University of Minnesota suggests that institutions are by far the most important factor. The authors show that "countries with good institutions tend to do all right with good or bad policies,"[48] and those countries lacking in quality institutions do badly, irrespective of the economic policy environment. Surprisingly, their study concluded that there is no clear connection between incomes and geography—other than the fact that geographic advantages typically lead to a good institutional setting.

Russia provides an excellent example of this point. The forest products company for which I worked for in the early 1990s was interested in examining the feasibility of building a pulp mill in Russia. This was the heyday of *glasnost* and *perestroika* (openness and restructuring) introduced by then President Gorbachev. Given the new open society, more books and newspapers were being published, producing a shortage of paper in the former USSR. We had a joint venture partner in Russia, and another partner in Canada—the latter manufactured pulp mill equipment. The role of our company was twofold: to provide mill design assistance and manufacturing expertise once the mill was operational; and, to market the pulp into the world markets for hard currency until the debt was substantially repaid.

In co-operation with our joint venture partners, we completed a preliminary feasibility study, but had to abandon the project for a variety of reasons. The foremost reason was the lack of predictability and stability of public policies, and the lack of understanding of basic, sound business practice on the part of the Russians.

They first offered us timber in a location a thousand kilometres from the site of the proposed mill. When we objected and cited this as a deal-breaker, magically and mysteriously timber tracts some 300 kilometres distance were identified—still a long way away. When we expressed concern about the health of these forests (many of the trees were decadent, i.e., they had some rot in their core), we were told not to worry, the rot would all be cut out and only the good wood would be shipped to the mill. The fact that there was an economic cost of doing this type of work didn't seem to be of great importance to the Russians.

In the middle of our feasibility study, the USSR disintegrated, and Mr. Yeltsin bolted from the Communist Party. Many of the officials with whom we had been dealing at the Soviet level suddenly reappeared as Russian bureaucrats. The rules of the game were constantly changing. Income tax rates, as well as rates of duties on imported machinery, were changing by the week.

Our repeated requests for assurances from the highest level of the government for the continuous and guaranteed supplies of wood, energy, and chemicals seemed to fall on deaf ears. Who in their right mind would invest US $300 million in a pulp mill without a secure raw material supply? When we asked Canadian embassy officials in Moscow who we should seek assurances from for the supply of raw materials—the USSR, the Russian Federation, or local governments—they answered "yes!"

Controlled government prices were disappearing, but no one, including leading economists, could predict where prices were headed. As one can imagine, this played havoc with our financial plans and forecasts. At one point in our discussions in Russia, officials referred to a "super profits tax" that would be imposed if profits exceeded a return on investment of 20 per cent. It was difficult, if not impossible, to convince the Russian officials that our board of directors viewed our project as a high-risk venture and were expecting a short payback period.

The Problem of Partnerships

In many developing countries and emerging economies, joint ventures with local partners are encouraged as the way to do business and at many levels this makes good sense. In seeking ways to reduce poverty in developing countries by creating economic activity, joint ventures and partnerships are an excellent way of reducing the risk associated with corrupt states. However, joint ventures with companies or organizations in foreign countries typically create unique challenges.

In my business experience with joint ventures in Russia and China, one of the more difficult areas was the consideration of in-kind contributions by foreign partners, and the valuation of these assets. Often, joint venture partners in countries like China and Russia, especially in the 1990s, had very little to bring to the table as their contribution to the joint-venture project.

In the mid-1990s, I was an executive officer with a Canadian company formed by business colleagues of mine at the time, who had a joint venture partner in Shenyang, China. Our mission was to build a medium-density fibreboard (MDF) mill in China to capitalize on the growth of the middle class in that country and the increasing demand for housing and furniture. MDF is used in the manufacture of furniture and in the production of moulded door skins that are used for doors for houses and garages. The project ultimately came into being—not as an MDF mill but as a moulded door skin plant (more value-added). During our initial discussions with our joint-venture partner in China, our Chinese partners had very limited access to financial capital and so they offered up in-kind contributions in lieu of cash. These in-kind items consisted of a manufacturing plant (old and outdated) and assorted pieces of equipment (some not relevant to the project at hand). Our partners tried to have us accept these assets at overvalued prices as a proxy for their equity contribution. Clearly, this was a thorny part of our negotiations and one area where we could not agree. Fortunately, other solutions were found.

In Russia, we encountered similar problems with our joint-venture partners in that country. We encountered overvalued in-kind contributions together with attempts to include items in the joint venture capital expenditure budget (CAPEX) that were not legitimate project costs. These items included a power grid which would benefit the area generally above and beyond the pulp mill, and items like a school, hospital, and nursery—costs that in Canada would in most instances be covered by the state.

All the Russian players wanted a piece of the hard currency receipts that would be generated by the sale of the pulp in world markets. We actually developed a hard currency cash flow model in addition to the normal versions to ensure that the hard currency was rationed in the best possible way. Even with that, we had to tell the Russians that the vast majority of the pulp would have to be exported outside of Russia for at least 10 years to satisfy the debt holders. This was not exactly what they had originally intended because they wanted to create a more robust domestic supply of paper; however, the Russians realized they had little choice and they reluctantly accepted this reality.

Investing and forming partnerships in developing countries can be problematical where contract law is weak and where intellectual property rights are not adequately protected. Contracts can often not be enforced, especially when officials in government and/or the judiciary have been bribed. Corrupt officials may also turn a blind eye to patent and trademark infringements. Key individuals participating as joint venture partners may seek personal financial contributions in the form of bribes to maintain their commitment to the joint venture or to keep the project moving forward. The valuation of joint-venture partner contributions and defining the scope of the project can be frustrating (and costly). Fortunately, in my international business dealings, I have never been asked for a bribe but I gather from my former business partners that the project in China which did get launched ran into problems with corruption many years later.

All in all, partnerships in developing countries need to be approached with a great deal of caution and pragmatism. Many have been burned and more will be hurt in the future.

Bureaucratic Corruption

In many developing nations, petty bribery and corruption at the middle management and junior levels of government are often countenanced and encouraged to supplement low wages and salaries. This practice unfortunately encourages a culture of corruption and adds to the cost of doing business in corrupt countries. Ironically, more regulated economies are more prone to petty bribery and corruption because there are more steps along the way for approvals, and hence more opportunities for officials who have some decision-making discretion to seek bribes.

In the late 1980s, I had the opportunity to stay with some Canadian friends in Thailand. These friends had lived in Thailand for some years, so they knew the area well. I had the opportunity to play golf with a retired deputy minister in the Thai government. He was a very genial fellow and we had an enjoyable round of golf. On the way to the golf course, we were pulled over for speeding—a very common occurrence in Thailand. The police constable came over to the rolled-down window of our car and showed off a very large and impressive book of speeding tickets. Our driver sorted the whole affair out in a few minutes with a bribe in lieu of the bother of writing up a ticket. I was told that tickets are rarely, if ever, issued by police officers in circumstances like this. Police officers are paid extremely low wages and are expected to make most of their income through bribes. It is the accepted practice. I wondered at the time why the government didn't pay better wages and use the ticket reve-nue to defray the costs—perhaps a small step towards mitigating the culture and psychology of bribery.

Similar scenarios are also played out throughout the developing world. Once, when I was visiting Mexico, our guide told me that in Mexico police officers are not paid much and most don't have much education. According to the guide, the police live on bribes. The guide also made the point that this seems to be the way that the politicians like things to be, that is, keep them ignorant and silent.

The result of all this is that there is often little respect for the rule of law, leaving citizens little option but to turn to other means of governing. This is certainly true in the case of the corruption-laden Mexican police force that has allowed a $7 billion-a-year drug trade market to flourish. This lack of legitimacy among the police in the country has led the military to take on the task of controlling the drug trade, with one-third of the military's budget being devoted to the anti-drug effort and 25,000 Mexican soldiers involved in drug control operations. The enormous profits from drug trafficking pro-vide the means for traffickers to buy political protections, as cocaine traffickers spend as much as $500 million a year on bribery (which is more than double the budget of the Mexican attorney general's office). The report by Mexico's interior ministry estimated that by

1995 there would be about 900 armed criminal bands in the country with 50 per cent comprised of current or former police officers.

Mexico has responded to the drug corruption scandals by firing or transferring individual officers, or disbanding entire agencies and creating new ones. However, this has done little to solve the problem, as many fired police officers were rehired in other regions of the country and hundreds more reinstated after challenging their dismissals in court.

As I said, I had the chance when in Thailand to play a round of golf with a retired deputy minister—an individual who had had a very successful career in the public service of Thailand. Having spent much of my career before politics in the forest sector, I enquired about the recent ban on logging in Thailand. Earlier that year torrential rains and floods had virtually wiped out a number of villages in Thailand, which precipitated the ban. Logging and over-cutting were blamed for most of these mishaps. My golfing partner told me that in northern Thailand the logging concessionaires were very accommodating with the government forestry officers. They were frequently told that they had two options when presented with a logging plan for approval: they could either accept the logging plan (which was made easier with a handsome bribe), or they could enjoy a float down a local river as a corpse! The result, not surprisingly, is massive areas denuded by clear cuts with little or no consideration of land erosion or soil impacts. I was told that the Thailand Forest Service offices in Bangkok were the most opulent of all government departments. I presumed that some of the forest industry largesse found its way through these channels as well.

Bribes paid to officials may also introduce greater health, safety, and environmental risks when rules are ignored after money has changed hands. The reason is that bribes are often paid to relax rules and regulations meant to protect the public. A country's citizens are then exposed to greater risks while others benefit financially. If bureaucrats were paid more, they might not need to accept bribes. This is the direction we should be heading in.

Business Corruption

Corrupt businesses add to a culture of corruption in a society and, coupled with corruption in the public sector, exact a toll on society and its citizens. In Chapter 5, I discuss the role of corporations on the supply side of corruption—or as payers of bribes. Corporate fraud, like the well-publicized cases of Nick Leeson and the US $1.4 billion futures contract speculation fraud which led to the collapse of Barings Bank in the United Kingdom, and the more recent example of the allegedly fraudulent trader Jerome Kerviel who caused Société Générale in France to lose US $7 billion, certainly adds to this problem.

Corporate governance failures are also cause for concern because well-developed, efficient capital markets are a pre-condition to strong and sustained economic growth. When appropriate checks and balances on corporate behaviour are lacking, corporate governance failures in the vein of Enron and WorldCom in the United States can be the result. These household names have become synonymous with unbridled and unchecked greed.

In the wake of these and other corporate scandals, investors world-wide have become increasingly sceptical—and cautious—about financial markets that have breached their trust and scuttled their confidence.

In Canada in the last decade we unfortunately have had our share of delinquent corporations: Bre-X Minerals, YBM Magnex, Phillip Services, Livent Inc., Laidlaw, Cinar, and Castor Holdings, to name just a few. In the United States the response to corporate governance problems was the passage of the Sarbanes-Oxley Act of 2002. In short, this Act requires a new oversight board to monitor the accounting industry, tougher penalties against executives who commit corporate fraud, and increases in the Securities and Exchange Commission (SEC) budget for auditors and investigators to oversee the industry.

There are as many definitions of corporate governance as there are players. Milton Friedman, economist and Nobel laureate, provided one of the earliest definition. According to him, corporate governance is the conducting of "business in accordance with owner or shareholders' desires, which generally will be to make as much money as possible, while conforming to the basic rules of the society embodied in law and local customs."

The Toronto Stock Exchange (TSE) defines corporate governance as "the process and structure used to direct and manage the business and affairs of the corporation with the objective of enhancing shareholder value, which includes ensuring the financial viability of the business."

In short, corporate governance is more than just improving financial performance. It provides a sound system of checks and balances to supervise senior management and fosters a culture of transparency and trust between the primary corporate players and investors.

In my judgement, corporate governance is enhanced when there is an independent board of directors and independent audit committee; where the role of chairman and CEO are split; where there is effective oversight of the accounting and auditing firms; where there are appropriate sanctions and penalties for executives convicted of corporate malfeasance; and where there is transparent oversight covering executive compensation, including stock option schemes. In Canada, corporate governance would benefit if we had one national securities regulator. We need to keep pushing for this notwithstanding the reluctance of certain provinces.

The principles of good corporate governance apply equally in developing economies, the difference being the stage of development and the business practice environment. When I worked with a major international accounting firm in Johannesburg in the mid-1970s, I examined the audited financial statements of a company in Mozambique. On the balance sheet was an amount in escudos captioned as "deferred expenses—representation costs." Upon further enquiry of the company's auditors, who had given a clean, or unqualified, report on the financial statements of the company, I discovered that these amounts represented outlays or bribes paid to various public officials over a period of time. They had been capitalized as an asset of the company on the rationale that they represented an enduring and lasting future benefit for the company. They probably did! Needless to say, we wrote off these assets on the consolidated financial statements of their parent company in Johannesburg.

This same holding company had previously gone through some incredible gymnastics to obtain a dividend from their wholly owned subsidiary in Mozambique. A bit of history first. In 1974, the Portuguese government was overthrown by Samora Machel and the Mozambique Liberation Front (Frelimo). The left-wing government nationalized almost everything, save the clothes that people were wearing. The most stringent foreign exchange controls were implemented. Remitting dividends to non-resident shareholders outside of Mozambique became a nightmare. To some, however, a problem is simply a solution waiting to be found. The holding company, through its control of the board of directors of the company in Mozambique, declared a dividend in escudos, which they promptly exchanged for South African rand on the black market. A private aircraft, which had landed on a landing strip at a remote location in Mozambique, soon collected the individual with a briefcase full of South African rand, and flew the dividend back to Johannesburg and into the hands of the chief financial officer of the holding company. Lo and behold, funds had been repatriated against all odds (and against all the laws of Mozambique). This transaction presented the auditors in Johannesburg with somewhat of an ethical dilemma— but only for a short time. The moral of the story: truth and justice can be relative concepts.

In Thailand, I believe the financial crisis that country faced in 1997–8 was caused largely because of the cronyism in their banking system. By cronyism in this context I refer to the granting of loans based on relationships, and the creation of private personal advantage, over rational lending policies. This invariably leads to bad loans, followed by huge write-downs and losses. Japan is another good example of this.

On a visit to Rio de Janeiro, Brazil, some years ago, a professional colleague advised me that most large companies had full time "expediters" on staff. Their role was exclusively to clear the path, by bribing public officials through the government bureaucracy for export permits, work permits, import permits, and myriad other necessary approvals essential when doing business in that country. Imagine the economic cost of such an infrastructure and non-productive, time-consuming processes.

Businesses that are not corrupt often suffer in environments where corruption is common, as the experience of George Cohon, the founder of McDonald's Restaurants of Canada, shows. It took him seven years to establish the first McDonald's hamburger outlet in Moscow. To his credit, neither he nor his officials ever entertained discussions about bribes. Perhaps that is why it took so long to bring his project to fruition. His strategy was, and is, to build a ruble business, and to integrate backwards into McDonald's traditional supply chain. By building a ruble business, he created more support in Russia for his enterprise, and he waited for the ruble to be convertible and/or to participate in the limited auctions of hard currency. It would appear that his strategy was a successful one.

These examples illustrate how corruption impedes the economic growth of developing countries on two levels. First, it robs the revenue of business owners in developing countries by claiming a portion of their profits through the payment of bribes. In countries such as Indonesia, businesses, especially small ones, are forced by public officials to pay bribes in order for the enterprise to remain in business.[49] These payments can raise the cost of doing business in some countries by as much as 20 per cent of the operating costs.

Secondly, the uncertainty of widespread corruption can act as a deterrent for potential investors.[50] Corruption can reduce foreign direct investment because it has the same effect as a tax—the less predictable the level of corruption (the higher its variance), the greater its impact on foreign direct investment.[51] A higher variance would have corruption behave like a random tax, thus deterring investors. In fact, IMF economist Paolo Mauro (1996) finds empirical evidence that corruption lowers economic growth.[52] Using the Business International Indices of corruption, Mauro finds a one-deviation improvement in the corruption index causes investment to rise by five per cent of the GDP, and the annual growth rate of GDP per capita to rise by half a percentage point.[53]

It should be noted, however, that up until the 1997 financial crisis, it appeared that some countries in Southeast Asia were growing economically despite their corrupt governments. Developing countries with corrupt practices such as Indonesia, Thailand, and Korea were just some of the countries thought to have grown economically while tolerating corrupt practices.[54] It was argued that in places such as Indonesia where corruption was institutionalized rather than random, corruption actually allowed the country to continue to grow economically. Researchers Leff (1964) and Huntington (1968) argue that the high rates of growth in corrupt countries in Southeast Asia were possible because corruption in the form of bribery actually enhanced capital flows by removing government red tape that prevented investment.[55]

Although these corrupt countries had satisfactory economic growth, they became susceptible to economic collapse. Eventually corrupt practices feed on themselves and multiply, producing higher illegal pay-offs, until growth is undermined.[56] For instance, if five to 10 per cent of the value of public projects go towards bribes, this may create pressures to increase payoffs to 10 to 15 per cent, leading to a self-destructive cycle. Costs from these activities suggest that corruption, despite cutting through bureaucratic red tape, actually has a negative impact on the rate of growth of countries.

Corruption also distorts the allocation of resources by reducing government expenditure on education, health, and infrastructure maintenance, preventing the advancement of developing countries. Clearly, corruption is not something a country will grow out of. Without significant reforms, countries affected by corruption will continue to experience impeded financial flows.

Corruption and Society

In a December 2005 document, "Controlling Corruption: A Handbook for Arab Politicians," a number of negative impacts of corruption on society were identified. I believe it is an interesting and quite comprehensive list of negative factors.

Corruption:
- ► Substitutes personal gain for public good;
- ► Prevents or makes it more difficult for governments to implement laws and policies;
- ► Changes the image of politicians and encourages people to go into politics for the wrong reasons;
- ► Undermines public trust in politicians and in political institutions and processes;
- ► Erodes international confidence in the government;
- ► Encourages cynicism and discourages political participation;
- ► Can contribute to political instability, provoke coups d'état, and lead to civil wars;
- ► Perverts the conduct and results of elections, where they exist;
- ► Keeps the poor politically marginalized;
- ► Consolidates political power and reduces political competition;
- ► Delays and distorts political development and sustains political activity based on patronage, clienteles and money;
- ► Limits political access to the advantage of the rich;
- ► Reduces the transparency of political decision-making.

This summary demonstrates how corruption can permeate an entire society and the damage it can cause. The impact of corruption goes beyond costs to the economy. Corruption attacks democracy itself and can undermine institutions and the attitudes of a country's citizenry.

Many individuals with idealistic notions of fighting corruption get caught up in the endless cycle of corruption once they are elected. Many of them quickly forget the very reason they sought public office and reinforce the old adage—if you can't fight them, join them.

For politicians in Mexico, when it comes to dealing with the drug lords, the choices are very clear—take the money and run and turn a blind eye; or have you and your family face the consequences of violence turned against you. It becomes even more difficult for a politician attempting to fight the drug lords when the police themselves are corrupt, and when judges are also bribed. It takes a brave politician to buck this trend.

Corruption is not only related to regular crime, however; the downing of a Russian passenger airliner in August 2004 by terrorists highlights how corruption and terrorism can be linked. It is alleged that the terrorist who blew up one of the planes was initially denied boarding the aircraft because of some irregularities with her documentation. However, a bribe approximating US $50 was paid—allowing her to board the aircraft and eventually blow it up, causing the death of 46 people.

In conclusion, corruption has enormous implications for developing countries. It undermines democratic processes, carries with it a huge economic cost, and corruption can lead to political unrest. But corruption also impacts countries with more developed economies and it is this to aspect that we now turn our attention.

CHAPTER 4

Consequences of Corruption for Developed Nations

Developed countries are not immune from corruption—it is more a question of order of magnitude, and the level of damage that corruption can cause in the respective jurisdictions. Many or all the negative consequences associated with corruption for developing countries apply to the more developed economies. There are, however, some additional and unique considerations for the industrialized world. There is an economic cost of bribery that is reflected in a higher cost of doing business in corrupt countries. This limits levels of foreign direct investment by developed countries in developing and emerging economies. Corruption in developing countries has undoubtedly changed world migration patterns as people flee their home countries out of disgust and/or the desire to improve the quality of their lives. They may flee their country of birth if they are being persecuted for exposing corrupt practices, or when bribery has caused greater health, safety, and environmental risks.

Exporting Corporate Corruption

The Organization of Economic Co-operation and Development (OECD) estimated in 1998 that product counterfeiting and piracy represented five to seven per cent of world trade. Counterfeiting refers to the unauthorized reproduction of goods protected by intellectual property right. It is generally associated with trademark violations, whereas piracy refers to copyright infringements. Once upon a time, these types of products were primarily associated with items like fake Rolex watches, fake Gucci handbags, and phoney Nike sports apparel, sold at flea markets or in underground markets. When the police turned up, vendors scurried to wrap up their goods and disappear (until the police vanished around the corner). Today the problem is much more widespread and complicated. It is now a worldwide industry involving a vast array of products ranging from clothes to medications, multimedia, batteries, electronics, toys, cosmetics, and parts for vehicles, ships, and aircraft. China is now producing complete cars that are counterfeit. Manufacturers are using blueprints and plans stolen or otherwise obtained without authorization, to produce identical replicas of known brand names of cars manufactured in North America, Europe, or Asia at a fraction of the cost because of their low labour costs. Toyota, Honda, and BMW have already been victims.

Profit margins are large for producers and distributors of counterfeit and pirated goods. Because sanctions or penalties are not severe, it is not surprising that organized crime is increasingly involved. There is an economic cost associated with counterfeit and pirated goods as well as a cost to society in terms of health and safety. The economic cost is largely felt by the owners of the intellectual property rights whose products are being counterfeited or pirated. Investments they have made in developing, producing, and bringing these products to market are being undermined. There is an economic cost to society as a whole to police and prosecute these crimes. More must be done to counter the growth in these products; this struggle requires more attention from authorities in nearly all jurisdictions in the world, and certainly Canada is no exception. In 2007, two standing committees of the House of Commons in Canada, the Standing Committee on Public Safety and National Security

(I serve as vice-chair of this committee), and the Standing Committee on Industry, conducted hearings on this topic and submitted reports to Parliament and to the Government of Canada calling for aggressive action to deal with the mounting problem of counterfeit and pirated goods.

I made the following comments in a debate on counterfeit goods in the Parliamentary Assembly of the Council of Europe in Strasbourg on April 20, 2007:

> In Europe it is estimated that there was a 100 per cent increase in the number of seizures of counterfeit goods entering the EU between 2001 and 2002. This follows an estimated 900 per cent increase in the number of seizures between 1998 and 2001. Figures published by the European Commission at the end of 2003 show that customs seized almost 85 million counterfeit or pirated articles at the EU's external border in 2002 ...
>
> According to the World Heath Organization, in developed countries counterfeit pharmaceutical products account for less than one per cent of the market value—but 50 per cent of the drugs sold over the internet are counterfeit. In less developed economies, fake drugs can make up to 50 per cent of the market ... Not all counterfeit and pirated goods originate from Asia. The European Commission reports, however, that 66 per cent of the counterfeit goods seized in Europe in 2002 came from that part of the world. In Canada, and in Europe, organized criminals are manufacturing counterfeit and pirated goods domestically—right in our own countries ...
>
> Counterfeiting causes job losses and lowers government tax revenues. The OECD and the European Commission estimated some years ago that counterfeit goods are responsible for the loss of 100,000 jobs each year in Europe ...
>
> The common perception that counterfeiting and piracy are victimless crimes is one of the factors contributing to the increase in counterfeit and pirated products. The public-at-

large is generally unaware of the scale of, and the risks associated with, counterfeit goods.

Now what does all of this have to do with bribery and corruption you ask? Well, it is true that not all counterfeit and pirated goods are the product of bribery—but some are.

In a well-publicized case from July 10, 2007, China executed its drug and food safety director after he was convicted of taking bribes to approve fake medicines that killed an unknown number of people. He was the most senior official in China to be put to death since a deputy head of parliament was executed in 2000 on similar charges. During his tenure from 1998 to 2005, the drug and food safety director's agency approved six medicines that turned out to be fake, and the drug makers used falsified documents to apply for approvals. One antibiotic alone caused the deaths of at least 10 people. Mr. Zheng was convicted of taking bribes worth some 6.5 million Yuan (Can. $1 million) from eight companies, and of dereliction of duty.

A spokesperson for the State Food and Drug Administration said at the time, "The few corrupt officials of the SFDA are the shame of the whole system and their scandals have revealed some very serious problems."

There have been other similar cases. The discovery of tainted pet food, poisonous toothpaste, and Thomas the Tank Engine toys painted with lead has caused an international uproar. There are also cases of electrical products flowing into Canada, bearing the forged mark of the Canadian Standards Association, that are unsafe and likely to cause a short-circuit and start a fire. A woman in British Columbia died after taking counterfeit medicines that she had bought over the internet.

There are other examples where the actions of corrupt officials, many in developing economies where corruption and bribery are the norm, are jeopardizing the health and safety of others. The problem is not limited to the citizens of the corrupt nations.

Economic Migration

Why do people leave the country of their birth in search of the Promised Land? If such a paradise were at home, would they emigrate?
Some understandably leave because they are legitimate refugees,
fleeing from repressive regimes, civil war, and the like. Some wish to
be re-united with family members who have already left their home
country and settled in a new land. The predominant reason, however,
for uprooting from one's home country, where one is familiar and
comfortable with the language, religion, and culture, is economic in
nature. People leave because the economic prospects in their own
country are seen to be inferior to those in another. Corruption and
income inequalities in their home country are contributing factors
too. A recent working paper prepared for the United Nations High
Commissioner for Refugees (UNHCR) describes these trends:

> The number of long-term international migrants (that is, those
> residing in foreign countries for more than one year) has
> grown steadily in the past four decades. According to the UN
> Population Division, in 1965, only 15 million persons fit the
> definition, rising to 84 million by 1975 and 105 million by 1985.
> There were an estimated 120 million international migrants in
> 1990, the last year for which detailed international statistics
> are available. An examination of data from selected countries
> of in-migration indicates that international migration contin-
> ued with about the same rate of growth in the 1990s. As of
> the year 2000, according to estimates prepared by this author
> for the International Organisation for Migration, there are 150
> million international migrants.[57]

The report continues:

> Between 1965 and 1975, the growth in international migration

(1.16 per cent per year) did not keep pace with the growth in global population (2.04 per cent per year). However, overall population growth began to decline in the 1980s while international migration continued to increase significantly. During the period from 1985 to 1990, global population growth increased by about 1.1 per cent per year, whereas the total population of international migrants increased by 2.59 per cent per year. Even with the numbers of international migrants large and growing, it is important to keep in mind that fewer than three per cent of the world's population have been living outside of their home country for a year or longer. The propensity to move internationally, particularly in the absence of compelling reasons such as wars, is limited to a small proportion of humans. International migrants come from all parts of the world and they go to all parts of the world. In fact, few countries are unaffected by international migration. Many countries are sources of international flows, while others are net receivers and still others are transit countries through which migrants reach receiving countries. Such countries as Mexico experience migration in all three capacities, as source, receiving and transit countries.[58]

The report highlights the fact that in recent years there has been a very significant increase in the number of people leaving poor countries and ending up in richer ones. Traditional destinations like Canada, the United States, and Australia are being replaced by Europe, the Persian Gulf, and East and Southeast Asia. Notwithstanding these trends, in the early 2000s, more that 46 million international migrants were living in the USA, France, Germany, Canada, Australia, and the United Kingdom, representing a 25 per cent increase in just 10 years. Refugees fleeing from oppressive (and often corrupt) regimes contribute to these increases, as well as unauthorized migration. In many cases, this illegal immigration is facilitated by professional rings specializing in human trafficking.

This migration comes at a great social and economic cost as the following commentary in a UNHCR report indicates:

> There is no question that the number of those seeking asylum in developed countries increased substantially over the past two decades. In 2000, just over 400,000 persons applied for asylum in the fifteen countries of the European Union (EU), double the number in 1980, but down from a high of 700,000 in 1992. With the increase in asylum seekers comes an increase in expenditures to pay for refugee status determination procedures and for the social assistance provided to asylum seekers. By one estimate, that expense among developed countries around the world reached $10 billion in 2000. When only one-quarter of asylum seekers is ultimately granted refugee status, as happened in the EU in 1999, governments balk.[59]

In my riding of Etobicoke North in Toronto, according to the 2001 census, 56.5 per cent of the population were recent immigrants to Canada. The largest of these groups was from South Asia (India, Pakistan, Sri Lanka, etc.). While it is true that some of these people emigrated to Canada because of conflicts in their home country (this is particularly true for the many Tamils in my riding from Sri Lanka), the majority came to Canada in search of a better life and improved standard of living. We are blessed with their decision to make their new home in Canada because they add character and diversity to our Canadian mosaic, but one can't help but wonder if corruption and poverty in their home countries were factors in their decisions, and if they would have preferred to stay in their countries of birth had it not been for the lack of opportunity and injustice they experienced. I have heard countless anecdotal stories from individuals who were tired and utterly discouraged by the levels of poverty and corruption in countries like India and Pakistan and how this prompted them to seek a better life in Canada.

Their loss is our gain, but in the big picture this type of migration should cause us to reflect on the social and economic costs associated with trends like this.

It is not only those who have suffered as a result of corruption who flee developing nations; corrupt leaders, once discovered, will often try and make a hasty escape to another country. Forged documents, if needed, are never a problem for individuals like this—they are well versed in how bribes work. Certainly we know that many of the so-called Russian mafia have ended up in Canada and other countries in the West. People like this always have convincing stories to tell and any money they try to launder into Canada will only be considered to be illegally obtained if it arose from an activity that would be illegal in Canada. In some cases, this is difficult to prove because funds derived from corruption have often been authorized by state authorities.

But Canada is not alone as beneficiaries of Russian mafia largesse. "The deputy chairman of the Central Bank of Russia stated that in 1998 alone, almost US $70 billion was transferred from banks in Russia to banks in Nauru."[60] (Nauru is a tiny island and tax haven in the South Pacific.) Russian money has fled elsewhere also. "According to some estimates, from 1986 until 1999, there may have been as much as US $500 billion looted from the country by corrupt politicians, intelligence officers and organized crime."[61]

Some corrupt officials will arrive in Canada and claim refugee status on the grounds that their safety is at risk and that they would be subjected to torture and perhaps death if they returned to their home country. They might claim the reason for this is the political views they hold and perhaps political activism (always non-violent) against the new ruling party. They are not likely to indicate to Canadian (or any other country's) immigration officers that they had to quickly leave their home country because of their corrupt activities. Fortunately Canada's immigration officers and the Immigration and Refugee Board (IRB) often are not convinced in cases like this and immigration is denied—but I am sure that many slip between the cracks. In fact, some years ago law enforcement officers described to me how many of the so-called Russian mafia had regrettably ended up in Toronto and were engaged in a variety of criminal activities. The violence and brutality that these criminal elements wreaked on each other and on innocent victims was a stark reminder to me of the need to keep people like this out of Canada. I was told also how Russian criminals in Canada make Italian mob types look like Boy Scouts. For the Russians, breaking knees and bones constitutes unnecessary delay. Getting in the way of the Russian mafia often is terminal.

Perhaps my cynicism shows, but I have read through a number of IRB appeal transcripts during the last dozen years. I recall my experience of attending a meeting of the Immigration and Refugee Appeal Board in Toronto. To be a "fly on the wall," I needed the approval of the IRB, and the lawyers on both sides, which in this case was the lawyer for the appellant arguing against his client's deportation, and the federal government lawyer, arguing the opposite.

The individual in question (let's call him Mr. Ahmed) was from Ethiopia. His lawyer argued that he should be granted refugee status because returning to Ethiopia would put him at grave risk including the possibility of execution by government authorities in that country. On the other hand, the federal government lawyer argued that, notwithstanding such risk, he should be deported anyway because he himself, prior to leaving Ethiopia, had been involved in tyrannical acts and crimes against humanity in his home country. Under Canadian, and perhaps international law, such a case can be made and a refugee claim quashed in circumstances like this.

Mr. Ahmed acknowledged that during the rule of known dictator and despot Halie Selassie, he had worked in a political, non-violent way (according to him) as part of a group intent on the overthrow of President Selassie. He was a banker at that time. When President Selassie was finally replaced by Mengistu, Mr. Ahmed (according to his submissions) was asked to join President Mengistu's secret police—in the accounting department. Mengistu was overthrown himself in 1991. Suddenly all those involved with Mengistu's regime, which turned out to be even more violent, brutal, and corrupt than the Selassie regime, had worked in the accounting department. Federal government lawyers successfully challenged his credibility and he was deported back to Ethiopia—to an uncertain fate. One tyrant replaced by another. Does this sound familiar?

Often expectations are very high when political leaders campaign, and win elections on platforms to clean up corruption, and then fail to do so or become co-opted by the forces of corruption themselves. Mwai Kibaki of Kenya and Cory Aquino of the Philippines are good examples of this. In 1986 Corazon Aquino focused her presidential campaign on the misdeeds of Ferdinand Marcos and his cronies, but ultimately she failed to deliver. Ferdinand Marcos embezzled US $5–$10 billion from the Philipino people. Mwai Kibaki promised to clean up the government in Kenya, yet following his election he was considered more corrupt than his predecessor.

Crime and Terrorism

In September 2002, I accepted an invitation from NATO to address a group of Eastern European parliamentarians in Kiev, Ukraine, on the topic "Money Laundering and Corruption as New Threats to National Security." While I was initially surprised by the choice of the topic for my speech, the more I thought about it the more easily I began to connect the dots. Corruption can result in the destabilization of society and money laundering can compromise international financial markets. So in that sense, they are both threats to national and international security. Corruption can create a feeling of hopelessness within a population which can lead to political unrest. Elements in a corrupt military can be persuaded to sell weapons of mass destruction to unstable states and/or terrorists. Indeed, this was, and is, a concern in the context of the Russian military after the break-up of the former Soviet Union—especially given Russia's nuclear weapons capability and its corrupt military.

Corrupt officials and law enforcement officers can also be susceptible to turning a blind eye to drug trafficking, trafficking in human beings, and to the production and distribution of counterfeit and pirated goods. It has been shown that terrorist activities can be funded from money laundered from illegal acts such as these:

> In 2004, the secretary-general of Interpol told reporters in Brussels that there is "a significant link between counterfeiting and terrorism in locations where there are entrenched terrorist groups." Interpol found that some of the suspects involved in the sale of fake car brakes in Lebanon had links with terrorist groups. Militants in Northern Ireland and Colombia have also been linked to counterfeiting, according to Interpol.[62]

The linkage between money laundering, international development assistance, and terrorism is complicated. US Congressman Barney Frank told a May 10–11, 2003, Parliamentary Network of the World Bank conference that it is a mistake to justify more foreign aid using the security argument that more aid will make for a safer world. He suggested that this rationalization could attract a "belligerent rather than a benevolent response" from donor countries like the United States. The point that Congressman Frank was making, I believe, is that we need to address the underlying issues associated with terrorism. Throwing money at the problem will not work. In fact, development assistance from donor countries can potentially be diverted to terrorist activities if the recipient countries harbour resentment and hate towards the West.

We hear this argument sometimes surfacing in the context of Sri Lanka and the dispute between the Sinhalese government and the LTTE, or Tamil Tigers, when funds ostensibly destined for humanitarian aid are allegedly diverted to the LTTE to support their military activities. Likewise, questions were raised about the humanitarian aid that flowed to Southeast Asia following the December 26, 2004, flooding caused by the largest earthquake to strike the planet in more than a generation. In Sri Lanka, for example, the Tamil populations complained that the assistance was flowing to the Sinhalese-controlled areas with much more ease and speed than the aid targeted for the Tamil areas.

The financing of terrorist activities, and related money-laundering activities, threatens the peaceful co-existence of countries and people around the world. The events of September 11, 2001, clearly demonstrated this.

The nature of the linkage between poverty and terrorism is unclear. However, the terrorist attacks targeted at innocent Americans by Muslim extremists on September 11, 2001, cannot be justified using any reasonable criteria. While the immediate and medium-term response must be, and has been, an outright attack on terrorism, we should also be asking ourselves—what are its causes? What motivated the perpetrators to commit themselves to certain death? What cause or purpose motivated them to make the ultimate sacrifice? Commentators and experts have advanced various hypotheses. These people are Islamic fundamentalists who are determined to destabilize the United States for political reasons, say some. The individuals, say others, are responding to the call for a Jihad against the impure and against the excesses of Western society. Islamists have attacked the American way of life. Yossef Bodansky suggests that:

> Followers of the Ayatollah Khomeini in Iran view the United States as a land preoccupied with the adulation and worship of money, and Majid Anaraki, an Iranian who lived for several years in southern California, described the United States as a "collection of casinos, supermarkets, and whore-houses linked together by endless highways passing through nowhere, all dominated and motivated by the lust for money."[63]

Still others speculate that the motivation is to draw attention to the plight of the Palestinians. Many theories abound.

"Poverty", Mahatma Gandhi once said, "is the worst form of violence," and some have argued that terrorism is a violent response to terrible poverty. However, Stewart Bell, in his book *Cold Terror*, argues that "the root cause of Islamic terrorism is not poverty, nor is it, as Chrétien has also suggested, Western arrogance and greed—it is that a group of fanatics wants to convince Muslims that theirs is the one true faith and that it is their duty and right to take over the world by force."[64]

"Europeans prefer to say that the root cause of terrorism is poverty—or the unresolved conflict in Palestine, which they accuse Mr. Bush of having dangerously neglected during his first term."[65] President George Bush argues that the primary cause of terrorism is the failure of democracy to take root in the Middle East.

While we may never know the real motivation for such terrorist actions (indeed the individuals involved may not know clearly why they did what they did), in my view, the reasons for this type of behaviour are more profound and more fundamental. It has to do with the growing impatience and frustration of those who "don't have" with the gap between the realities of their own lives and the lives of those who "have." I believe it is derived from the classical "have/have not" tension.

Former US President Bill Clinton, in his autobiographical book, *My Life*, asserts that one of the five priorities that the United States should be pursuing is to "make more friends and fewer terrorists by helping the 50 per cent of the world not reaping the benefits of globalization to overcome poverty, ignorance, disease and bad government."[66]

We know intuitively that where there is no hope, people will turn to desperate acts. They consider they have nothing to lose—and perhaps something to gain. There are some, however, who are motivated to become a suicide bomber based exclusively on ideology. While there are no magic solutions, to the extent that rampant corruption can contribute to poverty and this feeling of despair, we should be paying attention to this problem.

CHAPTER 5

Transnational Corporations and Corruption

In speaking with MBA classes at Royal Roads University, I have frequently used a case study that I prepared for them. The scenario is as follows:

You are the newly appointed director for business development (Asia) for a major multinational telecommunications company that is very anxious to do more business in Asia, especially in Indonesia, Malaysia, and Thailand. After many months of missed business and close calls, you have presented a major proposal for business to a state-owned Indonesian company. The amounts involved are in the millions and this piece of business would put your company on the map (and would significantly accelerate your own career advancement). After many months of meetings, your company is advised that you are short-listed for the award of a contract. There is only one other company still in the running. You are called to a meeting with the executive of the Indonesian company—the individual who will essentially choose the winning bidder. You and he are the only two at the meeting. He tells you that your company can be awarded the contract but there is a catch—one million dollars would need to be deposited into a Swiss bank account of his choosing (for his personal benefit). What do you do?

This case study always results in a very interesting discussion. Something that surprises me is that many MBA students do not realize that paying the $1 million bribe would constitute a criminal act under Canadian law. Apart from the illegal nature of the bribe, some students argue that what is being requested is unethical and must be rejected—end of story. The prevailing view that emerges, however, is that the bribe should be paid as long as the multinational telecommunications company's business case can absorb a charge of this magnitude, that is, the operating profit margin after paying the $1 million will still be within an acceptable range. The argument is often made—understandably—that if their company does not pay the bribe, the other company will, or another company will be sought who will play the game.

This is the problem, or part of the problem. If international businesses as a whole do not all agree to a common code of business ethics that precludes paying bribes, there will always be some who will engage in this type of activity—to the detriment of the others. I will come back to this later. Interestingly, it is sometimes argued that corruption is a cultural matter or endemic in certain societies. Maybe so, but that doesn't make it right. It just indicates that it will be more difficult and take more time to root out. The INDEM Foundation in a 2001 report entitled *Russia Anti-corruption Diagnostics: Sociological Analysis* argues, "Corruption is little more than a social phenomenon, admittedly a very significant and harmful one." This argument, while interesting, is more a play on words than a substantive comment on what corruption really is and what havoc it can wreak. The key words here, in my opinion, are "very significant and harmful." This is the key issue that causes people like me to attempt to reduce global corruption.

What follows is an actual bribery story involving a large Canadian company. On September 17, 2002, Canadian engineering group Acres International was convicted by the Lesotho High Court of paying bribes to win contracts on a $12 billion dam project. Acres was charged with paying a bribe of nearly $266,000 to the chief executive of the Lesotho Highlands Water Project. Acres' defence was that they were not responsible for the payments to Mr. Sole as these were made via an intermediary through a "representation agreement." The judge described this arrangement as a deliberate strategy to cover up the bribe payments. Earlier in May 2002 the former chief executive of the Lesotho Highlands Water Authority was found guilty by the Lesotho High Court on 13 counts of bribery. He was convicted on 11 counts of bribery and two of fraud for accepting about £3 million in bribes over more than a decade from an array of European, Canadian, and South African firms in return for contracts worth hundreds of millions of pounds. When his trial began, the prosecution said that as the chief executive of the Lesotho Highlands Development Authority, Sole was at the centre of a web of corruption. Bribery became a standard business practice as he handed out contracts to build dams to supply water and electricity to neighbouring South Africa. The prosecution said that the chief executive of the Lesotho Highlands Water Authority maintained at least three Swiss bank accounts into which bribes were paid in sterling, French francs, German marks, and dollars. Payments by particular consortiums coincided with the awarding of contracts to those companies. According to the charges on which he was convicted, the biggest payments were made by the Lesotho Highlands Project Consortium, which was headed by the French company Spie Batignolles, which included Balfour Beatty as a partner. The prosecution said that it deposited more than £1 million into the chief executive's accounts over three years.

Acres' argument that the payments to Mr. Sole were made via an intermediary through a "representation agreement" are weak at best and dishonest at worst. Unless an agreement such as this specifically excludes the payment of bribes, there is an unwritten expectation that the "facilitator" will do whatever is required, short of overtly criminal acts, to secure the contract or project. For a company like Acres, it is a way of distancing their bid or proposal from the unsavoury aspects of doing business in corrupt countries. These practices, however, are no less defensible. To deal with corruption effectively, we need to focus on both parties to the bribe—the giver and the taker.

Corruption: Supply and Demand

Those who offer or give bribes are just as much the problem as the takers of bribes. The Organisation for Economic Development and Co-operation (OECD) recognized this and in 1997 introduced the Convention on Combating Bribery of Foreign Officials in International Business Transactions. The following year, the Corruption of Foreign Public Officials Act was passed in Canada prohibiting Canadians from bribing foreign officials in the course of doing business (domestic officials were excluded, although it is, of course, also illegal to bribe Canadian officials).

Bribery and corruption have both a demand and a supply side. It is therefore important for businesses to refuse to offer bribes. In this regard, the Canadian business community adopted an International Code of Ethics for Canadian business, which contains, amongst other things, a commitment to the following values: human rights and social justice; wealth maximization for all stakeholders; the operation of a free market economy; and, a business environment that mitigates against bribery and corruption.

At the 2005 session of the World Economic Forum in Davos, Switzerland, some 47 large multi-national corporations agreed to a pact declaring zero-tolerance against the paying of bribes. More companies are needed to sign on to this initiative, however, including mining and oil and gas companies, which were noticeably absent in the original group. This is an important development which will grow over time. Companies will need to become accountable to their zero-tolerance commitments. With concerted action and coordinated efforts, progress can be made in limiting or eliminating the supply-side of bribery and corruption.

A test for measuring how well the companies in different countries are doing in complying with this pact can be found in Transparency International's "Bribe Payers Index," which ranks countries according to their perceived levels of bribery on a scale of zero to 10 (0 representing very high levels of bribery and 10 negligible levels) as perceived by exporters. In its 1999 report, Sweden, Australia, and Canada received scores of eight or better, while Malaysia, Italy, Taiwan, South Korea, and China scored less than four.[67] More recently, Scandinavian countries have improved in their performance, Canada has slipped somewhat as result of a program scandal, and Somalia has displaced Bangladesh as the most corrupt country in the world.

In the war against drugs we often hear about the need to focus on the supply side or the demand side—or, that we need to attack both ends. Bribes are not unlike a habit-forming narcotic. Power does corrupt, and as we have heard, absolute power corrupts absolutely. In the fight against corruption, we must address those who would pay bribes and those who would accept them.

Dealing with Those Who Offer Bribes

Governments, NGOs, and the private sector are aware of the problems associated with corruption, and various initiatives have been launched over the years to battle it. How effective have they been? This is difficult if not impossible to say because corrupt activities are clandestine and there is no way to measure accurately whether the volume of corruption globally is growing or shrinking. As the eternal optimist, I would like to believe that this interest is having some impact. If nothing else, these measures should have some deterrent value. Here is a quick inventory of some of the steps taken by NGOs, international bodies, and the private sector to combat corruption.

The United Nations Convention against Corruption was adopted by the UN General Assembly on October 31, 2003. It includes measures on prevention, criminalization, international cooperation, and asset recovery. The treaty entered into force on December 14, 2005. As of January 2007 there were 140 signatories. The convention is ratified, accepted, approved, or acceded to by 83 countries, including Canada.

The 1997 OECD Convention on Bribery mentioned earlier is now signed by 35 countries and states that "enterprises should not, directly or indirectly, offer, promise, give or demand a bribe or other undue advantage to obtain or retain business." Regrettably, about a third of the signatories to this OECD convention are performing below standard (including Luxembourg, Britain, Italy, and Japan), a third is performing adequately, and a third is performing well, according to a recent assessment by the OECD. Clearly, more needs to be done to implement this convention.

The Parliament of Canada implemented its commitment to this OECD Convention in 1999, when it passed into law the necessary legislation, The Corruption of Foreign Public Officials Act. Also, in 1991, Canada ended the tax deductibility of bribes in international business transactions. Surprisingly, this practice has not been eliminated in many other countries.

The Foreign Corrupt Practices Act in the USA, which was passed in 1977, outlaws the payment of bribes by American firms to foreign officials, political parties, party officials, and candidates. However, at the rate of less than two prosecutions per year on average since the law was passed, one has to question the effectiveness of this legislation.

Member states of the Council of Europe have signed a convention on laundering, search, seizure, and confiscation of the proceeds from crime and on the financing of terrorism.

There are other initiatives designed to make payments from corporations to governments more transparent. One such effort is the Publish What You Pay campaign, a coalition of over 200 NGOs worldwide that is calling for the mandatory disclosure of the payments made by oil, gas, and mining companies to all governments to extract natural resources. This campaign was launched by George Soros and was founded by Global Witness, the Open Society Institute, Oxfam, Save the Children UK, and Transparency International UK.

Another drive has been organized by the Extractive Industries Transparency Initiative, whose objective is to "increase transparency over payments and revenues in the extractives sector in countries heavily dependent on these resources."

The Revenue Watch Institute states that its mission is to improve democratic accountability in natural resource-rich countries by equipping citizens with the information, training, networks, and funding they need to become more effective monitors of government revenues and expenditures.

Another idea has come forward from Paul Collier, an economics professor at Oxford University. He proposes that we seek the pledges of countries to have firms like Deloitte & Touche audit their natural resource revenues, and how these revenues are allocated.

While the objectives of initiatives like the Extractive Industries Transparency Initiative, Revenue Watch, and the idea proposed by Paul Collier are laudable, it is hard to imagine what positive results the Publish What You Pay initiative can practically achieve. Amounts paid to developing countries for royalties and resource rents are one thing. Such disclosures might be more readily forthcoming and useful. But what would motivate corporations or individuals to disclose amounts they have paid to governments, government officials, or elected individuals in the form of bribes or "facilitation fees"? Likewise, what would motivate government officials or elected individuals to disclose these same payments? I have witnessed first hand the negative reaction from the leader of a corrupt nation to this proposition. Corporate leaders will react the same way if they are involved in bribes and corruption. What do they have to gain by disclosing amounts they have paid in bribes?

Instead, governments must act to prevent corruption, and parliamentarians are increasingly involving themselves in the fight against bribery, corruption, and money laundering.

Parliamentarians understand first hand the destabilizing influence of bribery and corruption, and the economic costs associated with it. All they have to do is listen to their citizens and taxpayers. Parliamentarians understand also how the financing of terrorism is a threat to international security. Governments must be held more accountable by parliamentarians and legislate whatever is required, respecting the privacy and human rights of citizens, to stamp out corruption, terrorist financing, and money laundering. Parliamentarians can work together and with multilateral organizations find the solutions to these very difficult problems.

Elected officials have a large responsibility to take steps to ensure that bribery and corruption are not accepted as societal norms. This can be accomplished in a number of ways. First and foremost, they must lead by example; that is, as elected people, they should reject bribery and corruption and refuse to be a party to it. Elected officials can take a number of other steps—for example by ensuring that public servants are paid an adequate wage and have reasonable job security—so they can have the confidence to reject bribes. In some countries, such salaries and wages are kept deliberately low because public servants are expected to take bribes. This approach has to stop. Citizens are paying for this either way—either as an "on-site" user fee or as a general tax.

There are also many ways in which parliamentarians can demand greater accountability from the executive branch of government. While it is true that legislators are not immune from corruption, it is typically the executive branch of government (the president, prime minister, and cabinet ministers) that is more prone to be corrupt. After all, these are the individuals who have the primary decision-making responsibilities in their respective governments. Those outside of government seeking favours and personal advantage know this and will, from time to time, attempt to bribe these individuals to influence decisions in their favour. It is the role of parliament to hold the executive branch of government accountable and this is why parliamentarians have a very important role to play in the fight against corruption.

In my work with the Global Organization of Parliamentarians Against Corruption (GOPAC), I have had the opportunity to meet many parliamentarians who are committed to the fight against corruption—some at great personal risk and cost. I recall, in particular, a Zimbabwean member of parliament who is active in exposing the corrupt activities of the Mugabe regime and who is dragged off to jail most weekends for questioning. To her credit, she is continuing the fight.

It has become apparent to me that many parliamentarians do not fully appreciate the powers they have to fight corruption in their respective jurisdictions. Admittedly in some jurisdictions it is easier than in others. Often party discipline is very strict in a number of developing countries, making it very difficult for members on the side of the government to raise questions about corrupt activities of their own ministers. Parliament typically controls the purse strings of governments and it is in this role in particular that legislators can exert their pressure. Parliaments also pass laws and this is another way parliamentarians can influence the direction their countries take, by legislating against corruption and money laundering, and stipulating appropriate sanctions. To make this work, however, the judiciary of the country must be above reproach and free from corruption. Many parliaments and governments have established anti-corruption commissions or agencies—with varying degrees of success. To achieve success, these bodies need the complete support of the government (executive branch) and this is not always forthcoming. Steps and measures are sometimes taken to give the impression that the government is interested and is acting when often the reverse is true.

One place where action is being taken, however, is South Africa. The Republic of South Africa has developed an interesting model for ensuring enforcement of anti-corruption measures: the Scorpions. This group, created in 2001, is a multi-disciplinary agency that investigates and prosecutes organized crime and corruption. With a staff of some 2,000, it is a unit of the National Prosecuting Authority of South Africa. By February 2004, the Scorpions had completed 653 cases, including 380 prosecutions, of which 349 resulted in convictions—a highly successful conviction rate of 93.1 per cent! When I visited South Africa in September 2006, the anecdotal evidence gleaned from conversations with average citizens was that the Scorpions were serving a useful purpose and were achieving results. Even Jabob Zuma, the newly elected leader of the African National Congress and heir apparent to President Mbeki, has recently been charged with fraud, tax evasion, and money laundering.

In Canada, our parliament is designed along the lines of the parliament in Great Britain (the Westminster model), which means we have an emphasis on party discipline. Notwithstanding this, I was able to introduce in the Parliament of Canada, initially against the wishes of my own government, Bill C-212, An Act Respecting User Fees. After a two-year debate, my private member's bill was enacted by parliament and brought into force in March 2004. The intent of this legislation is to bring greater transparency and accountability and parliamentary oversight to federal government departments and agencies when they attempt to recover costs through user fees.

User fees take many different forms and are meant to defray some or all of the costs of a service provided by government presumably in the public interest, but which also provides a specific service to the client (for example licence fees, registrations, etc.). In 2003/4 these user fees amounted to approximately $6 billion across the entire federal government. These fees, while not taxes per se, are akin to taxes and they are priced by monopolies. If you want a new drug approved in Canada one can't shop around for the best deal—you are obliged to work with Health Canada. Likewise, if you want a Canadian passport you must deal with the Department of Foreign Affairs.

I have always pointed out that I support the federal government's objective to recover costs through user fees for private goods or proprietary services. The focus of my private member's bill was:

► The need for more parliamentary oversight when user fees are introduced or changed;
► The need for greater stakeholder participation in the fee-setting process;
► Improved linkages between user fees, and federal department and agency performance specifications and standards;
► The requirement for more comprehensive stakeholder impact and competitiveness analysis when new user fees, or fee increases, are contemplated;
► The goal of increased transparency with respect to why fees are applicable, what fees are charged, what costs are identified as recoverable, and whether performance standards are being met;
► The need for an independent dispute resolution process to address the complaints or grievances of the payers of user fees;
► The need for an annual report outlining all user fees in effect that would be tabled in the House of Commons, and referred to the appropriate Committee of the House (Finance).

I believe my bill will accomplish these objectives, and at the time of writing, federal government departments and agencies were in the process of implementing the spirit, intent, and letter of this new law of Canada. This legislation somewhat limits the ability of the executive branch of government, and at the same time it empowers parliamentarians. Small steps are sometimes needed to accomplish the overall mission. Parliamentarians can make a difference.

In 2007, on behalf of GOPAC, I met with the International Public Sector Accounting Standards Board at their meeting in Montreal and asked them to demand more transparency of natural resource revenues in the public accounts of nations and sub-national governments. If acted upon, this would better hold governments to account for these sizeable revenues. This idea builds on the so-called revenue curse which recognizes that for many developing countries there is a heavy dependency on natural resource development and a corresponding risk that these revenues might be prey to corruption.

For the Thirteenth Annual Session of the Organization for Security and Cooperation in Europe (OSCE) Parliamentary Assembly in July 2005 in Washington, DC, I presented a resolution addressed to the problem of money laundering, as well as the following one, which addressed corruption. Both these resolutions were strongly encouraged and supported by the United States Senator from Maryland, Hon. Benjamin L. Cardin, in his capacity as the then Chair of the General Committee on Economic Affairs, Science, Technology and Environment of the Parliamentary Assembly of the OSCE.

This OSCE Parliamentary Assembly Resolution on the fight against corruption made the following declaration:

- ▶ Urges parliamentarians of the OSCE participating States to strengthen their efforts to combat corruption and the conditions that foster it;
- ▶ Urges the parliaments of OSCE participating States, which have not yet done so, to ratify the United Nations Convention against Corruption as soon as possible, in order to ensure its rapid entry into force, and implement it fully;
- ▶ Calls upon parliamentarians of participating States to promote a positive framework for good governance and public integrity
- ▶ Urges parliaments of participating States to make better use of existing international instruments and assist each other in their fight against corruption;
- ▶ Recommends that parliaments of participating States promote the best practices against corruption identified by the OSCE's Office of the Co-ordinator for Economic and Environmental Activities;
- ▶ Urges parliaments of participating States to adopt clear and balanced legislative procedures for waiving parliamentary immunities, and to support the establishment of efficient mechanisms for

monitoring declarations of income and assets by parliamentarians, ministers, and public servants; and

▶ Recommends that the General Committee on Economic Affairs, Science, Technology, and Environment collaborate with other parliamentary associations and the Global Organization of Parliamentarians against Corruption in developing a program for parliamentary action against corruption and a document describing the role of parliamentarians in the fight against corruption.

I was encouraged by the fact that both resolutions were passed. We are continuing to follow up to ensure that these resolutions don't die on the vine but become living, breathing documents.

Laws, treaties, and resolutions are one thing, but it is action that will turn the tide against bribery and corruption. Shining more light on the problem will assist in making government actions more transparent. We should also never underestimate the role that individual parliamentarians can play in holding their governments accountable. Results can be achieved if there is political will. Without that, much of the work is mere window dressing. The time for action is now.

CHAPTER 6

Money Laundering

Money laundering is a technique for making illegally obtained funds accessible for the personal use of perpetrators without being traceable back to their illicit source—often by transferring the funds across international borders to legitimate financial institutions. It is estimated that worldwide money laundering approaches $1 trillion per year (about the same size as Canada's entire GDP). In a recently published book, *Money Laundering in Canada*,[68] the authors argue at length that there is no reliable way to estimate the volume of money laundered internationally or domestically, and that there is no evidence that anti-money-laundering legislation, policies, and regimes are having any impact in reducing money laundering. It seems to me, however, that if you can't measure money laundered volumes, it is impossible to measure the impact of anti-money-laundering initiatives. Everything can't be measured. Focusing on the proceeds of crime and the laundering of money is an important piece in the fight against crime, terrorism, and corruption.

Parliamentarians I have met from around the world who are concerned about corruption, and fighting to do something about it, view money laundering as inextricably linked to the challenge of reducing or eliminating corruption. The proceeds from corruption and other crimes are often laundered to make the funds more accessible to the perpetrators. Corruption is often associated with organized crime and, increasingly, terrorism.

In my work on the fight against corruption and money laundering, parliamentarians in corrupt countries have pointed out on a number of occasions that they understand the need for, and they are committed to, the fight against corruption, but they cannot help but become dismayed and discouraged when they witness the unimpeded flight of corrupt funds from their country to safe havens. They are right to be concerned because it is only by fighting both corruption and money-laundering activities that any success can be achieved. Slowing down or eliminating the laundering of corrupt money will serve as a serious disincentive to corrupt activities.

Effective anti-money-laundering regimes have the effect of constraining corrupt activities by reducing the outlets and means to benefit from these crimes. The chain, however, is only as strong as its weakest link, and this is why it is important for all countries to implement effective anti-money-laundering regimes. As the minister of finance for Swaziland, the Honourable Majozi Sithole pointed out at a 2003 conference: "Money laundering can only be fully addressed by countries collectively, as criminals operate without regard to national boundaries. Any weak links in the anti-money-laundering chain will be exploited."[69]

Those who launder money use many different techniques. In a 2004 study of RCMP "proceeds of crime" cases in Canada,[70] the use of nominees[71] ranked as the number one method for laundering money; this was followed by legitimate revenue (laundering money through legitimate businesses); layering (creating various layers of financial and commercial transactions); smurfing (spreading cash across different accounts); structuring (a variation of smurfing); undervaluing assets; use of fraudulent information/alias; internal conspiracy/corruption; and others.

In the late 1990s, the OECD launched an initiative to fight harmful tax competition. This initiative originally began as an attack on offshore banking centres like those found in the Bahamas, Switzerland, Luxembourg, and other locations. Countries in Europe were also concerned that tax subsidies offered by countries to attract new investment were creating a race to the bottom. They were worried that companies would shop around for the best economic incentive package that various jurisdictions might offer, and in the competition to win the new investment, government revenues would be severely reduced. The other concern was focused on the growing trend for funds in the industrialized economies of member countries of the OECD to find their way to offshore banking centres as a means of evading taxes.

Once it became clear that it was difficult, if not impossible, to determine what level of taxation, per se, was competitively harmful, the focus of this exercise shifted to a demand for greater transparency from the offshore banking centres, or tax havens. It is difficult, for example, to make a reasonable assessment of whether or not the rates of taxation in a country like Ireland, where corporate and individual income tax rates are low, are harmful and non-competitive. It may well be that the rates in Ireland are set at a very appropriate level, and those in other countries in the industrialized world set at levels that are too high. It is fair, however, to insist on greater transparency and better disclosure of financial information so that those taxpayers that are suspected of evading taxes in their home country can be examined and the structure of their financial holdings and transactions can be subjected to greater scrutiny.

Achieving greater transparency in tax havens is a daunting task, however. Countries like Switzerland have built their reputations on the confidentiality of client information. Recent interest in terrorist-financing activities has had the result of improving tax haven transparency. Over the years, I have found that whenever I have spoken to groups of parliamentarians about the need to fight corruption and money laundering, the subject has generated much interest and subsequent follow-up. The most vociferous sceptics of plans to fight money laundering are those elected individuals from jurisdictions like Luxembourg and Switzerland—countries that benefit greatly from their respective banking communities. Needless to say, they are opposed to further anti-corruption measures and make great attempts to describe the measures their countries have implemented to combat money laundering. In one sense, they are correct: Since 9/11, offshore banking centres and tax havens have been co-operating more fully with law enforcement agencies and intelligence operations.

Recent interest in terrorist-financing activities, however, has had the result of forcing an improvement in tax haven transparency. Proceeds from crime—especially drug trafficking funds—elicit greater cooperation from tax haven authorities. It is more difficult, however, to induce tax havens to be more forthcoming with information when tax evasion and corrupt activities are the primary concern—but progress is being made.

This lack of co-operation makes the tracing corrupt funds a daunting task since the audit trail in most cases is highly complex and convoluted. The problem is compounded by the fact that what is considered a corrupt activity in one country may not be considered such in another country. After the break-up of the former Soviet Union in the early 1990s, Russia embarked on an aggressive program of privatization. Many of these privatizations were corrupt by Western standards. Certain individuals and groups, or so-called political elites, were provided with advantages in the privatization processes. The executive branch of the Russian government sanctioned these processes. Should the funds that eventually flowed offshore (some to Canada) from the profits of these "bent" privatizations be considered corrupt funds? The criterion used in Canada's anti-money-laundering regime is that money can only be considered proceeds from crime if the offence is a criminal offence under the laws of Canada. So would the proceeds from a bent privatization in Russia qualify? While there are no easy answers, the vast majority of laundering activities associated with illicit drugs, terrorist activities, and corrupt practices are defined similarly as criminal acts in different jurisdictions.

Of course, even when the laws are clear, exposing corruption and prosecuting money laundering becomes almost impossible when those indulging in illegal activities are the leaders of a state.

Politically Exposed Persons

Corruption fostered by politically-exposed persons (PEPs) such as politicians and bureaucrats has the potential of perpetuating global corruption. With access to vast amounts of profits and with the co-operation of institutions such as offshore banks, these individuals are frequently able to evade compliance with anti-money-laundering laws.

When corruption reaches into government, it becomes difficult to expose the guilty politicians or high-ranking officials who are illegally enriching themselves at the expense of the development of their state. In addition to the challenge for law enforcement posed by politically exposed persons caught up in potential money-laundering operations, it is often difficult for legislatures to enact legislation that addresses corruption and money laundering—because parliamentarians may realize that they could be exposing their own wrongful acts by voting for a particular piece of legislation.

The steps followed by these corrupt individuals in laundering their ill-gotten gains usually follows a set pattern, beginning with the movement of large amounts of illegal funds into trust accounts.[72] This is followed by the creation of companies to provide a layer of obscurity, as well as the naming of nominee directors, who contribute nothing to the company, and are used, instead, to issue money to the true beneficial owner.[73]

Another strategy involves three phases. The first is the placement step, which involves putting the funds generated from a crime into a financial system either directly or indirectly.[74] The second involves layering, which involves a complex network of financial services and trusts where multiple transactions are used to eliminate an audit trail.[75] Finally, there is the integration stage, in which politically exposed persons take the successfully obscured funds and put them back into the economy as legitimate funds.[76]

Money laundering can also cause corruption to bleed into banking institutions, which in some cases aid corrupt leaders. Such was the case with the Chilean dictator Augusto Pinochet, who illegally profited from his citizens with the help of Riggs Bank in the United States. The practice of institutions such as banks turning a blind eye to how some of their wealthiest customers obtain their fortunes allowed for the corrupt dealings of Pinochet to continue, long after his term in office.

Riggs began its banking relationship with Pinochet in 1979; this relationship lasted until 2004. Throughout Pinochet's alleged crimes against humanity, Riggs helped the tyrant set up two offshore corporations in the Bahamas which allowed him to open corporate accounts in order to provide him with easy access to his money.[77] Despite the fact that Pinochet had international arrest warrants issued for him that ordered all bank accounts be terminated, Riggs continued to open accounts in the name of Pinochet's Bahamian corporations.[78] In December of 2001, media outlets began advertising Riggs' relationship with Pinochet, citing the fact that the bank was holding over $1 million in a bank account for him. Riggs, in response, altered the names on the personal account, deleting any reference to Pinochet in the titled holder of the account and prevented any electronic searching or tracking of his account and finances.[79] After more than two decades of aiding Pinochet's scandals, Riggs decided, in 2002, to close his accounts, sending $6 million directly to Pinochet.[80]

As well as aiding dictator Pinochet, Riggs continued to aid corruption in the developing world by ignoring its obligations under the anti-money-laundering laws in its banking institutions in Equatorial Guinea. Riggs managed one of the most corrupt banking institutions in the developing world, allowing suspicious transactions to take place without notifying authorities. This included having the Equatorial Guinea president bring in suitcases of banknotes worth

US $13 million without accounting for its origin, and allowing Riggs' bank managers to profit over $1 million in oil revenues. The growing scrutiny surrounding the bank's dealings eventually led to Riggs closing all of its Equatorial Guinea accounts in February 2004.

Further scrutiny of the bank's operations eventually resulted in Riggs Bank, a venerable institution that dated back to 1836, becoming involved in one the America's highest-profile investigations involving money laundering.[81] This eventually led to record fines being imposed on the bank for its unlawful actions and the eventual sale of the bank to PNC Financial Services Group Pittsburgh.[82]

Although money is often laundered through banks, corrupt money can also be laundered in a variety of other, ingenious ways. In the April 10, 2004, edition of the *National Post*, it was reported that Zimbabwe's finance minister, Christopher Kuruneri, was building a 10,000-square-foot home in an exclusive area just outside of Cape Town, South Africa. The cost of the house was estimated at $6 million once completed. "Among the many interesting aspects of this tale is that Mr. Kuruneri is responsible for Zimbabwe's foreign currency laws, which place strict limits on the export of the country's limited supply."[83] Of course, the finance minister argued that he was building this home using funds that he accumulated in the private sector before his election—funds that stayed outside of Zimbabwe and were therefore not subject to the foreign currency rules. Not a totally implausible story, but one that was at odds with the rumour that the house was actually being built for his boss, Robert Mugabe.

In a 2004 study of RCMP "proceeds of crime" case files, it was shown that although deposit institutions were the predominant recipient of the proceeds of crime, other sectors were also implicated including the insurance industry, motor vehicle and real estate dealers, criminal companies, currency exchange dealers, marine vessel dealers, jewellery/gems/gold/coin dealers, the security industry, and other sectors (e.g. casinos and lotteries).[84]

In summary, money laundering is a big business that is growing as criminals, terrorists, and corrupt leaders increasingly try to hide the true source of their nefarious activities. Money launderers are very creative in the ways they launder their proceeds of crime. And there is no sector of the economy that is immune. Without effective anti-money-laundering legislation, policies, sanctions, and an adequately resourced financial intelligence unit, criminal elements will not be constrained in the ways in which they distribute their illegal proceeds. There is a very real deterrent value to effective anti-money laundering-initiatives. We will now turn our attention to this aspect.

Anti-Money-Laundering Initiatives

The central focus of anti-money-laundering initiatives (AMLI) is to reduce the motivation for economic crimes by making it more difficult for criminals to access the proceeds of their illegal activities. AMLI are important to discourage the supply of funds to international terrorists and criminals. Impeding the international flow of such funds reduces the means available to terrorists and criminals, and identifying their sources discourages their funders.

The principal global initiative to reduce money laundering to date has been the formation of the Financial Action Task Force on Money Laundering (FATF). Formed in 1991 by the G-7, FATF is an inter-governmental body whose purpose is to develop and promote policies to combat money laundering. FATF is closely associated with the OECD and its members, and its secretariat is located in the OECD offices in Paris. The FATF currently consists of 29 countries and two international organizations. Its membership includes the major financial centre countries of Europe, North and South America, and Asia. It recommends 40 actions—recently updated—for governments. These policies aim to prevent such proceeds from being utilized in future criminal activities and from affecting legitimate economic interests. Most OECD countries have accepted these.

The recommendations include:

► Making money laundering a crime;

► Requiring financial institutions to: know their clients; maintain records; and exercise due diligence regarding suspicious transactions;

► Requiring governments to: monitor cross-border transport of cash and report aggregate flows to the IMF and BIS (Bank for International Settlement); ensure financial institutions have appropriate capacity; and cooperate internationally on information, investigation and prosecution.

FATF has a peer review process to assess the degree and quality of member's compliance with its recommendations.

Parliamentarians, knowing that accountability promotes transparency and good governance, are now coming together to form an organization to combat, and speak out, against corrupt activities. The Global Organization of Parliamentarians Against Corruption (GOPAC) was founded in 2002 at a conference hosted by the Canadian House of Commons and Senate. GOPAC has over 700 members around the world, organized into regional and national chapters. This organization is the umbrella organization to motivate, support, and organize regional chapters around the world such as North American Parliamentarians Against Corruption (NAPAC), Latin American Parliamentarians Against Corruption (LAPAC) Southeast Asian Parliamentarians Against Corruption (SEAPAC), African Parliamentarians Network Against Corruption (APNAC), Arab Region Parliamentarians Against Corruption (ARPAC), Caribbean Parliamentarians Against Corruption (CaribPAC), European Parliamentarians Against Corruption (EPAC), North East Asian Parliamentarians Against Corruption (NEAPAC), and Newly Independent States Parliamentarians Against Corruption (NISPAC). Other chapters are being formed on a regular basis.

A chapter has also been formed in the Russian Federation named Parliamentarians for Parliamentary Control. In fact, a few years ago, a colleague of mine from the House of Commons in Canada, John

Williams, and I met with members of the State Duma in Russia on the topic of governance; and this dialogue is continuing amongst parliamentarians and with Canada's auditor general and Russia's Accounts Chamber. The Canadian International Development Agency (CIDA) through the Parliamentary Centre in Canada is supporting this work.

The mandate of the regional chapter of GOPAC in North America, North American Parliamentarians Against Corruption, or NAPAC, is to:

▶ Build the capacity of parliaments to exercise accountability with a particular emphasis on financial matters;
▶ Share information with international parliamentarians about lessons learned and best practices;
▶ Undertake projects and organize workshops focused on reducing corruption and promoting good governance; and
▶ Cooperate with International Financial Institutions (IFIs) and organizations in civil society to build on current information and research that is applicable to parliamentarians.

GOPAC has identified the fight against money laundering as a priority of the organization. I have been asked to lead this initiative by bringing together a team of 12 or so parliamentarians from around the world—those interested in fighting money laundering.

The objectives of this initiative are:

▶ To engage parliamentarians from around the world in the anti-money laundering (AML) agenda by developing a better understanding of how money laundering occurs and launching an international initiative to combat it; and
▶ To build political support to effectively implement practical mechanisms to combat money laundering.

The ultimate result that GOPAC is seeking to extend the anti-money-laundering regime beyond its current focus—principally in Europe and North America—and to develop effective strategies that parliamentarians can execute (e.g. promotion of international treaties) to combat money laundering.

The GOPAC team will work with AML experts and organizations (such as FATF) associated with the OECD and the International Monetary Fund to develop an approach to combating money laundering and promote its practical implementation.

GOPAC's approach to building integrity in governance is to bring together political will and expertise to empower parliamentarians in all countries. Such an approach, especially on a matter where there are regional differences and sensitivities, takes time to develop the necessary understanding, build consensus, and guide implementation.

GOPAC proposes, therefore, to begin by ensuring that the team fully understands the current international approach and its implications before beginning to assess the impediments and special features of their regions that could hinder or require adjustments prior to implementation. These will be documented for discussion and resolution. After such background work, the team will shift its focus to developing a coherent global strategy that is sensitive to these differences and develop an approach to implementing a global AML regime. This includes developing tools and supporting materials for parliamentarians. The final step is communicating the approach internationally, including through GOPAC. We anticipate that GOPAC would formally adopt the approach and lead its implementation.

The work will proceed through four distinct stages, beginning with an orientation and training session for the parliamentarians who are members of the GOPAC anti-money-laundering task force. This will be followed by the development of position papers. A report will be prepared with a set of anti-money-laundering initiatives for parliamentarians, together with a set of tools designed for parliamentarians to accomplish these objectives. The final phase will be the discussion and adoption of the report at a global conference of GOPAC.

FATF is the recognized source of expertise on money launder-ing. Our GOPAC project, accordingly, will establish arrangements with FATF in order to benefit from its expertise and advice. Where individual governments are willing to provide access to their experts, the project will use such services as needed. In addition, individual experts will be retained on contract to undertake needed tasks and draft the planned reports.

Parliamentarians can play a vital role through their influence on legislation, by vigorous oversight of government activity and support of parliamentary auditors, and perhaps most effectively through per-sonal leadership. They can engage the public and help build the polit-ical will to act. However, to do so, they must understand how money laundering occurs and the mechanisms for its mitigation. They also need the support of recognized experts and a global voice. GOPAC provides the global voice and the proposed Anti-Money-Laundering Initiative can help provide the understanding and expertise.

AMLI and Anti-Terrorism Initiatives

Canada's parliament ratified the United Nations International Con-vention for the Suppression of the Financing of Terrorism with the enactment in December 2001 of an anti-terrorism bill. As parlia-mentary secretary to Canada's minister of finance from 1999 to 2001, I had the responsibility and honour to shepherd our government's anti-money-laundering legislation through our parliament. This leg-islation, the Proceeds of Crime (Money Laundering) and Terrorist Financing Act, initially enacted in 2000, led to the creation of Cana-da's anti-money-laundering agency, the Financial Transactions and Reports Analysis Centre (FINTRAC), which started up in Novem-ber 2001. FINTRAC is currently monitoring any suspicious finan-cial transactions, as defined by regulation and guidelines. In October

2001, FINTRAC was given added responsibilities and resources to combat the financing of terrorist activities in Canada. Canada is now largely compliant with the anti-terrorism financing standards announced by the Financial Action Task Force, the G-7 institution that combats money laundering.

When enacting Canada's anti-money-laundering regime, the government's attitude was that the reporting of transactions should extend to all financial intermediaries and all possible parties who might be involved in money-laundering transactions, including banks, foreign exchange dealers, accountants, lawyers, and many other categories. The view was, and is, that any groups that were exempted would become a natural target for money launderers.

However, these initiatives have not been without controversy. The anti-money-laundering legislation raised a number of concerns with respect to privacy issues, which had to be dealt with very sensitively. The anti-terrorism legislation raised the ire of many who believed, and still believe, that their human rights were infringed upon. This is the careful work that legislators must perform in order to achieve a balance between these sometimes competing objectives.

Measuring results and evaluating the effectiveness of FINTRAC is a daunting task, but one that must be pursued. It is a difficult task to link data supplied from FINTRAC to law enforcement agencies in Canada, to ultimate arrests and convictions. With the passage of time, more of this will be able to be done; however, the connections are in some cases tenuous.

Also in 2001, the G-20 finance ministers and central bank governors, led by Canada, agreed to an Action Plan on Terrorist Financing at their meeting in Ottawa on November 17, 2001. This plan commits member nations to:

► Implement the relevant United Nations Security Council Resolutions and Conventions to freeze terrorist assets and stop the financing of terrorism;
► Work with international bodies to promote the adoption, imple-

mentation and assessment of standards to combat abuses of the financial system, including terrorist financing and money laundering;

▶ Provide technical assistance to countries that need help in developing and implementing necessary laws, regulations and policies to combat terrorist financing and money laundering; and

▶ Establish Financial Intelligence Units and facilitate the exchange of information on terrorist financing and money laundering.

These plans have largely been implemented by the G-20 countries.

In July 2005, I presented the following resolution against money laundering at the Thirteenth Annual Session of the Organization for Security and Cooperation in Europe (OSCE) Parliamentary Assembly in Washington, DC. This resolution was adopted by the OSCE Parliamentary Assembly.

The OSCE Parliamentary Assembly:

▶ Urges parliaments of participating States, which have not yet done so, to adopt anti-money laundering laws along the framework developed in the FATF 40 Recommendations, and consistent with the United Nations Office on Drugs and Crime Model Money-Laundering, Proceeds of Crime and Terrorist Financing Bill 2003;

▶ Calls upon parliaments of participating States to ensure that adopted legislations are expeditiously enforced, and that the enforcement is adequately monitored by parliamentary bodies;

▶ Encourages parliamentarians to participate in the efforts made by parliamentary associations and international organizations such as the Global Organization of Parliamentarians against Corruption in the fight against money laundering; and

▶ Recommends that the General Committee on Economic Affairs, Science, Technology, and Environment collaborate with FATF in identifying parliaments of participating States that have not adopted adequate anti-money-laundering laws, or do not have the appropriate tools to monitor the efficient implementation of anti-money laundering laws, and report annually to the Parliamentary Assembly.

Realistically, resolutions like this one are largely symbolic but they are important nonetheless because the debate on, and approval of, these proposals focus the attention of parliamentarians, the media, and the general public on the nature of the problem and they serve as a call for action. The objective is to place money laundering on the public policy radar and agenda.

In Mexico City, on March 2–3, 2006, the Global Organization of Parliamentarians Against Corruption (GOPAC) and the Senate of Mexico hosted an Anti-Money-Laundering Training (AML) workshop for Latin American and Caribbean parliamentarians. This seminar brought together parliamentarians from across the Latin American and Caribbean region to the Senate of Mexico (Mexico City) for a two-day capacity building seminar on anti-money-laundering initiatives and combating the financing of terrorism. The seminar was funded by the Canadian Department of Foreign Affairs, Human Security Program, and Scotiabank, and was hosted by the Senate of Mexico. Under the leadership of Senator César Jauregui and me, and with contributions from a number of technical experts, parliamentarians undertook discussions on anti-corruption, AMLI and Financing of Terrorism (FT), and the role/importance of parliamentarians, as well as a comprehensive approach to the UN international treaties and conventions and FATF recommendations. The emphasis of the program on the one hand was on improving the understanding on the part of parliamentarians of money laundering, its impacts, and international and national initiatives in the region to combat it. On the other hand, it was to develop an understanding of what parliamentarians could do to help combat money laundering.

The result we were seeking from the seminar was to have participants develop and propose an action plan for the Latin American and Caribbean regions for consideration by the Latin American Parliamentarians Against Corruption (LAPAC) and the Caribbean Parliamentarians Against Corruption (CaribPAC) chapters, and if accepted, implemented by those chapters.

Participants concluded that the best way to achieve this result would be to develop a single resolution proposing a series of actions at both the global and regional levels. The resolution produced by the end of the seminar was signed by nearly all of the parliamentary participants present.

The resolution adopted by the participants from the GOPAC Anti-Money Laundering Seminar for Latin American and Caribbean Parliamentarians:

▶ Recognising that the fight against money laundering is common to all countries of the world and that the fight against money laundering needs to be global in nature;

▶ Recognising that money laundering is a problem that affects the democratic system and social and economic development of all our countries;

▶ Recognising the need to create common standards, adopt best practices and encourage cooperation amongst states and financial institutions;

▶ Recognising that the fight against money laundering needs to be assumed preferably by parliamentarians and parliaments of the Latin American and Caribbean region;

▶ Recognising that the Inter-American Convention Against Corruption does not specifically address money laundering.

Resolve to:
▶ Strongly encourage the Global Organisation of Parliamentarians Against Corruption (GOPAC) Anti-Money-Laundering Initiative, to work with experts in the field to create an international treaty which when adopted would ensure harmonization of AML legislation throughout the world;

► Such a treaty would incorporate standardized best practices from around the world;

► Work with organizations such as GOPAC, LAPAC, CaribPAC and their associated organizations to build political will to fight corruption and money laundering and implement common international strategies;

► Work with organizations such as International Compliance Association, Financial Action Task Force and their associated organizations on increasing the technical capacity to fight corruption and money laundering;

► Work with parliamentarians from across the globe to raise awareness amongst citizens and the media of the harmful effects of the crime of money laundering and corruption and the role of parliamentarians in reducing the problem;

► Legislate to achieve the recovery of the proceeds of these illegal activities;

► Recommend a review of the Inter-American Convention Against Corruption to include a more explicit acknowledgment of the need to implement anti money laundering regimes;

► Investigate including corruption and the laundering of money as international crimes.

The resolutions that were adopted in Mexico City were important in themselves but what was equally powerful was the media coverage of the event. The efforts of Senator César Jauregui of Mexico paid off as the national and local media provided extensive coverage of our meetings in Mexico City and the passing of the resolution. This type of media attention raises the level of consciousness of the public of the level of corruption and money laundering, and also of the remedies that are needed to address these related problems. Public awareness usually results in pressure on elected officials and a call to action. If nothing else, when parliamentarians convene to discuss corruption and money laundering, a more knowledgeable public results and citizens become more engaged in the issues.

With respect to the specific resolutions adopted in Mexico City, three require some elaboration. The first resolution calls for GOPAC to investigate the adoption of an international treaty on money laundering that would lead to a harmonization of anti-money-laundering initiatives worldwide. Money launderers move their activities into those jurisdictions where the anti-money-laundering legislation and enforcement is weak. An international treaty or convention, with the means to enforce, could go some way to closing these gaps.

As a follow-up to the meeting in Mexico City, GOPAC has drafted an international treaty on money laundering for consideration by its members. However, in negotiating an international convention, there is a danger that the standards that FATF is striving to have adopted worldwide will be weakened to fit the lowest common denominator. Clearly, this would be counterproductive and is to be avoided at all costs. In this regard, the FATF needs to broaden and extend its influence so that all countries will employ the needed international anti-money-laundering standards.

In Mexico City, parliamentarians resolved to legislate to recover the proceeds of corrupt activities that have been laundered to conceal their source. This is becoming a bigger issue, and one where expertise is developing quickly. GOPAC is pursuing this with the offshore and international banking community.

GOPAC has concluded that designating corruption and money laundering as international crimes against humanity, while perhaps laudable in its intent, may be over-reaching and very difficult to achieve. While it is true that the impact on citizens of corruption and money laundering are very negative and pervasive, it may not be possible or appropriate to put these crimes on a par with genocide and mass murder.

The resolutions which follow were adopted at the 2nd Global Conference of the Global Organization of Parliamentarians Against Corruption (GOPAC) that was held in Arusha, Tanzania, September 20–23, 2006. This very successful conference had approximately 300 individuals in attendance—mostly parliamentarians from around the world and members of GOPAC. The conference was organized into eight working groups. I had the honour to chair the anti-money-laundering workshop, so the resolution that was adopted by this working group (task force) is presented here also.

2nd Global Conference, Arusha, Tanzania
CONFERENCE DECLARATION

The Global Organization of Parliamentarians Against Corruption held its 2nd global conference in Arusha, Tanzania, from September 20–23rd. At that conference the delegates, after vigorous debate and discussion, set out a clear vision for the organization.

GOPAC is an organisation committed to leadership for results and has resolved to set up global task forces to energize the debate on issues such as:

Parliamentary Oversight
Parliamentary Immunity
Codes of Conduct for Parliamentarians
Access to Information and Media
International Conventions Against Corruption
Anti Money Laundering
Resource Revenue Transparency
Development Assistance Loans and Grants

GOPAC is speaking to the world, saying that these serious political issues need to be addressed. We are prepared to address them.

We call on all governments and other organizations who are committed to good governance, improved prosperity and better lives for their citizens and society to join forces with GOPAC to achieve these objectives.

The anti-money-laundering resolution adopted in Arusha, Tanzania, committed GOPAC to the following:

- ► To extend the GOPAC global Task Force of GOPAC members to guide this work and advise the GOPAC Executive of further steps needed as well as how this can complement Control of Terrorist Financing initiatives;
- ► To encourage training of parliamentarians in all chapters to expose larger numbers of parliamentarians to the issues and steps governments and parliamentarians need to take—based on the pilot training initiatives GOPAC has undertaken in cooperation with the World Bank, the International Monetary Fund, and the International Compliance Association;
- ► To develop awareness amongst GOPAC members of the FATF 40 + 9 recommendations;
- ► To seek "observer" status in the FATF;
- ► To examine the benefits of drafting and encouraging the adoption of an International Convention Against Money Laundering while encouraging countries to ratify and implement the UN Convention Against Corruption;
- ► That GOPAC begin dialogue with the offshore and international banking community to: (a) better understand what the community is doing to fight money laundering and the financing of terrorism, and; (b) develop protocols specifically on fighting the laundering and the recovery of corrupt money and assets.

The GOPAC resolutions adopted in Arusha, Tanzania, in September 2006 were most encouraging and covered the full landscape of the problems and issues. For each of the eight working groups (now task forces), an action plan is being developed, resources are being sought, and results are expected when GOPAC hosts its Third Global Conference in late 2008 in the Middle East. As I have been asked to lead the task force on money laundering, I have chosen to focus on the resolutions of this working group that were adopted unanimously in Arusha.

With these resolutions, GOPAC has committed itself to creating awareness amongst its members of the 40 + 9 recommendations of the FATF. GOPAC acknowledges that the FATF is the anti-money-laundering standard-setter. GOPAC has begun to build more awareness by encouraging its regional chapters to create linkages with the FATF-style regional organizations, which are present throughout the world, and begin working with these organizations to develop and implement anti-money-laundering strategies.

GOPAC has formally submitted a request to the FATF for observer status on the Financial Action Task Force. This would allow parliamentarians a more direct role and impact on the development of anti-money-laundering standards and implementation tools.

At present, though, GOPAC, as stated in the last anti-money-laundering resolution passed in Arusha, is committing itself to dialoguing with the offshore and international banking community with the objective of limiting or eliminating the laundering of corrupt funds through financial institutions such as these. GOPAC has begun this process by contacting the Offshore Group of Banking Supervisors (OGBS).

The stated aim of OGBS is to participate with relevant international organizations in setting and promoting the implementation of international standards for cross-border banking supervision, and for combating money laundering/terrorist financing and encourage members to apply high standards of supervision based on internationally accepted principles. In a letter I wrote to Mr. Colin Powell, the chair of OGBS, I indicated that parliamentarians throughout the world have expressed a strong desire to obtain further information and training in money laundering; in particular, I stated that they would be interested in knowing what legislative and other tools are available to them so that they can assist in the reduction or elimination of money laundering in their respective countries. I asked

Mr. Powell if GOPAC could work with his organization to achieve the same degree of enhanced co-operation that his members have accomplished in the fight against terrorist financing and drug crimes, and enhance this co-operation to the fight against the laundering of corrupt money. OGBS understands the benefits of working together, and they are anxious to participate in a meeting GOPAC is organizing with the offshore banking community to map out a program to better address the fight against the laundering of corrupt money, and the recovery of stolen assets.

GOPAC is continuing its dialogue with the Offshore Group of Banking Supervisors as a result of this letter. We have come to the realization that we must deal with the governments in the offshore banking jurisdictions and in this connection we are working with the IMF on a proposal to begin a dialogue with these countries with the objective of improving the detection and recovery of laundered corrupt funds.

It should be noted that achieving full co-operation with the offshore banking community in denying safe haven to the corrupt is a challenging task. Many issues arise. For example, many tax haven countries, by virtue of their own legislation, are able to invoke non-co-operation if a request breaches confidentiality agreements—on the basis that complying with the requested information would run contrary to that country's national interest. Likewise, many offshore banking jurisdictions insist on "dual criminality,"[85] meaning that the offence alleged by the country requesting the co-operation must also be an offence in the jurisdiction where the bank is located. The "double jeopardy"[86] argument may also be raised.

Another problem is that states pursuing corrupt individuals in an attempt to recover stolen assets may, from time to time, embark on fishing expeditions where they draw on vague allegations and circumstantial evidence that a corrupt leader has embezzled funds and deposited them in an offshore bank. The offshore banks reasonably expect some specificity to the request for information but it is unreasonable for the bank to ask for the numbers of specific bank accounts

from the complaining government officials. If the government officials trying to recover the missing funds had the bank account numbers, the problem would generally be much closer to being solved.
Usually, the trails to the missing money are not so strong. Having
said that, the offshore bank must be careful also not to comply with
a newly elected government that is on a politically inspired "witch
hunt" to discredit the outgoing administration. Differences in evi-
dentiary procedures also abound, and there are other issues. Notwithstanding the challenges, there seems to be some goodwill to
co-operate and GOPAC is pursuing this aggressively.

There is a growing appetite for stronger action against corruption
and related money laundering. These initiatives take time to develop
and evolve, however. For example, at the January 2004 Summit of
the Americas in Monterrey, Mexico, the *Globe & Mail* reported that
"U.S. diplomats arrived in Monterrey with a controversial plan to act
against countries regarded as corrupt, including barring them from
future America's summits."[87] The plan was not approved, however,
because of the perceived difficulties in arriving at a set of criteria,
which would dictate which countries were corrupt and which were
not. The countries represented at the summit did agree, however, to
discuss at future meetings corruption fighting measures. Incremental progress is better than no progress at all.

CHAPTER 7

Aid, Development and Corruption

The terms development aid, overseas development assistance, development co-operation, international aid, overseas aid, and foreign aid are often used interchangeably. The terms describe aid given by governmental and non-governmental agencies to support the economic, social, and political development of developing countries.

Issues surrounding concepts like conditionality (making loans or grants on the condition that the recipient country implement certain social or economic policies) and questions about tied aid (tying the supply of the aid to companies or organizations from the donor country) have been hotly debated over the years. Questions also about the definition of aid, and whether it should include military assistance and debt, have been around for some time, as has the need to differentiate between humanitarian aid (short-term relief from crises) and long-term aid (assisting countries with structural change)

What has not been much discussed—at least until recently—is how corruption affects aid. In fact, it was not that long ago that the use of the term "corruption" was not considered politically correct in development assistance circles. Paul Wolfowitz, the former head of the World Bank—and a man with governance and management problems of his own—ran up against this bias in his attempts to have the bank lead the fight against corruption. It can be argued that he was forced to resign his position at the bank because of his aggressive stance on the subject. Now, however, the majority of people realize that the efforts to alleviate poverty in developing countries is being hindered by corrupt practices in recipient countries, and that it is necessary to battle those practices in order to ensure that aid actually goes to help those for whom it is intended.

Official Development Assistance (ODA) Trends

There are many challenges with international assistance. How can the priority needs of the developing country be identified? Is it better to provide goods and services to those in need, or is it better to provide the means for producing those so that inhabitants of developing countries can provide for themselves? Should aid be tied to suppliers from the country supplying the aid? Will the aid get through to the intended recipient? How effective will the aid be in reducing poverty?

As always, setting targets is important. At the Millennium Summit in September 2000 in Monterrey, Mexico, world leaders adopted specific and quantifiable development goals. Subsequently, the United Nations published eight Millennium Development Goals in the September 6, 2001, Report of the UN Secretary General on the road map for implementation of the UN Millennium Declaration.

The eight goals are:

► To halve, between 1990 and 2015, the proportion of people living on less than US $1 a day; and to halve, between 1990 and 2015, the proportion of people suffering from hunger;
► To ensure that, by 2015, all children can complete primary schooling;
► To eliminate gender disparity in primary and secondary education, preferably by 2005, and at all education levels no later than 2015;

▶ To reduce by two-thirds, between 1990 and 2015, the mortality rate for children under 5 years old;

▶ To reduce by three-quarters, between 1990 and 2015, the maternal mortality ratio;

▶ To have halted and begun to reverse by 2015 the spread of HIV/ AIDS; and to have halted and begun to reverse by 2015 the incidence of malaria and other major diseases;

▶ To integrate the principles of sustainable development into country policies and programs and to reverse the loss of environmental resources; and to halve by 2015 the proportion of people without sustainable access to safe drinking water;

▶ To develop a global partnership for development including through trade openness and debt relief.

These were ambitious goals. It has been argued by some that they are unrealistic and not attainable. Countries like Ghana, however, have indicated that they are on track to meet their Millennium Development Goals—seven years ahead of the 2015 target. In a United Nations report in 2005 monitoring progress on the Millennium Development Goals,[88] some progress was noted, but in a number of areas progress is slow. The report highlighted that in fact the number of poor in Africa is rising and the decline in hunger in the developing world is slowing. More than one quarter of the children in the developing world are still malnourished.

In two areas, however, there is good news. Firstly, there was a decline in extreme poverty in Asia during the 1990s. Secondly, there has been progress achieved in primary school enrolment in five regions of the developing world—Latin America and the Caribbean, Eastern Asia, Commonwealth of Independent States (CIS) Asia, Northern Africa, and South East Asia. According to the UN progress report, reaching the HIV/AIDS goals can be achieved, but efforts need to be accelerated and actions scaled up (including, I suspect, expediting the shipment of HIV/AIDS drugs to Africa).

Personally, I do not believe that the global targets, however noble and ambitious, can be achieved and I believe it is wrong to commit to goals that cannot be reached. Something I learned very early in my management career was that organizational goals and objectives must be realistic and achievable. To create unrealistic goals is to threaten one's credibility and limit the buy-in of those who will have the responsibility to attain these goals. My point with respect to poverty reduction is that elected officials should avoid the temptation to generate photo opportunities to announce goals and objectives that are not attainable.[89]

Assistance from the developed world to developing nations has been growing in absolute terms, but shrinking in relation to the income capacities of donor countries, in the last few decades. While Overseas Development Assistance (ODA) totalled some US $104.4 billion in 2006—an increase over 2005—this is almost entirely due to debts written off for a handful of countries like Iraq. The same figure for global ODA for the year 2000 was US $53.7 billion; however, this year-over-year increase is still way below the agreed 0.7 per cent target outlined in the United Nations Millennium Development Goals. The leading donor countries, comparing ODA with national incomes, are Sweden, Luxembourg, Norway, the Netherlands, and Denmark. In 2006, these five countries exceeded the 0.7 per cent United Nations target, and they were the only countries that achieved it. Less generous countries in 2006 included Greece (0.16), USA (0.17), and Italy (0.2).

In 2003, Canada donated 0.29 per cent of GDP.[90] This represents a decline in Overseas Development Assistance (ODA) of more that 34 per cent since 1991/92, when it peaked at 0.49 per cent of GDP. More recently, countries like Canada have committed to higher levels of assistance, but there is some serious catching up to do. In the 2002 Speech from the Throne, the Government of Canada committed to doubling its Overseas Development Assistance by the year 2010. For Canada to reach the 0.7 per cent of GDP target by 2015, additional spending of some $41 billion would be required. This is a large sum for a country like Canada and therefore the United Nations target will not soon be reached.

Equating development assistance to a country's GNP is important because in absolute terms an amount like the US $104 billion sounds like a huge amount, and it is, but by relating it to GNP one can compare the level of assistance with what a country can afford (the measure or proxy being gross national product which measures a country's output). World GDP, which is in the vicinity of $55–$70 trillion, is almost an unimaginable amount which loses meaning when looked at in absolute terms. This same approach is also often used when examining the debt levels of countries by equating these amounts to a percentage of GDP rather than examining the debt in absolute terms. Another perspective is gained by comparing total aid to other benchmarks, like the level of agricultural subsidies worldwide and funds expended annually throughout the world on defence spending. In 2002, agricultural subsidies totalled some US $311 billion, or approximately five times total ODA. Some US $800 billion was spent on military equipment and operations in 2002—or nearly 16 times the amount spent on foreign aid.

It is argued by Canada's Coalition to End Global Poverty that Canada, like the UK, USA, Sweden, Switzerland, Denmark, Belgium, Italy, Luxembourg, Greece and Austria, amongst others, should enact legislation to govern Overseas Development Assistance. Others, like the Aid Effectiveness Discussion Forum, contend that Canada should reverse the trend of channelling the vast majority of its development budget through multilateral agencies—the World Bank, UNICEF, the African Development Bank, the Red Cross and others—and foreign governments, and, instead, increase its bilateral spending. While I am not so convinced that we should legislate our approach to ODA, I support the move to more direct funding by the Canadian International Development Agency (CIDA), which is, after all, Canada's lead agency for development assistance. Indeed, it is their mandate to support sustainable development in developing countries in order to reduce poverty and to contribute to a more secure, equitable, and prosperous world.

Too often, though, funding is channelled through multilateral agencies because they are seen as being able to offer a solution to concerns about the aid getting directly to the individuals who are most in need, rather than being wasted or siphoned off by corrupt officials. However, in adopting this approach, we lose control of our own programs and have to rely on the good work of these agencies. Canada could have more targeted impact if it carefully chose solid bilateral efforts. Bilateral aid, or direct aid from country to country, is sometimes not possible, as, for instance, when a failed state or a hopelessly corrupt state is the recipient of aid, but we should promote direct aid wherever possible. For example, bilateral aid to a country like Somalia at this time would be very difficult given the political turmoil in that country and the level of corruption that exists. This should not stop the larger agencies with on-the-ground resources in Somalia from assisting the Somali people who are in desperate need of support.

A recent trend in aid assistance has been the development of debt relief programs. Since many developing nations suffer from debt loads so heavy that they are required to devote significant portions of their national budgets simply to payment of interest—to the detriment of investment in social programs and infrastructure—debt relief provides a solution that can provide real assistance to the citizens of those countries.

The Heavily Indebted Poor Countries (HIPC) debt relief program was initiated by the G-8[91] in 1996 and is administered by the International Monetary Fund (IMF) and the World Bank. The IMF was established to promote international monetary co-operation, exchange stability, and orderly exchange arrangements; to foster economic growth and high levels of employment; and to provide temporary financial assistance to countries to help ease balance of payments adjustment. The World Bank focuses on the achievement of the Millennium Development Goals that call for the elimination of poverty, and on building the climate for investment, jobs and sustainable growth.

The HIPC program aims to reduce the external debt of the world's poorest, most heavily indebted countries to sustainable levels. It provides substantial debt relief to these countries that undertake to implement critical social and economic reforms and use the benefits of debt relief to reduce poverty. To date, US $51.1 billion (number in reference to "HIPC Initiative: changes and estimates of Potential Costs by Creditor Group")[92] has been dealt with in this manner, with Canada's then finance minister, Paul Martin, leading the way.

Much more still needs to be done to provide debt relief to poor countries. Members of parliament from Zambia, who were visiting Canada in 2003, pointed out that their country was still very heavily burdened with paying down their debt with fully 5.4 per cent of its GDP in 2004 devoted to servicing these debts. This is a decade after plans were set in motion to cut the debt burdens of more than 40 heavily indebted poor countries. "Paying for debt will absorb 7.4 per cent of the entire market output of Malawi and a fifth of the output of the tiny state of São Tomé."[93]

Where finances are being redeployed to anti-poverty programs, as in Mozambique, rapid progress is being made in the numbers of children having regular primary education. The proportion of people living on less than US $1 a day has fallen from about two-thirds to about half.

The North-South Institute, in its brief to the House of Commons Standing Committee of Finance in 2002, argued that the debt burden of HIPC countries should be reduced by a further 30 per cent. In their judgement, the architects of HIPC set the level of debt sustainability too high in a context of falling commodity prices and international recession. The status of commodity prices is different today, so the conclusion might be different given their strong performance—and the same applies to the risk of worldwide recession. However, the need to more aggressively reduce the debt of poor governments who are committed to good governance is clear.

Problems with Aid

To be effective, aid must reach the intended target. To reduce or eliminate a developing country's debt is only justifiable if the debt service resources that are thus freed up are reassigned to more productive poverty reduction uses. Debt reduction programs must go hand-in-hand with good governance, otherwise debt will pile up again as corrupt leaders skim off resources once more. Likewise, direct development assistance must be able to address the real needs of citizens—not the greed of corrupt leaders. Lack of good governance in many developing countries is resulting in many donor countries ceasing to transfer aid money directly to recipient countries; many instead are moving the development assistance through multi-lateral organizations like UNICEF or the World Bank who have more resources on the ground to adequately monitor how aid is dispersed.

Aid promised on the condition that the developing country commits to a set of public policies acceptable to the donor country or multilateral agencies such as the World Bank, is often the way in which development projects or financial assistance packages from the IMF proceed.

This policy of "conditionality" is also a highly contentious one, and one that has created much negative publicity for organizations like the IMF and World Bank. In a June 2002 address I made at the Parliamentary Assembly of the Council of Europe, I commented on the role of the World Bank and IMF:

> Globalization is a frequently used word, which means very
> different things to different people. To some, globalization
> is the natural and obvious extension of a shrinking world,
> faster communications and the tearing down of tariff protec-
> tion walls. Most, if not all, economists would argue that the
> elimination of tariffs has the effect of significantly increasing
> incomes and wealth. To others, globalization is the monopo-

lization of income and wealth creation by multinationals and political elites—to the detriment of the many.

The more recent debate on globalization contains some ironies. The Breton Woods institutions, namely the International Monetary Fund and the World Bank, were created to help all countries share in the benefits of global trade and commerce. This may be hard to believe as we have witnessed the protests during the last few years by so-called civil society at meetings of these institutions. I say so-called civil society because some of these groups, albeit a minority, support violence to achieve their objectives—not exactly a civilized response however noble the objective.

Where have we gone wrong as elected representatives to allow that level of distrust and lack of confidence, by some, in our international financial institutions? Is it a lack of transparency by these institutions that has led to misunderstandings or have the actions, or lack of action, by the international financial institutions been the cause of this level of animosity?

The role and reform of the international financial institutions have been a long-standing Canadian concern. Indeed Canada made international financial issues a central focus of a previous G-7/G-8 summit, which it hosted in Halifax in 1995, and Canadian parliamentarians also made a number of reform proposals in preparing for that summit...

Canada's former finance minister, Paul Martin, has provided leadership and energy to the Heavily Indebted Poor Countries Initiative, but more needs to be done. We need to understand better what factors determine the sustainability of debt levels. We must provide assistance to poor countries in identifying debt capacities, and with debt management strategies. Transparent and accountable governance, and anticorruption measures, need to be at the forefront of debt forgiveness...

The work of achieving a sound, equitable, socially and environmentally sustainable international economy is far from over. The IMF and the World Bank must continue to adapt and to reform themselves so that they are more transparent and accountable, and therefore better able to respond to the critical developments and new challenges which have been so astutely identified by the rapporteur. "Cookie cutter" solutions will no longer work. IFI's will need to play the innovative and global public interest role that is expected of them.

As parliamentarians we can, and should, play a key role in this evolution.

There are many examples of aid gone wrong. It was reported that in Somalia, during the civil war in the late 1980s and early 1990s, the warlord Mohamed Farrah Aidid, leader of Habr Gidr, a powerful Somalia sub clan, blocked aid to millions of Somalis and contributed to the starvation of many. This phenomenon has been repeated in many countries, many times.

In the English-speaking world, Ryszard Kapuściński is best known for his reporting from Africa in the 1960s and 1970s, when he witnessed first hand the end of the European colonial empires on that continent. In his book on Africa, *The Shadow of the Sun*, Kapuściński describes the typical African warlord this way:

> The warlord—he is a former officer, an ex-minister or party functionary, or some other strong individual desiring power and money, ruthless and without scruples—who, taking advantage of the disintegration of the state (to which he contributed and continues to contribute), wants to carve out for himself his own informal mini state, over which he can hold dictatorial sway. Most often, a warlord uses to this end the clan or tribe to which he belongs. Warlords are the sowers of tribal and racial hatred in Africa.[94]

Kapuściński goes on to say:

When we hear that an African country is beginning to totter, we can be certain that warlords will soon appear on the scene. They are everywhere and control everything—in Angola, in Sudan, in Somalia, in Chad. What does a warlord do? Theoretically he fights with other warlords. Most frequently, however, he is busy robbing his own country's unarmed population. The warlord is the opposite of Robin Hood. He takes from the poor to enrich himself and feed his gangs. We are in a world in which misery condemns some to death and transforms others into monsters. The former are the victims, the latter are the executioners. There is no one else.

He concludes: "Whoever has weapons has food. Whoever has food, has power."

Warlords are certainly not limited to Africa, however. Afghanistan provides another good example of a country where warlords have enormous power and sway.

Corruption not only plagues governments of the developing world, it can seep in to the most respected and "legitimate" institutions, such as the United Nations. When the UN's controversial Oil for Food Program was investigated, members of the UN and program advisors were accused of profiting illegally from the program.

The tangled web of corruption, bribery, and money laundering began in 1996 when the Oil for Food Program was created in response to the abject poverty of the Iraqi civilians—a combined result of the corrupt dictatorship of Saddam Hussein and the sanctions placed by the UN on Iraq. Following the Iraqi invasion of Kuwait, the sanctions barred UN member states from trading with Iraq in an effort to force the country to disarm.[95] In order to prevent severe suffering to ordinary Iraqis, the UN created the Oil for Food Program which allowed the Iraqi government to sell small quantities of oil on the world market in exchange for basic necessities such as food, medicine, etc.[96]

According to the Independent Inquiry in to the Oil for Food Program, money from some of the sales and transactions of the program never reached the hands of the poor Iraqi citizens. One of the most detrimental allegations is against the former executive director of the program, Benon Sevan, who was accused of obtaining more than $147,000 in kickbacks.[97] The Independent Inquiry Committee, led by Paul Volcker, which looked into the UN Oil for Food Program, revealed that Sevan benefited from the program through the sale of oil allocated by Iraq and that he had knowledge that some of the oil was purchased by paying an illegal surcharge to Iraq, which was in violation of the United Nations rules of the program.[98]

Although Sevan denies all allegations, Alexander Yakovlev, a former senior contracts officer for the program, has admitted to the corrupt dealings of the UN.[99] Yakovlev has pled guilty to money laundering and accepting bribes from UN vendors.[100] The Independent Inquiry found that more than $1.3 million was wired into an account for a dummy firm called Moxyco that Yakovlev established in 2000 in the island of Antigua.[101]

There were allegations of former UN Secretary General Kofi Annan's involvement in, and knowledge of, the illegal transactions. Further to this, Annan's son was allegedly implicated because he was working for a Swiss company that was also under investigation for abusing the program.[102] In the end, investigators concluded that there was not enough evidence to show that Annan knew of a contract bid by his son's employer, but they were critical of Kofi Annan's management of the organizational crisis. Although no convictions were made against Annan, his failure to detect or stop the abuses of UN advisors and vendors weakens the creditability of the UN and proves no institution is immune to corruption. Following the release of the investigator's report, Kofi Annan accepted the criticism, but at the same time he expressed relief that he had been exonerated of committing any wrongdoing by the independent inquiry.

These developments are damaging to the reputation of the UN and will require severe internal modifications to prevent fraudulent activity in the future.

Even when aid does reach its intended target, however, the results can be disappointing. The traditional approaches to overseas development assistance that have evolved over the years do not appear to have had the intended impact. Direct international aid is based on the philosophy that it is better to "give the fishing rod, not the fish," so that people in poor countries can learn to fish for themselves—but giving someone something can only help if that person values it.

In the late 1980s, management consulting projects took me to the Northwest Territories of Canada. Here I learned at a practical level what I had known intuitively; that is, the importance for people who are in receipt of aid, of any description, to take an interest and make their own commitment to any supported projects and initiatives. At the time of my visits to Yellowknife in the Northwest Territories, the Northwest Territories Housing Corporation had two distinct housing programs for aboriginal Canadians. One program could be characterized as a typical social housing program—fully subsidized housing for poor aboriginal families. The second program was what was referred to as the "sweat equity" program. In this program, the Northwest Territories Housing Corporation provided the building materials to an aboriginal individual who was willing to build the house for himself or herself—hence the term "sweat equity." I was told that the houses occupied in the first category were in a state of disrepair, whereas the sweat-equity houses were well maintained and cared for. This is not surprising when you think about it. Given human nature, people are more inclined to care for things when a part of them is injected into the project. I believe there are lessons to be learned here in our approach to international development aid. It is better when the local aid recipients are partners in the enterprise or project.

Another good example of local empowerment and civic society is in the Brazilian town of Porte Allegri. In brief, a new constitution was drafted for the city, which gave more power to local government, and for citizen councils to have more input into the policies and programs of their federal government. Through a series of assemblies, delegates were chosen to represent the 16 districts in the Porte Allegri area. The citizens themselves were able also to decide how the budget would be spent. Since 1988, the city has made a significant dent in poverty with 98 per cent of the residences currently having running water, paved roads, higher enrolment of education, and a reduction in corruption.[103] These results underline the importance of community-tailored solutions, rather than the traditional macro-oriented, top-down approaches which often neglect how and why poor people are doing what they are doing.

Often such top-down approaches involve what is known as "tied aid," where the aid is tied to the procurement of related goods and services from the donor country. This is still a contentious area for debate. My own view is that tied aid is acceptable, provided pricing and quality are competitive. Canada's tied aid program has been delivered by CIDA Inc., an arm of the Canadian International Development Agency. Development experts at Canada's embassies and missions abroad speak consistently of the positive aspects of CIDA Inc. projects. These projects have often involved small- and medium-sized enterprises in Canada and, given our large multi-cultural community, this program seems to be a natural for our country. We are able to draw on the knowledge and experience of our local population of the customs and traditions of the countries of their birth and translate this into highly productive and mutually beneficial development projects.

The effectiveness of international aid is a vexing question. Former World Bank president James Wolfensohn has claimed, "We're in the poverty reduction business." Some years ago, as members of a sub-committee of the House of Commons Standing Committee on Finance studying the effectiveness of aid through multilateral organizations such as the World Bank and the Inter-American Development Bank,[104] I travelled to Washington, DC, looking for answers. We met with many individuals and organizations, but one particular meeting stuck out in my mind. Robert McNamara, after serving as secretary of defence under President Kennedy and President

Johnson from 1961 to 1968,[105] was president of the World Bank from 1968 to 1981. While he was emphatic on the criteria that should be used to evaluate the effectiveness of development aid—the reduction of poverty—he struggled with the related question of how to best measure this. He talked of the challenges of doing this because of measurement problems, but, more importantly, the difficulty of isolating other variables, such as political upheaval, conflict, and weather and its impact on crops, that might occur at the same time as the aid is being supplied. If a country has shown no progress in reducing poverty and during the same period being examined that same country has experienced civil war, drought, and other mishaps, how does one measure the impact of all these events separately on poverty-reduction efforts? How can one say definitively that a reduction in poverty is the result of development assistance or other factors, such as bumper crop years or a more positive political climate? If someone like Robert McNamara, who headed the World Bank for 13 years, was unable to answer these questions, evaluating the impact of development aid is surely a difficult pastime.

However difficult it is to measure progress in the alleviation of poverty, we must continue with this fight. Not to do this would be unconscionable. We need an equal determination, nonetheless, to constantly challenge the way we try to assist those who are in a state of poverty. The systems in place and the practices currently employed are not working very well and need to be fixed. Thinking "outside the box" is not a concept that should be limited to the private sector—it is equally applicable in the area of public policy and programs. My contention is that we need to be doing this in the area of development assistance if we are truly to break the poverty cycle in the underdeveloped world. That is what this work is all about.

CHAPTER 8

Development and the Market

It is my view that world poverty can be attacked in a number of ways. The potential solutions are not limited to reducing or eliminating corruption; although I contend that the fight against corruption is a key piece of this strategy. Reducing trade barriers, both tariff and non-tariff, in the developed economies would assist those in emerging and developing economies to expand the markets for their products, in particular agricultural products, and industrial products like textiles. The World Trade Organization (WTO) Doha "Development" Trade Round is attempting to bring some consensus on how these trade barriers can be reduced. The challenges are enormous and positive results have not been forthcoming to date. As a result, many poor countries are limited in their ability to sell many of their agricultural and industrial products into these markets. The potential for economic activity and jobs in the developing world, which would assist in alleviating poverty, are lost while an agreement is not reached.

As pointed out earlier, many developing countries rely on their natural resources to enrich their treasuries. If these precious resources are not managed in a sustainable way because of corrupt officials, they may not be available for their use in the future. This could have devastating affects on these economies and poverty-reduction efforts, notwithstanding efforts to diversify their economies.

The question of labour standards is also an important one. How do you uplift a citizenry of a country that is at a different stage of development than the jurisdictions where their products are sold? Should they expect the same wage rates, benefits, and protections under labour laws that exist in the developed world? If they do, will fewer be employed and more left in poverty?

One could assume wrongly that international financial markets do not impact on the poor. But the reverse is true. The international market meltdowns in Asia, Russia, and Mexico affected all citizens in those regions—not only investors, but the middle class and the poor as well. Friends of mine in Thailand who were small business operators were ruined economically during the 1997 East Asian Financial Crisis—a crisis which started in Thailand with the financial collapse of the Thai baht. Their company employed a number of individuals who lost their jobs.

Stability in international financial markets is an important cornerstone in the fight against poverty.

The Environment, Labour Standards and Trade Barriers

A great intellectual debate has raged in recent years over what are referred to as North/South issues. It is actually more than an intellectual debate—it has very serious practical ramifications for developing countries. In these debates, "North" refers to the predominately developed countries of the northern hemisphere, and "South" to the struggling countries of the southern hemisphere. The expression "North/South issues" refers to the economic disparities that exist between countries in the northern and southern hemispheres. The areas most frequently discussed focus on environmental standards, labour standards, and barriers to trade.

Environment

The environment, poverty reduction efforts, and corruption are closely intertwined. Less corrupt countries generally exhibit stronger sustainable development practices, and less environmental degradation. Poor countries are more focused on survival and economic growth, sometimes at the expense of the environment, and typically these same countries lack the resources to implement regimes that develop and execute sound environmental performance standards. Even with sound environmental regulatory regimes, enforcement may be an issue since the officials who monitor environmental performance are frequently corrupt. As a result, compliance with policies and regulations may be compromised.

Is it fair, it is asked, for developing countries to face the same environmental and labour standards as developed countries? In my view it is not fair to demand the same standards from developing countries in the short/medium term that the developed world has imposed on itself. It is impossible for the developing world to bear the cost of higher environmental standards at this stage of their growth cycle. Developed countries had the benefit of a lower bar as they developed and grew their economies. Although countries in the North have now improved their environmental standards, developing countries are still at an earlier stage of development. Tougher controls on effluents and smoke stack emissions impose a cost on struggling companies. It makes sense, therefore, that these rules be relaxed for developing countries until their industries reach the maturity of those in the developed world. Since most agree that strong economic performance is the best route to encourage investments in improving environmental performance, it is argued that those economies, with the passage of time, will be better positioned to make these investments if they are given more unfettered opportunities to grow in the short to medium term. This argument is behind the agreement at Kyoto (which did not receive support from the USA) to give some manoeuvring room to developing countries as they attempt to reduce greenhouse gases.

However, I also believe that it is true that environmental policies that enhance environmental performance and ensure that development is sustainable inhibit the potential for corruption. There is a strong relationship between the environment in the developing world and corruption. It appears that whenever development planning in the environmental area fails to meet both the needs of the local and global communities at stake, corruption often follows: desperately poor people are forced to deforest land, poach, or engage in other activities that result in environmental destruction. The tolerance of corruption alongside these activities becomes necessary in order to survive.

A good example of how poverty, corruption, and environmental degradation all intertwine in the developing world involves Nigeria's Ogoni people, whose homeland has been despoiled by those involved in the search for oil in that country. It is alleged that the level of corruption that has accompanied the discovery of this oil in 1958 has been significant. Not only have the Ogoni people been displaced and nearly eradicated in the process of this quest for oil by Royal Dutch Shell, but the Ogoni have not shared in the oil revenues in any meaningful way. In addition, the level of environmental degradation in the Niger Delta region of southeast Nigeria has been significant. Ken Saro-Wiwa, an Ogoni activist who for years led the fight against the Nigerian administration (led at that time by the dictator Ibrahim Babangida), wrote extensively on this matter. Saro-Wiwa's book, *A Month and a Day: A Detention Diary*, is an excellent chronicle of his last years, leading up to his death sentence in 1994.

When looking at the relationship between poverty and the environment or poverty and corruption, the theory adopted by most international institutions has been that they are directly linked to each other. Before it is possible to alleviate the destruction of the environment or curtail corrupt, illegal actions taken by people living in developing nations, it is necessary to focus on alleviating poverty first. People living in poverty are faced with little choice in the decisions they have to make in order to survive. A United Nations Development Program (UNDP) report stresses the importance of community-based solutions in addressing poverty: *Poverty and Environment: Priorities for Research and Policy*, prepared for the UNDP, by Tim Forsyth and Melissa Leach. While this report focuses solely on the environment, it does advance a new way of thinking about poverty and development, one that puts an emphasis on the local rather than the universal experience of poverty. For instance, it looks at the use of community-based solutions to poverty as apposed to solutions rendered by governmental institutions which often restrict indigenous freedoms, or in some cases fail to immediately relieve the conditions of poverty in local communities.

Corruption in the environmental sector is distinct from any other forms because of its link to large sums of formal and informal revenues that are derived from natural products. This is especially true in developing countries that are rich in natural resources and whose economies are largely based on resource extraction. Nations such as Indonesia, Nigeria, Sierra Leone, and Colombia are highly dependent upon natural resources and are countries that Transparency International 2000 describes as losing billions to natural resource related corruption.

Environmental-related corruption manifests itself in two ways: on the one hand, natural resources have a high value on the black market, which allows public officials to make profits from illegally issuing access to them, such as issuing false permits to overlook illicit consignments of endangered wildlife species. Another common source of corruption is related to the poor funding and weak environmental policies of the resource-rich developing countries. Without sufficient conservation programs or institutions in place, there is little environmental management or control. This opens the door to corrupt activities because a relaxation of the environmental rules, which are often not well articulated, usually benefits the project promoter. The latter could be motivated to pay a bribe to derive a positive outcome. According to the 2001 Environmental Sustainability Index, there is a high correlation between the level of corruption and environmental outcomes: the higher the level of corruption in a country, the lower the level of environmental sustainability.

The link between the environment and corruption is best illustrated by the environmental disasters of Mexico. The former president of Mexico, Vincente Fox, described in his speech at the National Accord for Transparency and Combating Corruption in 2001 how corruption thrives in the environmental sector because of private interests that have dominated the administration. These have granted forest, fishing, and hunting permits on a discretionary basis in favour of companies that recklessly exploit Mexico's natural resources. This practice has resulted in environmental inspections that allow illegal poaching, logging, and discharges in return for bribery and nepotism. These corrupt actions are fuelled both by the lack of accountability of government officials, and the low salaries paid to officials, which entices inspectors and wardens to allow private groups to take resources illegally for bribes. This has produced environmental policy failure in Mexico and the depletion of essential resources, such as timber; Mexico now has the third-largest deforestation rate in the world.

Corruption in Mexico's enforcement agencies has been increasing. In 1996, it was estimated that 70 to 80 per cent of the judicial police were corrupt.[106] This widespread corruption has led Mexican citizens to lose faith in their government. Mexican citizens have been forced to tolerate corrupt government officials. "In Mexico, they have a saying that they use when they are offering you a bribe: *Plomo o plata?*—'Lead or silver?' What it means is that if you don't take bribes, they will shoot you. Well, at least you get the option."[107]

Corruption in the environmental sector has also plagued Russia. The World Wildlife Fund (WWF) estimates that Russia loses over US $1 billion due to illegal forest harvesting, processing, and trade. As a result of the corruption in forest practices, the country suffers from great loss in biodiversity and has lost many of its valuable forests, which in turn has caused major changes in various microclimates. When in Russia in the early 1990s, I became aware of vast tracts of forests where the conifer species had been harvested, leaving the less desirable hardwoods standing, which, by the time we examined them, were largely decadent. To address this, WWF implemented the Russian Forest Program in 1994, which initiated a monitoring organization of illegal deforestation, and which has found more than 24 cases of illegal logging. In 2002, WWF commissioned a study by the Department of Natural Resources of Primorskiy Krai, which revealed that illegal logging in Primorskiy Krai constituted from 30 to 50 per cent of the total amount of harvested timber that was exported every year. The study concluded that there were insufficient enforcement measures to fight forest crime and in order to combat corruption in the natural resource sector, legislation and policies that clearly stipulate environmental control need to be enforced. As well as having an effective monitoring system, the country must also utilize public, private, and civil input in order to create a system of incentives and sanctions to reward compliance with policies. Simply banning corruption in the developing world is not enough to deter people from gaining access to the black market.

Labour Standards

It is ironic that insisting on labour standards in the developing world that are equivalent to those in the developed world may slow down global poverty-reduction efforts. Raising the level of labour standards in developing countries is a contentious issue, as it is feared that it may cause immediate economic harm to the developing countries by eliminating their competitive advantage of having cheap labour. Some researchers and social scientists argue that allowing appalling working conditions to occur in the developing world will create a race to the bottom in the deterioration of labour standards. An example cited that illustrates this concept is the competition between China and Mexico for the North American apparel market. Despite the outstanding employment growth in these sectors, apparel workers in these countries have experienced very limited wage growth, and the conditions in which they work are barely liveable.

Some make the same argument for labour standards that is made for environmental standards: The developing world cannot bear the cost of a higher hurdle of tougher labour standards at this stage of their growth cycle. Developed countries had the benefit of a lower bar as they developed and grew their economies, so these rules should be relaxed for developing countries until their industries reach the maturity of those in the developed world. Many ask why minimum wage laws, the abolition of child labour, and other labour standards should apply to developing countries. Won't applying the more rigorous standards of the developed world, it is asked, translate into fewer jobs in developing countries and/or a diminishment of their competitiveness? How can foreign companies operating in the "developed world" justify their sweat shops in "third world" countries?

While I know that many or most trade unions do not support relaxing any of these rules, I am reminded of the scores of black Africans in South Africa who worked for very low wages during the repressive apartheid era. Higher wages would certainly have reduced their numbers. During this same period Africans from countries to the north flocked in great numbers to Johannesburg—the "city of gold." The same can be said about the use of child labour in countries around the world. What realistic other options do they have? Their cheap labour is surely the source of their products' comparative advantage in world markets.

What is needed, perhaps, is a South-South agreement between countries of the developing world that would ensure governments, trade unions, and workers of the developing world regulate the minimum labour standards through a social clause.[108] Southern countries as a bloc could negotiate with the North to set a minimum living wage in accordance with each country's own standard of living. Anita Chan and Robert Ross, in their article "Racing to the Bottom: International Trade without a Social Clause," describe this agreement as the solution to prevent further deterioration of labour standards in the South. They argue that if labour standards are allowed to remain static in the developing world, there is a risk that fewer employees will be able to reap the benefits of their work, because their governments will insist on having the believed competitive advantage of cheap labour. Many studies, including one by Lawrence (1995), find that wage disparities have widened over the past 20 years, and that there has been a significant increase in poorly paid jobs.[109]

One way of ensuring higher standards of labour for the South is to link trade with labour standards, which would set a minimum wage, limitation of work hours, as well as occupational health and safety regulations. Canada did this when the Liberal government came to power in 1993 on the promise to renegotiate the North American Free Trade Agreement (NAFTA) that had been agreed to by the Conservative government during their 1988–1993 mandate. Rather than revise that agreement, the North American Agreements on Labour and Environmental Cooperation were negotiated and implemented in parallel to the NAFTA. These were designed to facilitate greater co-operation between the partner countries in those areas and to promote the effective enforcement of each country's laws and regulations. The idea was that improved working standards and environmental standards would go hand-in-hand with more trade amongst Canada, USA, and Mexico.

The jury is still out as to whether these labour standard and environmental standards objectives have been met, but the results have not been earth-shattering. In an article by Janine Jackson for *FAIR* (Fairness and Accuracy in Reporting), the author had this to say: "1997 marks three years since NAFTA took effect, and, by any standard, the results are decidedly less rosy than proponents predicted. Many of the critics' concerns for workers' wages and rights—on both sides of the border—and for environmental protections are now verifiable."[110]

While many authors note the opposition from countries in the

South to this initiative (most notably from the All China Federation of Trade Unions, which rejects two core labour standards: freedom of association and the right to collective bargaining), there are other Asian trade unions, such as the Korean Confederation of Trade Unions (KCTU) and the Malaysian Trade Union Congress, that support having labour standards and trade linked, although they are against the inclusion of a minimum wage. However, the opposition to higher standards of labour in the developing world is usually based on the belief that there will be a massive job loss that will accompany regulated labour standards, because of the competitive advantage lower standards of labour have in the South over the North. Thus it is not surprising that proposals made for upgrading labour standards are not welcomed by developing countries.[111] Such opposition has resulted in an alliance between Western bankers, multinationals, employers, and governments in the South in favour of unrestricted trade without labour conditionality. Opposing them are Western labour NGOs, human rights groups, and trade unions in opposition.

To determine whether or not labour standards have an impact on the competitiveness of various countries, Professor André Raynauld of the University of Montreal conducted an analysis to determine the effects of the labour standards on the economy. In his analysis Raynauld divided countries into two groups: high- and low-standard countries. This division was based on the United Nations human-development index, with the top 20 countries of the index defined as the high-standard countries while the rest were characterized as the low-standard countries. A statistical analysis was then conducted to determine whether high-standard countries suffered as a result of the more stringent labour standards they applied. The findings were that between 1970 and 1993 none of the 20 countries with high standards had experienced any drop in export market share. Among the 145 low-standards countries, only 23 (16 per cent) had their export share increase over that period. Raynauld's findings indicate that labour standards have had no significant negative impact on the competitiveness of the developed countries, which is also the conclusion reached by the OECD's 1994 Employment Outlook Study,[112] which also found no correlation between labour standards and overall trade performance.

With regard to foreign direct investment (FDI) inflows, Raynauld used the same index to calculate FDI inflows, and found that labour standards did not have any major negative impact on high standard of living countries. Despite the notion that high labour standards would result in FDI being relocated to low-standard regions, only two of the low-standard countries saw their share increase. Further findings from Raynauld's study reveal countries with low wages as a result of low labour standards, also have significantly lower productivity. This suggests that it may also be in the interest of investors to pursue higher labour standards, in order to yield more productivity.

According to these findings, adopting higher labour standards is not only a matter of human rights—a living wage to provide a decent standard of living should be a norm that is enjoyed in every social setting, regardless of whether one lives in the North or the South. Adopting higher labour standards is also a benefit to all of society as the health and occupational safety benefits enjoyed by workers will yield greater productivity and as a result, may promote higher educational achievement which is valuable to the whole of the country.

Notwithstanding these sound arguments, my own view is that the developed world should encourage in an evolutionary way, rather than a revolutionary way, improvements in environmental and labour standards in developing countries.

Jeffrey Sachs is an acknowledged world expert on poverty reduction. He is Special Advisor to United Nations Secretary-General Ban Ki-moon on the Millennium Development Goals, and has spent 25 years advising governments and NGOs on poverty reduction strategies. In his book *The End of Poverty*,[113] he describes the extreme poverty in Bangladesh and how many Bangladeshi women in Dhaka, the capital of Bangladesh, have lifted themselves out of poverty, and made themselves more independent, by working long hours for low wages in the garment factories. These sweatshop jobs are a target for public protesters around the globe—but the women who work there, while acknowledging the arduous conditions and poor pay, see these jobs as the first step out of extreme poverty. When Jeffrey Sachs interviewed these workers, they asserted that these garment factory jobs were "the greatest opportunity that these women could ever have imagined, and that their employment had changed their lives for the better."[114] Sachs goes on to say:

> Some rich-country protesters have argued that Dhaka's apparel firms should either pay far higher wage rates or be closed, but closing such factories as a result of wages forced above worker productivity would be little more than a ticket for these women back to rural misery. For these young women, these factories offer not only opportunities for personal freedom, but also the first rung on the ladder of rising skills and income for themselves and within a few years, for their children. Virtually every poor country that has developed successfully has gone through these first stages of industrialization.[115]

In our zeal to help workers who receive sub-standard pay (by Western standards), in our attempt to raise the bar of environmental performance too quickly, we may inadvertently push people back into poverty. While focusing attention on these issues can have positive affects, we should not, in my view, be arbitrary and prescriptive in the responses we propose. Better labour and environmental standards which are harmonized with the developed world as a *quid pro quo* for international recognition, however well intentioned, will act against their best interests. We need to keep the pressure on countries in the developing world to improve their labour and environmental standards over time—with realistic goals and a timetable that is reasonable and pragmatic.

Trade Barriers

In the quest to reduce or eliminate world poverty, the attack must be multi-pronged and multi-dimensional. Focusing on corruption in developing countries, while important, will not be sufficient in and of itself. This is why trade barriers evidenced by tariff and non-tariff barriers—those that diminish the ability of developing countries to sell their products and services into Europe and North America—must also receive our close attention. These constraints result in developing countries being unable to reap the benefit of this economic activity—jobs and prosperity. Developing countries that have achieved the greatest success in alleviating poverty are the same countries whose economies have grown through trade.

We need to extend duty-free and quota-free access to the economies of developed countries from the Least Developed Countries (referred to as LCDs) and identified by the UN as the 49 poorest countries in the world. For countries like Canada, this should also include supply-managed agricultural products (dairy, poultry, and eggs).

In 2001, the World Trade Organization (WTO) launched a broad round of talks in Qatar to lower global trade barriers. The Doha round, as it has come to be known as, called on the industrialized world to provide lower-cost access to patented medicines and to reduce or eliminate distorting agricultural subsidies. The Doha round of trade talks has now collapsed, with the result that many countries are now more aggressively pursuing bilateral arrangements. This development is very unfortunate, because developing countries need new markets for their products. Huge agricultural subsidies in Europe and the United States distort the international agricultural markets and create an uneven playing field between industrial countries and developing countries.

So, what does all this mean? It means that there are many reasons why some nations are poor. It also means that we need to deal more effectively with world poverty—and there are many ways of doing this. We need to find new solutions and approaches. We need to boost the levels of overseas development assistance from the more developed economies of the world. We need to remove trade barriers to give greater assess to world markets for the products of the least-developed countries. We need to think very pragmatically about the issues that surround labour and environmental standards. But the part we need to really focus in on, in my judgement, is corruption. To do otherwise is to miss one of the key, if not the most important, impediments in the fight against world poverty.

International Financial Markets and their Impact on the Poor

Stable international financial markets provide an important economic pre-condition for poverty-reduction efforts. While these markets are often seen as the playground for the rich and famous, when the markets fail, it is frequently the middle class and poor who are most affected. This is especially true in developing nations. A look at the global financial crises of the mid-1990s illustrates this point clearly.

The mid-1990s witnessed a number of global financial crises—in Mexico, Asia, and Russia—that rocked the world's financial markets. The primary cause of the Russian financial crisis of 1998 was the fall of oil prices, but it was precipitated primarily as a result of non-payment of taxes by the energy and manufacturing industries. By August 1, 1998, there were also approximately $12.5 billion in unpaid wages owed to Russian workers. A $22.6 billion International Monetary Fund and World Bank financial package was approved on July 13, 1998, but it was later revealed that about $5 billion of these international loans were stolen upon the arrival of the funds in Russia on the eve of the meltdown.

The stabilization package that was implemented in Mexico in 1995 achieved its intended results, but at a huge cost—not to the country's corrupt elites or foreign lenders, but to the country's middle class and poor. The resulting recession caused a reduction in average wages of almost 15 per cent. Fallout from the Asian financial crisis of 1997 had the same effect. Thailand's unemployment rate doubled. In Indonesia, millions lost their jobs, and at the same time the prices of basic staples like chicken and rice rose by nearly 100 per cent, resulting in riots in the streets.

In aiding countries such as Mexico and Indonesia, the International Monetary Fund (IMF) provides economic remedies, but many times in the past, the cure for the disease is often worse than the illness itself. The IMF has come to understand this and is attempting to move away from a "one size fits all" approach. They are modifying their concept of conditionality (i.e. the terms and conditions of their financial assistance) by both reducing the number of conditions and focusing on those actions that are required for macroeconomic stability and growth. This has been accompanied recently by a greater degree of transparency in the work and activities of the IMF. Both these developments are positive

The run on the Thai baht, which essentially precipitated the Asian financial crisis of 1997, is an interesting and important phenomenon to examine, especially since it was preceded by a period of unprecedented economic growth in that country. Some argue that the collapse of banking systems in Thailand (like that of Japan) was the result of cronyism—a form of corruption where loans are granted in return for personal favours. Others argue that the problem was more technical in nature—a run on the currency by speculators, which caused a severe downward spiral, resulting in the devaluation of the baht. Accepting this latter theory leads one to consider policy measures like the Tobin Tax, a global tax aimed at reducing speculative flows in currencies.

Global taxes have also been considered as a means of reducing poverty. France introduced an air tax in 2006, the proceeds of which will be used to fight AIDS in Africa. Other similar initiatives include an environmental tax on fuel, a tax on weapons sales, and an international super-lottery. The United Nations terms these initiatives "innovative sources of financing for development."

The Tobin Tax, named after James Tobin, was introduced in concept in 1972. Put simply, Tobin's idea was to create a small tax on international transactions. His idea stemmed from the volatile reality of financial markets, which are notorious for being characterized by a surge in buying, followed by a panic of selling which results in market crashes.[116] This has been especially harmful for people of the developing world, as seen with the Mexican peso crisis of 1994–5 and the Asian crisis of 1997–8.[117] In both these instances, the volatility of the financial market left these nations with high unemployment and stunted development.

Tobin's argument for a Currency Transaction Tax (CTT) rests on its ability to create stability, efficiency, and self-determination of nations.[118] First, Tobin has proposed a CTT of 0.5 per cent, which would stabilize markets by preventing speculators from buying and then quickly reselling large amounts of foreign currency. Secondly, to ensure efficiency, the proposed CTT would also be highest for short-term holdings and lowest for long-term investments, encouraging investors to make long-term commitments in these countries that are desperately needed for continued development.

Tobin also argues that the tax will prevent the IMF's one-size-fits-all way of dealing with lenders, which left countries such as Mexico, during the peso crisis, in a depression with high unemployment and 60 per cent interest rates. The CTT however, would be adaptable: if a country finds its currency threatened it could raise its CTT to a higher level to counteract the speculators, instead of raising interest rates. Such was the case in Chile, which, during the 1980s, faced a current account deficit and an over-valued exchange rate. Rather than raise interest rates, the country implemented a transaction tax of 1.5 per cent on incoming investment, resulting in an economic recovery and so averting a Mexican-like crisis.

Finally, it is argued that the Tobin Tax will help spread the ideal of democracy by giving those whose lives are most affected by the consequences of financial outcomes a greater say in financial transactions. This promotes the fundamental principle of democracy and self-determination. Unless citizens of each nation feel they have a stake in their economy, they will resist reforms necessary to develop it. The revenues derived from the CTT would empower nations to help themselves. Proponents of the Tobin Tax suggest that half the revenues from the CTT (the revenues from just a 0.1 per cent CTT is estimated to be over US $200 billion), would provide enough money to developing nations to aid poverty eradication and social development—with money still left over for environmental protection.

Opposition to the Tobin Tax comes from nations who fear the tax will restrict their freedom. Countries that would lose from a CTT are nations such as Switzerland which have harboured offshore facilities as tax havens, and have established a reputation of money-laundering sanctuaries since the 1930s. More significant, however, is the USA and UK opposition to the tax. Thatcher's implementation of the UK Banking Act removed all distinction between offshore and onshore markets, which transformed the UK into a crucial market with ex-British colonies such as Bermuda and the Cayman Islands as important offshore markets. This, coupled with the expansion of the New York market, has resulted in London and New York accounting for almost half of the world's foreign exchange since the year 2000. Unfortunately, the enormous influence of the US and the UK has meant that their opposition to the Tobin Tax is an opposition for all.

To get co-operation from nations on the tax, Tobin suggests making it a condition of membership to the IMF. In doing this, agreement among the members to levy the tax would result in the IMF acting as the administrator and establishing the rules of conduct. Tobin suggests that the wealthiest countries such as the UK, the USA, Germany, and Japan would earmark most of what they collect in revenues for "international purposes," such as financing the United Nations Development Program. Others argue that the IMF lacks legitimacy for governing the Tobin Tax, and the way to garner co-operation amongst nations is to create a new organization called the Tobin Tax Organization (TTO) which would be an independent body that collects and allocates the revenues from the tax.

In any event, co-operation among some nations has already begun. In Canada, for instance, a campaign led by the Halifax Initiative (a coalition of environment, development, and social justices groups) gave support to Canadian MP Lorne Nystrom's 1998 motion in the House of Commons, which encouraged the government to enact a tax on financial transactions in agreement with the international community. A signed Citizen's Declaration on the Tobin Tax was presented to Finance Minister Paul Martin, and the motion was passed in March 1999. Canada became the first parliament in the world to announce its intention to work towards adapting the Tobin Tax. With the continued co-operation of other countries, the Tobin Tax has the ability to empower the vulnerable and lead the path towards economic and democratic changes in the developing world. The real challenge is to ensure that, if the Tobin Tax is enacted, all countries adopt it—otherwise transactions will be directed to those jurisdictions where the tax is not in place. This is the real challenge with the Tobin Tax—making it universal.

Other international taxes to fight world poverty have been discussed and proposed. More recently, France, Brazil, and Chile got together with then UN Secretary-General Kofi Annan to promote a global tax, levied by the airline industry, to combat world poverty. New UN Secretary-General Ban Ki-moon would appear to support global taxes also. A declaration was signed in the summer of 2005 by 110 mostly developing countries supporting this tax which would augment the overseas development assistance coming from countries around the world. While this idea has some merit, the way it is proposed could hurt an already damaged airline industry which is only beginning to recover from the events of 9/11.

Considering all these examples and arguments, is it possible to avoid this type of major financial and economic collapse? This is a tall order perhaps, given the complexity and size of the challenge.

Initiatives have been launched by the international community and others are being debated.

With the encouragement and support of Rt. Hon. Paul Martin, P.C., M.P., then Canada's minister of finance, the Group of Twenty (G-20) finance ministers and central bank governors was established in 1999 to bring together systemically important industrialized and developing economies. The G-20 was created as a response both to the financial crises of the late 1990s and a growing recognition that key emerging-market countries were not adequately included in the core of global economic discussion and governance. The inaugural meeting of the G-20 took place in Berlin on 15–16 December 1999, hosted by the German and Canadian finance ministers.

The members of the G-20 are the finance ministers and central bank governors of 19 countries: Argentina, Australia, Brazil, Canada, China, France, Germany, India, Indonesia, Italy, Japan, Mexico, Russia, Saudi Arabia, South Africa, South Korea, Turkey, the United Kingdom, and the United States of America. The European Union is also a member, represented by the rotating council presidency and the European Central Bank. Together, member countries represent around 90 per cent of the global gross national product, 80 per cent of world trade (including EU intra-trade) as well as two-thirds of the world's population. The G-20's economic weight and broad membership gives it a high degree of legitimacy and influence over the management of the global economy and financial system.

While the G-20 started out as a forum for finance ministers, Paul Martin promoted the idea of expanding the concept to the level of first ministers (i.e. prime ministers, heads of state). The G-20 will assist in anticipating, and preparing for, international financial crises. As well, it is engaged in preventative work by proactively putting in place the policies and institutions necessary for good governance and sound fiscal and monetary policy in countries around the world.

A crisis of confidence exists for both public and private investors who might otherwise be interested in supporting development projects, but who are also very concerned about the quality of governance in many of the less developed jurisdictions. Until such time as confidence is regained, the developing world will have to focus on ways to generate more capital domestically—whether through public policies that encourage more savings or more employee share ownership and micro credit, through more developed local capital markets, or by freeing up "locked capital" in real estate. Foreign investors, both public and private, will want to see the citizens of less-developed countries invest in themselves. This will reduce risk, and over time reduce the extent of bribery and corruption.

At the same time, developing countries will need to more fully develop their institutions to support better governance. Institutions such as a strong parliament, which can better hold their executive branch to account, together with a free press, a corrupt-free judiciary, and auditor general-like agencies. Better and more transparent reporting of the income and assets of public officials would be a good step forward also. As well, reducing unneeded red tape helps to reduce the opportunities for bribery, as does paying bureaucrats a fair wage.

Developed countries should have mechanisms to reward countries that enjoin the fight against corruption, with tangible support, so that the word starts to spread that if you reduce or eliminate corruption, the developed world will recognize this in a tangible way.

The task is a big one. Why would we avoid doing the right thing because the job is not easy? The costs, not just economic, of inaction are huge. We need to question how this problem has been addressed up until now and find new ways to attack it. We owe it to ourselves and to the generations that will follow us.

CHAPTER 9

Governance, Development and Corruption

Only 10 years ago, the word "corruption" was not in the vocabulary of the World Bank. "Its staff spoke instead of 'implicit taxes' or 'rent-seeking behaviour' lest they be accused of meddling in politics."[119] Fortunately, James Wolfensohn, when he became president of the World Bank, decided that corruption had to come out of the closet and be dealt with. Political correctness, he decided, had to take a back seat to economy, efficiency, and justice. We must thank Mr. Wolfensohn for taking this stance—which at the time, and in that context, was very courageous.

This reticence in discussing corruption can also be seen in Jeffrey Sachs' book *The End of Poverty*,[120] where one cannot locate a reference to the word corruption in the book index. In fairness to Mr. Sachs, a world-leading thinker in the fight against poverty, his book does contain a chapter entitled "Myths and Magic Bullets," where three pages are devoted to corruption—under the heading Corruption is the Culprit. Three pages devoted to corruption in a book of 368 pages! In this part of his book he argues that in Africa corruption is used as an excuse not to fight poverty on that continent. He then argues that "Africa's governance is poor because Africa is poor."[121] In saying this, he makes the classic mistake of drawing a conclusion regarding cause and effect on the subject of the relationship between poverty and corruption. However, as I mentioned earlier, it is not known which causes which. No one knows this. I have come to the conclusion that since we will never know what the causal relationship is between poverty and corruption, we need to tackle both. We cannot, in my judgement, allow ourselves the luxury of avoiding dealing with corruption—the stakes are just too high.

The Relevance of Good Governance

Good governance is important in the public sector, the private sector, and in the not-for-profit sector. The culture of corruption is exacerbated when any one of these sectors has weak governance. Those impacted by bad governance vary based on the breadth of the sector. Corruption in national governments negatively affects all citizens of that jurisdiction, whereas the direct impact of corporate malfeasance is more limited. Collectively, however, the impact is cumulative when there is poor governance in any of these sectors.

Too often we learn that corporate managers, in their desire to inflate corporate profits, bend accounting rules or commit outright fraud. One could describe this type of behaviour as corporate corruption and it is just as offensive as corruption in the public sector. Often, members of the boards of directors of corporations are not independent of management and are not provided with the information they need to challenge management. As John Kenneth Galbraith asserts in his book *The Economics of Innocent Fraud*:

This fraud has accepted ceremonial aspects: One is a board of directors selected by management, fully subordinate to management but heard as the voice of the shareholders. It includes men and the necessary presence of one or two women who need only a passing knowledge of the enterprise; with rare exceptions, they are reliably acquiescent. Given a fee and some food, the directors are routinely informed by management on what has been decided or is already known. Approval is assumed, including for management compensation—compensation set by management itself.[122]

We have all read about rising executive compensation (often to ridiculously high levels) during periods of declining corporate profits and/ or falling stock market prices. Golden parachutes in the millions of dollars are typically available to down-sized executives concurrent with much stingier packages for other managers and workers.

The former chairman of the US Federal Reserve, Paul Volcker, rightly points a finger at the legal and accounting professions who have not been assertive enough, and whose principles have been subordinated to the will of investment bankers and senior management.

Corporate greed and malfeasance reinforce a culture of corruption and add to the challenge of eliminating corruption in both the private and public sectors.

The Role of Education, Communication and Collaboration

A 2007 report of the World Bank underlined the reality that it is not just poor countries who struggle with corruption and flawed government. It is a global issue. Developed countries can learn from developing countries as well. I recall at an IMF/GOPAC-sponsored workshop on the topic of the fight against money laundering in Nairobi for African parliamentarians, we learned much from our colleagues in Africa. One item that surprised me was the extent to which money was being laundered domestically in African countries and often being used to buy votes and favour in those countries. We had focused our discussion on the laundering of corrupt money offshore but after the session we appreciated that the problem (and potential solution) was two-fold. It is through dialogue and interaction that we learn from each other and are better able to move the policy agenda forward. In developed countries we have more experience with democratic institutions and market economies than do countries like Russia. By the same token, Russia can teach us much in the processes of decision-making in decentralized large economies.

Meetings such as these underscore the importance of creating dialogue between parliamentarians so that they can learn from each other, which in turn allows them to better serve their constituents and improve government. A perfect example of the fruits of this cooperation is the sharing of strategies for improving governance and combating corruption, both domestically and internationally. First let us examine the role of parliamentarians.

The institution of parliament has a key role to play in fighting corruption. Parliamentarians can hold the executive branch of government to account for their spending and administrative actions. This important role can be achieved in a number of different ways:

► Through debates and questions in the legislature itself;
► Through the work of an auditor general, or accounts chamber, that reports directly to parliament;
► By enquiry and investigative work by a public accounts committee of parliament.

At a Commonwealth Parliamentary Association Workshop held in Nairobi, Kenya, in December 2001 on the topic Parliamentary Oversight of Finance and the Budgetary Process which I attended, a general consensus was reached around the following points:

► Budget plans should be responsive to the priorities of citizens;
► The budget must have the approval of parliament;
► After the passing of the budget, funds expended must be accounted for to avoid the misuse of funds;
► Mechanisms in place to deter the misuse of funds must be adhered to.

These principles would be commonplace and the norm in countries like Canada—but in many countries in the world these standards are often not adhered to.

In addition to these oversights on budgets and finance, parliamentarians should use whatever power and influence they have to safeguard free speech, freedom of the press, and an active civil society of non-governmental organizations. In Canada, members of parliament on the government side shudder when the auditor general publishes his or her quarterly report because the media, the opposition parties, and the NGOs have a field day with it, embarrassing the government.

None of this is easy, especially in countries where the executive branch has most of the powers, constitutionally or by convention.

Parliament in Canada, and in most parliamentary democracies, has four separate and distinct responsibilities regarding its accountability over government:

- ▶ It approves legislative requests from government for programs and policies;
- ▶ The government has to seek authority from parliament (ways and means) for its policies on taxation in order to raise the funds necessary for government;
- ▶ The government must seek approval from parliament for spending authority (the Estimates process);
- ▶ Government is required to report to parliament and table a variety of reports on its performance.

This oversight role that parliament performs is absolutely crucial, and, if properly exercised, holds the government to account and should result in greater probity and prudence in its spending decisions. Corruption grows wherever accountability is weak.

Parliamentarians can also push for tax and regulatory reform. Those countries with more predictable regulatory regimes and lower levels of regulatory discretion have a better chance of minimizing or eliminating corruption.

Getting the institutions of government right is another area where parliamentarians can make a contribution. Corruption cannot be reined in by repression alone. Countries with presidential or semi-presidential systems have fewer built-in accountability mechanisms than parliamentary systems. International bodies can and do play an important role in the fight against corruption and money laundering. The Global Organization of Parliamentarians Against Corruption (GOPAC) has a number of very strong relationships with entities like the World Bank, the International Monetary Fund, the United Nations (in particular the UN Office on Drugs and Crime), US Aid, the Financial Action Task Force, the Organization of American States, the Inter-American Development Bank, and many others. By doing this, it is able to effectively and efficiently combine the technical and policy capabilities of organizations such as these with the legislative experience of parliamentarians. I have seen this work well, for example, at joint IMF/GOPAC workshops on the fight against money laundering directed at parliamentarians in developing and emerging economies. I am able to connect with parliamentarians at the political/legislative level, and the IMF is able to provide the technical and policy expertise needed to make these sessions very productive.

The Global Organization of Parliamentarians Against Corruption involves parliamentarians in the fight for better governance, as does the Parliamentary Network of the World Bank, which is growing in its influence and effectiveness.

The purpose of the Parliamentary Network of the World Bank (PNoWB) is to increase parliamentary involvement and effectiveness in the field of international development. The core mission of the PNoWB is fivefold:

▶ *Accountability:* To facilitate and encourage direct policy dialogue between parliamentarians and multilateral development institutions to provide greater transparency of World Bank policies and practices and increase collective accountability;

► *Advocacy:* To provide the members of the Network with a platform for coordinated parliamentary advocacy on international development issues;

► *Networking:* To encourage concerted action, early debate, and exchange of information among parliamentarians on major issues of international development, finance and poverty eradication;

► *Partnerships:* To take initiatives to further co-operation and encourage partnerships between parliamentarians and policy makers, the academic community, the business sector, and nongovernmental organizations on development issues;

► *Progress Review:* To promote the development of parliamentary mechanisms and practices for the effective democratic control of development assistance in all its phases.

To achieve these objectives, the PNoWB delivers these programs:

► *Annual Conference*: At least once a year the Network organizes a conference. This is organized in partnership with the parliament of the host country and the World Bank.

► *Field Trips:* The Network facilitates field trips for parliamentarians from donor countries to visit projects in developing countries. At the same time the Network organizes visits from parliamentarians from developing countries to parliaments in countries with well-established democratic traditions.

► *Website:* The Network has its own website in order to facilitate coalition-building and the exchange of information on international development issues among parliamentarians and multilateral institutions such as the World Bank (www.pnowb.org).

► *Consultations:* The PNoWB engages in consultations with the World Bank and other international financial institutions on their respective projects, programs, and research activities.

► *Training:* The Network seeks training opportunities for parliamentarians, in partnership with the World Bank Institute, amongst others, on the Bank's technical procedures.

▶ *Newsletter:* A newsletter is disseminated regularly to inform members about the activities of the Network and to raise its profile vis-à-vis third parties. The newsletter features, among other things, interviews with parliamentarians active in international development.

▶ *Research:* The Network encourages small-scale, parliament-specific research projects based on the needs defined by the members of the Network.

▶ *Partnerships:* The Network actively seeks opportunities to build partnerships with other international parliamentary networks to encourage cross-fertilization. In addition, the Network attempts to build bridges with other constituencies involved in international development (academia, NGOs, etc.).

This type of parliamentary interaction with the World Bank, and increasingly with other institutions like the International Monetary Fund, can be useful accountability mechanisms for elected officials. It provides them with an opportunity to engage in dialogue with these institutions and provide them with feedback on priorities and best practices.

We must never forget the purpose of agencies and parliamentary networks when they engage in work related to good governance. The goal is to reduce or eliminate corruption and money laundering so that the quality of life for citizens in developing and emerging economies is enhanced. Each stakeholder group brings its unique skills and experience to the table. Together the synergies can be significant. I have seen this at work. Measuring success is difficult, but the "do nothing" alternative is simply not acceptable to most.

The United Nations also has an important role to play in the fight against corruption and in improving the investment climate in developing countries, a perfect example of which is the UN Convention Against Corruption (UNCAC). As I pointed out in my April 28, 2004, remarks in the 2004 Ordinary Session of the Parliamentary Assembly of the Council of Europe during the debate on strength-

ening the United Nations, the UNCAC was signed by over 95 countries in December 2003 at a ceremony hosted by the government of
Mexico.

> Canada is committed to a multilateral approach to interna-
> tional security and the prevention of armed conflict. This is
> why we decided not to participate in the war against Iraq—
> because there was no international consensus to act militarily
> at that time. The Canadian public generally was very support-
> ive of this position, and continues to be.
>
> The United Nations is in need of reform, however. There are
> times when the United Nations seemed to be paralysed into
> inaction. Ten years ago, hundreds of thousands of Rwandans
> lost their lives in genocide, while the international community
> failed to act. Our own Lieutenant General Roméo Dallaire was
> very much at the epicentre of this tragedy. Secretary General
> Kofi Annan is aware of these structural and decision-making
> problems at the UN, and I applaud him for addressing this—
> especially with the High Level Panel on Threats, Challenges
> and Change.
>
> Canada has promoted the human security agenda which
> emphasizes that the security of individuals transcends national
> borders and requires the international community to act if it
> is at risk. There is a balance here, however, that needs to be
> carefully maintained to ensure that the sovereignty of nations
> is respected.
>
> When is it appropriate for a country, or the international
> community, to attempt to overthrow a despotic ruler in a
> failed or failing state when the personal security of citizens is
> threatened? What criteria should apply? In its reform agenda,
> the United Nations needs to address these vexing questions,
> and design a governance model that will facilitate timely and
> appropriate responses when the safety and security of our fel-
> low citizens of the world are at risk.

Reform of the UN Security Council must protect the role of middle powers—like many of the member states of the Council of Europe and Canada, while acknowledging the need for new permanent members ...

The area of so-called "soft" threats is one where the United Nations can play a larger role as well—principally through the Economic and Social Council or ECOSOC.

The United Nations Convention Against Corruption and the UN Commission on the Private Sector and Development are two very important recent initiatives focused in this area—but more needs to be done ...

I look forward to the reform of the United Nations and to the contribution that the Parliamentary Assembly of the Council of Europe can make to this transformation. The UN is a very important institution that deserves our full attention ...

The new anti-corruption convention deals with prevention and punishment of corruption in both the private and public sectors. The highlights of this convention are as follows:

▶ *Prevention:* Measures such as the establishment of anti-corruption bodies and enhanced transparency in the financing of election campaigns and political parties address both the public and private sectors. Requirements are also established for the prevention of corruption in the judiciary and in public procurement. The convention calls on countries to actively promote the involvement of non-governmental and community-based organizations as well as other elements of civil society, to raise public awareness of corruption.

▶ *Criminalization:* Countries are required to establish criminal and other offences to cover a wide range of acts of corruption. This includes not only basic forms of corruption, such as bribery and the embezzlement of public funds, but also trading in influence and the concealment and laundering of the proceeds of corruption.

► *International Co-operation:* Countries agree to co-operate in the fight against corruption, including prevention and investigation activities, and the prosecution of offenders. The convention also binds countries to render specific forms of mutual legal assistance in gathering and transferring evidence for use in court and to extradite offenders. Countries must also undertake measures to support the tracing, freezing, seizure, and confiscation of the proceeds of corruption.

► *Asset Recovery:* This is an important issue for many developing countries where high level corruption has plundered the national wealth, and where resources are badly needed for reconstruction and the rehabilitation of societies under new governments. Measures include the prevention and detection of transfers of illicitly acquired assets, the recovery of property, and the return and disposition of assets.

Winning the battle against corruption and money laundering requires an all-out effort by many players. A public more informed about the nature and extent of these problems, and the havoc they wreak, is a critical piece in this puzzle. It requires sustained pressure on governments, elected officials, corporations, and others. Non-governmental organizations like Transparency International, the United Nations, the World Bank, the IMF, the Financial Action Task Force, and countless others also have a key role to play in researching this topic, providing citizens and policy makers with good information and in advocating change. Parliamentarians, through groups like GOPAC, are able to demand greater transparency, oversight and accountability as it relates to corruption and money laundering, and to pass legislation and establish institutions to tackle these problems.

Having said this, there are no magic bullets, no instant solutions.

Realistically, corruption and money laundering will never be completely eliminated. With dedication and hard work, however, the fight against global poverty can be enhanced if we reduce the incidence of corruption. To do this, we need the courage and foresight to look at new ideas and we must dedicate ourselves to new solutions to these serious problems.

CHAPTER 10

Some Solutions to the Problem

We need to attack the challenges of poverty and corruption in different ways. The old methods have yielded some limited success in reducing poverty, but the results have been very modest. Conventional wisdoms need to be re-visited and new paradigms developed.

Here are some of the areas I believe we need to focus on if we are to significantly reduce poverty and corruption in the years ahead:

Make corruption a crime against humanity. When one evaluates the havoc that corruption wreaks on a nation, it is easy to understand why a parliamentarian from an African country at a meeting in Ottawa suggested that corruption should be designated by the United Nations as a crime against humanity. While it is always difficult and dangerous to equate economic crimes with crimes like genocide, murder, and rape, the negative impact that corruption has on a country's citizens cannot be underestimated.

Implement an international treaty to combat money laundering. While there have been a number of international conventions and treaties on bribery and corruption (e.g. UN Convention Against Corruption, OECD Convention on Bribery and Corruption), the

international efforts against the related problem of money laundering have been more regional (e.g. work of the Council of Europe).

One of the priorities of the Global Organization of Parliamentarians Against Corruption is to work towards an international convention or treaty against money laundering. The old adage "a chain is
as strong as its weakest link" certainly applies to money-laundering
activities, and criminals or corrupt leaders will always direct their
money-laundering efforts to those countries with the weakest legislative and regulatory environment. If all countries would make public
international commitments to combat this scourge, the noose would
be tightened further. This also includes the offshore banking centres and tax havens, because although many of them have improved
their efforts to combat money laundering, much more needs to be
done. An international convention on money laundering must build
on the Financial Action Task Force standards, and not dilute them
in any way. The notion of a convention should be abandoned if the
negotiated result is a reduction in these internationally recognized
standards.

*Require the mandatory disclosure of income and assets of public
officials.* Transparency is a very important tool in the fight against
corruption and money laundering. While it might appear naïve to
think that disclosure by public officials of their income and assets is
an achievable goal in some countries, it is most worthy of pursuit. In
most developed countries such mandatory disclosure requirements
are commonplace. In Canada, we have an ethics commissioner who
reports to parliament and who sets out the public reporting requirements of members of parliament (with a similar system for senators),
parliamentary secretaries, and members of cabinet. The ethics commissioner scrutinizes all the assets and liabilities of MPs and seeks
redress if conflicts of interest occur (e.g. blind trusts for parliamentary secretaries and ministers). Certain summary information is
maintained on a publicly accessible web site for all to see (although
some would argue the disclosure does not go far enough). This is

the information that the Ethics Commissioner of the Parliament of Canada scrutinizes and provides summary information to the public about:

Public Declaration of Gifts, hospitality or other benefits received;
Public Declaration of Liabilities;
Public Declaration of Outside Activities;
Public Declaration of Past Outside Activities;
Public Declaration of Recusal;
Summary Statement with Recusal;
Summary Statement with Recusal & Part III;
Summary Statemen.t

Reward and support jurisdictions that practice good governance.
We need to reward good governance, such as that of Ghana in Africa, which, under President John Kufuor's able leadership, has committed itself to fighting bribery and corruption. I had the great honour to meet President Kufuor when he came to Canada on a state visit in 2001.[123] We met at Rideau Hall and discussed a range of topics including agricultural opportunities in the Afram Plains of Ghana, a very large and fertile area in that country. The president's desire was (and is) to develop value-added and export opportunities in this area through public/private partnerships in an effort to promote economic development, and assist in the achievement of a sustainable national food supply for Ghana. We also discussed the availability of ferries that could serve on the huge Lake Volta in Ghana, a lake that extends into the vast interior of that country. Ferries were viewed, and perhaps still are, as a needed mode of transportation for people and goods to better connect the country. At that time I was aware of the "bargain-basement" sale of three large ferries by the British Columbia Ferry Corporation, so I put my Ghanaian friends in touch with the company that was responsible for their disposal. The three ferries in question were eventually sold for a grand total of some $10 million, even though they had cost the B.C. taxpayer about $400 million! Unfortunately a transaction could not be consummated

with the Ghanaian interests for a variety of reasons, including the need for major expensive retrofits to reduce the operating costs of the vessels, and the fact that the ships' draught exceeded the capacity of the lake in important locations. Finance was also a problem.

It was very frustrating to understand the many needs in a country like Ghana (one whose leader remains committed to good governance) and the inability to attract much-needed foreign capital. The contrast on continents like Africa is always so startling. Compare Ghana with Zimbabwe, for example. In an August 30, 2002, letter I sent to then Prime Minister Jean Chrétien, I referred to Zimbabwe as "Land Reform Gone Terribly Wrong."[124] I went on to say:

> The Government of Canada should be objecting in the strongest terms possible to the undemocratic and tragically misguided methods of President Robert Mugabe. Appropriate international action should be implemented in concert with the United Nations and the road to sensible land reform begun.[125]

In this same letter I offered my views on Somalia:

> Given our unique relationship with Somalia, Canada should be playing a stronger leadership role in the search for governance models and development assistance that will lead to lasting peace, stability, and democracy in Somalia and the Horn of Africa. We should also support and assist the Somali-Canadian Diaspora in their efforts to bring about peace and security in the area.[126]

And on Ghana:

> As part of the plan for Africa that was agreed to at the recent G-8 meeting at Kananaskis, Canada should support countries like Ghana who, under the capable leadership of President

Kufuor, has made great strides in eliminating bribery and corruption. Last year I submitted two proposals to you on behalf
of the Canada-Ghana Business Council—an organization that
I helped to form. The first proposal seeks funding for a high-
level Trade Mission from Ghana to Canada. The second initiative is the development of a "Doing Business in Ghana" guide,
a publication that would assist Canadian businessmen and
women in their business dealings in Ghana.

There are others who share my view that more needs to be done to
reward good governance. In October 2006 Mo Ibrahim, a Sudanese-
born millionaire, announced the creation of what he called the
world's biggest individual prize—US $5 million, spread over 10 years,
for the Sub-Saharan African president who, on leaving office, has
demonstrated the greatest commitment to democracy and good
governance. Hopefully this initiative will prove to be an incentive for
leaders to run "clean" governments, although the initiative has been
criticized already as a form of bribery itself.

On April 26, 2003, I hosted, together with the Canadian International Development Agency (CIDA) and the Somali Press, a Somalia Peace and Reconciliation conference in my riding of Etobicoke
North in Toronto. About 75 members of the Somalia Diaspora in
Toronto and elsewhere attended the conference and the group came
up with 13 recommendations. The conference's aims were to focus on
two primary objectives, namely:

- ► What can Canada do, or should be doing, to assist in the reconstruction of Somalia?
- ► How can Canada provide leadership in the international community to achieve the objectives of re-construction and re-develop-
ment in Somalia?

The report contained 13 different recommendations and concluded
with the following statement:

Canadians are an important resource for Canada and for the peace and reconciliation process in Somalia. As we wait for the results of the latest peace conference in Kenya, we must acknowledge that Canada could have a role in promoting peace and stability in the Horn of Africa. Canada's Somali-Canadian population would be willing to stand by the Canadian government's commitments to any involvement in the Somali peace and reconciliation process and indeed look towards Canada for a lead that could galvanize the inertia that characterizes the international community's position on Somalia.[127]

There is currently another interesting model in place which rewards good governance—the Millennium Challenge Corporation. In January 2004, the US Congress passed a new compact for global development and created the Millennium Challenge Corporation (MCC) which links greater contributions from developed nations to greater responsibility from developing nations. The Millennium Challenge Account (MCA) is the vehicle through which development assistance is provided to those countries that rule justly, invest in their people, and encourage economic freedom. An initial $1 billion in funding was committed for fiscal year 2004, and President Bush has pledged to increase funding for the MCA to $5 billion a year starting in fiscal year 2006, roughly a 50 per cent increase over then current USA core development assistance. The mandate of MCA is presented on its website. As is noted there, "The MCA draws on lessons learned about development over the past 50 years":

▶ Aid is most effective when it reinforces sound political, economic and social policies—which are key to encouraging the inflows of private capital and increased trade—the real engines of economic growth;

▶ Development plans supported by a broad range of stakeholders, and for which countries have primary responsibility, engender country ownership and are more likely to succeed;

► Integrating monitoring and evaluation into the design of activities boosts effectiveness, accountability, and the transparency with which taxpayer resources are used. [128]

It is based on these key principles:

► *Reduce Poverty through Economic Growth:* The MCC will focus specifically on promoting sustainable economic growth that reduces poverty through investments in areas such as agriculture, education, private sector development, and capacity building.
► *Reward Good Policy:* Using objective indicators, countries will be selected to receive assistance based on their performance in governing justly, investing their citizens, and encouraging economic freedom.
► *Operate in Partnership:* Working closely with the MCC, countries that receive MCA assistance will be responsible for identifying the greatest barriers to their own development, ensuring civil society participation, and developing an MCA program. MCA participation will require a high-level commitment from the host government. Each MCA country will enter into a public compact with the MCC that includes a multi-year plan for achieving shared development objectives and identifies the responsibilities of each partner in achieving those objectives.
► *Focus on Results:* MCA assistance will go to those countries that have developed well-designed programs with clear objectives, benchmarks to measure progress, procedures to ensure fiscal accountability for the use of MCA assistance, and a plan for effective monitoring and objective evaluation of results. Programs will be designed to enable progress to be sustained after the funding under the MCA Compact has ended.[129]

It has taken some time for the Millennium Challenge Corporation (MCC) to swing into action. In fact, the first grant under this program was only made on April 18, 2005, over one year after the MCC's inception. The first approval was a grant of US $110 million to the Republic of Madagascar. Some are saying that the criteria that are used to access funding under the Millennium Challenge Account are too subjective. For example, a country cannot qualify for aid unless it ranks in the top half quartile of the least-corrupt countries. Others argue that the Millennium Challenge Corporation encourages countries to reform so that they can qualify for its funding. This debate has led for a call to review this initiative by the US Senate who began hearings on this topic in the spring of 2005. I believe the Millennium Challenge Corporation is a good idea—we need more of them,

Build capacity in developing countries so that they can help themselves. As I indicated earlier, we can't solve all the challenges of the developing world without the active participation—financial and otherwise—of a country's citizens in their own economies. Would foreign investors, both public and private, considering Africa as an investment target like to witness Africans investing in Africa alongside their own capital? I would think so. I became aware of the critical importance of concepts like "sweat equity" and local investor participation when I was exposed to the Northwest Territories Housing Corporation in Canada's North. Their fully subsidized properties were often in a state of poor repair, whereas the sweat equity properties were well maintained. The lesson, in my judgment, is that you need local commitment, investment, and participation are needed for economic development initiatives to work effectively. It is also necessary to build capacity in developing countries in other areas—like an effective banking system, an independent and free media, as well as parliamentary accountability systems.

Encourage the formation of domestic savings and capital pools in developing countries. In the short to medium term, given the generally bad state of governance and corruption, it is necessary to be realistic about the appetite of the developed world to accelerate our aid to poorer countries. Taxpayers and voters in the developed world do not, and will not, support 40 to 60 cents of every aid dollar going to its intended purpose, with the balance lining the pockets of local officials and politicians and/or ending up in Swiss bank accounts. This scenario is simply not acceptable.

Investment capital will likewise have no incentive to flow to the developing world. For example, while foreign direct investment (FDI) rose to a record US $644 billion worldwide in 1998, FDI to Africa declined from $9.4 billion in 1997 to $8.3 billion in 1998. Africa's share decreased from two per cent to 1.3 per cent of global FDI.[130]

What can be done? It begins, I believe, with the goal of increasing the levels of domestic savings in countries in the developing world. Some countries are rapidly moving in this direction, as I learned at an Economic and Social Council meeting of the United Nations in Geneva in the year 2000 from the minister of finance and economic planning for Ghana. There is a wide range of public policies that encourage domestic savings—savings that can be invested in the developing economies.

As was noted in a February 2003 Canadian International Development Agency consultation document entitled *Expanding Opportunities: Framework for Private Sector Development*:

> Domestic savings, by far, represent the most important source of investable capital in all economies, typically accounting for well over 90 per cent of finance on a net basis. Foreign savings, whether public (as in development assistance), or private (as in foreign direct investment and private capital flows), can be important and can catalyze change, but in the bigger picture, it remains a "top-up," or complement, to domestic savings. While there are different behavioural attributes to different sizes of enterprises, in general, it is fair to say that the development of a vibrant, healthy and sufficiently diverse domestic private sector is generally seen as a precondition for attracting significant levels of foreign direct investment and integrating into the global economy.[131]

The UNDP report *Unleashing Entrepreneurship: Making Business Work for the Poor* notes that

> domestic resources are much larger than actual or potential external resources. Domestic private investment averaged 10–12 per cent of GDP in the 1990s, compared with 7 per cent for domestic public investment and 2–5 per cent for foreign direct investment (FDI). Second, when informal resources are examined, such as potential land value, the domestic assets that can be tapped are much larger than cumulative FDI or private portfolio flows. Third, unleashing the domestic resources in an economy—both financial and entrepreneurial—is likely to create a more stable and sustainable pattern of growth.[132]

One huge source of funds for individuals in developing countries is remittances from relatives abroad. These entail regular payments sent by immigrants in Canada or other developed nations to their relatives in, say, India.

> Most people remit just a few hundred dollars per transaction, but those contributions add up. Worldwide, remittances are now US $100 billion a year, according to Canada's federal finance department. The largest recipient, Mexico, now receives more than US $16 billion a year in such transfers. India, the second highest, gets more than US $10 billion, a figure that appears to be growing... Jamaica, with a gross domestic product of just US $11.13 billion last year—received US $1.5 billion in remittances from around the world in 2002.[133]

To put these remittances into some context, the annual remittances from expatriates living in Canada to individuals in Jamaica is about equal to the annual development assistance funding flowing from the Canadian International Development Agency to Jamaica each year (just over $13 million). These remittances are a form of development assistance and the funds are undoubtedly used primarily by the recipients for badly needed basic requirements like food, clothing, shelter, and education—but imagine if this flow of capital, or some of it, could be used as a source of capital for starting or growing small businesses in these developing countries.

To accomplish this objective, however, investors must have confidence in the laws and regulatory environment in the country in which they are planning to invest. C.K. Prahalad refers to the need for Transaction Governance Capacity.[134] By this he means the following:

> Fundamental to the evolution of capital markets and a vibrant private sector is the need for a transparent market for capital, land, labour, commodities, and knowledge. Transparency results from widely understood and clearly enforced rules. Transactions involving these rules must be clear and unambiguous. Ownership and the transfer of ownership must be enforced...TGC is the capacity of a society to guarantee transparency in the process of economic transactions and the ability to enforce commercial contracts.[135]

Business does not have a big appetite for uncertainty. For investment to flow the rules of the game need to be clear, understood, reasonable, and enforceable.

Expand micro credit—especially to women. Focusing on micro finance by providing access to affordable credit for new and expanding small businesses in poor countries is another important way in which to help alleviate poverty in developing nations. When I had the opportunity to represent Canada's then finance minister Paul Martin at meetings of the European Bank for Reconstruction and Development (EBRD) in 2001, the president of the EBRD at the time, Mr. Jean Lemierre, agreed with me that micro finance should be a priority—especially micro credit for women (not to be sexist, but women have a better track record with micro credit). The EBRD continues to promote and advance micro credit—advancing a small loan to a woman to buy a sewing machine or set of machines to start a small business, for example.

I have seen the power of women and sewing machines in my own riding of Etobicoke North in Toronto. A group of Somali immigrant women some years ago established Haween Enterprises (Haween is derived from the Somali word for women) with an initial donation of a few Singer sewing machines. The company has grown substantially and now provides sewing, cutting, and product development services for clothing and tote bags for schools, conferences, and other institutions.

The payoffs from investments like this can be enormous. As the Oxfam Great Britain policy department noted in 1999, "Increased household income is the single biggest factor in determining the rate of improvement in health and education status, pointing to the need for economic growth to be placed at the centre of poverty reduction policies."

One of the great micro credit success stories is the Grameen Bank in Bangladesh. In fact, the bank's founder, Muhammad Yunus, together with the Grameen Bank, were awarded the 2006 Nobel Peace Prize for their efforts to create economic and social development from below. This bank, which has grown from its start in 1976 to a portfolio of loans currently exceeding $1 billion to over two million borrowers, provides credit to the poorest of the poor in rural Bangladesh without the requirement for any collateral. It began by leasing underutilized fishing ponds and irrigation pumps and later expanded into venture capital and other businesses. Since the Grameen Bank (Grameen is the Bengali word for village) opened for business, 31 million people, three-quarters of them women and two-thirds classified as the "poorest of the poor," have received micro loans in more than 40 countries, according to the *No-Nonsense Guide to International Development*.

It has financed businesses that manufacture everything from cosmetics and candles to bread, umbrellas, mosquito nets, even mobile phones. And what about the loan repayment rate? Ninety-eight per cent, thanks in large part to the peer pressure that exists in villages to keep the community's reputation clean. Contrast that repayment rate to the 10 per cent recovery boasted by the Bangladesh Industrial Development Bank, which serves only people with property. No contest.[136]

The role of micro credit for women also brings to light the question of gender in development and the conflict between the WID (Women in Development approach) versus the GAD (Gender in Development approach). There is a division among scholars as it applies to the question of gender in development politics.

The WID approach focuses more on the "practical gender needs" of women, such as the basic need to adequate clean water, proper living conditions, employment, etc. Often international organizations like the World Bank have superficially tacked on these WID policies to development projects, without effective research and planning.[137] The GAD movement arose in 1986 by critiquing the WID approach as not sufficiently including women in development planning. The GAD approach believes that in order to make effective changes for women in development, planning needs to include politically empowering women.[138] This approach focuses on the "strategic gender needs" of women by creating a line of credit, abolishing domestic violence, eliminating inequalities in the division of labour (many countries in the developing world have legislation giving men a higher minimum wage then women), etc. The Grameen Bank is a good example of the GAD approach to women and development.

Unlock "trapped" capital in developing countries. In his book *The Mystery of Capital*, Hernando de Soto explores why capitalism triumphs in the West and fails everywhere else. He was led to conclude that, far being a cultural phenomenon, much of the failure can be attributed to the lack of legal property systems in many developing countries. He estimates that "the total value of the real estate held, but not legally owned by the poor of the Third World and former communist nations is at least US $9.3 trillion".[139] This is a staggering sum—nearly twice as much as the total value of all the companies listed on 20 of the world's main stock exchanges, including New York, Tokyo, London, Frankfurt, Toronto, Paris, Milan, the NASDAQ, and a dozen others.

This represents "dead capital." For example, "In Haiti ... 68 per cent of the city dwellers and 97 per cent of people in the country-side living in housing to which nobody has clear legal title. In Egypt dead-capital housing is home for 92 per cent of city dwellers and 83 per cent of people in the countryside."[140]

Irshad Manji, in her book *The Trouble with Islam*, describes dead capital this way:

Two examples of dead capital are black market businesses, which operate off the books and off the tax rolls, and proper-ties claimed by squatters, who have no clear title to the parcels of land on which they live. In each case, we're talking about assets that poor people can't afford to register legally because it takes too much government paperwork, time, and fees. Lose the red tape, de Soto has shown, and the capital of the enterpris-ing lower classes can explode into something truly construc-tive. Squatters can get collateral to secure mortgages and build less provisional lives. Cash-only businesses can expand into legal and value-added companies. Governments can thereby acquire taxable income. Everybody wins, particularly women and children. They're usually the ones who stay home in order to guard untitled land. Men, after all, must work. When prop-erty is documented, though, women can leave the premises to sell goods at the market, for instance, and children can go to school. After Peru implemented de Soto's ideas, school attendance rose by twenty-six per cent...[141]

What would the benefits be of freeing up this dead capital? In his book *The Fortune at the Bottom of the Pyramid*, C.K. Prahalad argues that "All forms of foreign investment in poor countries—whether aid, FDI by multinational firms (the private sector) or philanthropy—are but a fraction of the potential for capital that is trapped in these countries."[142]

The political elites in developing countries are concluding that if they have to rely on sources of finance outside their respective countries, they will only muddle along with no significant progress in uplifting their economies and the plight of their impoverished citizens.

Facilitate share ownership by employees. It is also important to encourage broad-based local ownership of companies in the developing world, through instruments like Employee Share Ownership Plans (ESOPs). In today's world, the flow of technology and information are just as important as the flow of goods and capital to developing economies. As Jeff Gates asserts in his book *The Ownership Solution*,[143] "For development to take root and for prosperity to be enjoyed by more than a financially savvy few, the financial value of that development must not only be captured for those *residing* in the developing country; it must also be captured for a *broad base* of those residents [italics are the author's]."[144] Wages alone may not be enough, especially in an age where manufacturing flows to the lowest cost area.

Employee share ownership is driven by the notion that employees who have a stake in their company will be more motivated to enhance productivity because they will be able to share in the rewards. They are also better connected to the nation's economic system. These employees also achieve greater job satisfaction. Unlike stock option schemes, which are targeted at management, ESOPs involve everyone in the firm, from the receptionist, to the inventory clerks, to the sales staff and senior management. It is an all-inclusive approach. Some years ago, a study was done of those companies listed on the Toronto Stock Exchange who were employee owned—and they exhibited a 34 per cent enhancement in productivity and return on investment compared with companies with no such employee share participation.

Employee share purchase plans, while a step in the right direction, do not offer the advantages of ESOPs because participation is voluntary.

Gates argues that ownership-transforming financing techniques, like ESOPs, will be necessary to accelerate growth in developing countries. Broad-based domestic ownership will assist in the development of the capital markets in those countries. The development of these markets will attract more outside investment as they acquire more liquidity and create exit strategy possibilities if required. Gates argues that development assistance tied to broad-based equity ownership would also address social justice concerns because of the greater inclusiveness of employee share ownership.

He argues, with merit, that we should be addressing root causes, not symptoms. Just as food is not the long-term solution to hunger, so is money not a cure for poverty. "A lack of money is a symptom, not a cause of poverty. Poverty is cured not with money but by gaining access to the productiveness—the skills and the tools—required to earn money."[145]

Stem the laundering of corrupt money. Parliamentarians from around the world with whom I have spoken have linked the need to fight corruption and money laundering simultaneously. Citizens and honest elected officials in corrupt countries are very dismayed when they witness the flight of corrupt funds, with impunity, to offshore banking centres in Switzerland, Luxembourg, the Bahamas, and the like. Making it more difficult to launder corrupt money will act as a deterrent to corruption—even if the impact is not a huge one. Countries around the world need to adopt the anti-money-laundering standards espoused by the Financial Action Task Force. This involves two parts that are inextricably linked together. Not only is anti-money-laundering legislation needed in countries around the world, but resources are needed to establish and operate a financial intelligence unit. One part of this equation cannot be put in place without the other. There is no point in legislating against money laundering without a financial intelligence unit to monitor monetary transactions and identify suspicious transactions. Likewise, establishing a financial intelligence unit without the authority of enabling legislation will result in a toothless tiger. International banks, especially offshore banks, must co-operate more fully in identifying and rejecting the flight of corrupt money. In addition, these banks must help in the repatriation of corrupt assets to the countries where they belong. Progress is being made on all these fronts, but more must be done.

Build a stronger role for parliamentarians in demanding greater accountability and transparency from the executive branch of government. Most parliaments have some type of separation of duties amongst the three main elements of governance—the executive branch, the legislative branch, and the judiciary. One key role for the legislature is to hold the executive branch (those who have been charged with the responsibility to run the day-to-day operations of the government and to provide the government with overall policy direction) accountable to the citizenry. While corruption is certainly not limited to the executive branch in many countries, heads of state, ministers, and other senior officials hold many of the levers of power and are most susceptible to bribes.

The legislature is able to, and should, put mechanisms in place to increase transparency and sanctions against corruption. This would include, but not be limited to, strong legislation making bribery and corruption illegal; an active, all-party, and independent public accounts committee of the legislature which is charged with examining the revenue and expenses of the government to ensure probity and honesty in the conduct of the affairs of government; an auditor general, or equivalent, who reports directly to parliament on the financial affairs of the government and issues an annual audit opinion on the government's financial statements.

Promote an independent judiciary, an independent auditor general (or its equivalent), and an adequately resourced anti-corruption agency. In some countries, the price of getting a judge to bring in a not-guilty verdict for someone charged with an offence is common knowledge. Kenya is a good example of this. Without an independent judiciary that is committed to the fight against corruption, there is little hope to stem the tide of bribery and corruption because corrupt officials must, from time to time, be brought to justice. With a corrupt judiciary, what are the chances of this happening? Besides, the judiciary set a very important example for society. If the judiciary is corrupt, what signal does that send? It reinforces the fact that bribery and corruption is an acceptable societal norm.

Institutions like Canada's auditor general, which reports directly to parliament and whose mission is to hold the government to account for the way it spends money and manages the affairs of state, is another important building block to greater transparency and accountability.

Some countries, like Russia, have formed anti-corruption agencies or commissions. This is to be encouraged, notwithstanding the limited success of organizations like this. Anything that shines more light on this problem is a positive step.

Help to foster freedom of speech and freedom of the press so that the media can focus attention on corruption. Freedom of speech and freedom of the press are also critically important ingredients in the fight against corruption, so that corrupt activities can be exposed to the public. The media can play an important role in exposing corrupt activities. To do so, the public needs to have confidence in the objectivity of the media and confidence that the reporting is not driven by partisan interests. Whistle-blower legislation can be a useful tool to encourage and protect officials in the government who are witnessing inappropriate behaviour in government and who report to the media. Freedom of expression and the press (in Canada this is guaranteed by the Canadian Charter of Rights and Freedoms) is a necessary requisite to this, as is a public that has a low tolerance for bribery and corruption. Sometimes the stories need to be "juicy" to get the media interested. But over time, if the reports are credible, the public's attention will be more easily focused on this type of activity.

In countries like Zimbabwe, it is difficult, if not impossible, for this to happen because of the strict controls on the press and freedom of expression generally. In countries like Russia, after decades of state-controlled newspapers like *Pravda* and *Isvestia*, Russians are sceptical of the objectivity of the media, even though direct state control of the media has been relaxed. In Canada, the role of the media in exposing government mismanagement and corruption are legendary. While difficult and challenging for the government in power, the freedom of the press and freedom of expression keep a check on the level of corruption. The media plays a key role in forcing transparency and accountability.

Encourage the involvement of the private sector in development initiatives, including public/private partnerships. The Commission on the Private Sector and Development, an initiative launched by the United Nations Development Program, was a high-level commission that was convened to provide analysis and evaluation of the key factors that are inhibiting the role of the private sector in development, and to develop strategic recommendations on how to promote strong indigenous private sectors and initiate concrete programs with the highest potential impact in private sector development.

The Commission was asked two basic questions:

▶ How can the potential of the private sector and entrepreneurship be unleashed in developing countries?
▶ How can the existing private sector be engaged in meeting that challenge?

In March 2004, the Commission released its report, *Unleashing Entrepreneurship: Making Business Work for the Poor.*

According to the Commission, the private sector can contribute to economic growth and empowering poor people by providing them with a greater array of cheaper goods and services. For the private sector to flourish, the following are needed:

▶ Access to finance;
▶ Knowledge and skills;
▶ A level playing field for firms competing in the domestic market.

The Commission recommended actions in three spheres: the public, the public-private, and the private. The Commission's recommendations are as follows:

PUBLIC SPHERE
▶ For governments in developing countries:
  ◆ reform regulations and strengthen the rule of law;
  ◆ formalize the economy (e.g. property rights along the lines proposed by Hernando de Soto);
  ◆ engage the private sector in the policy process.
▶ For governments in developed countries:
  ◆ foster a conducive international macroeconomic environment and trade regime (e.g. access to international markets for exporters in developing countries);
  ◆ redirect the operational strategies of multilateral and

bilateral development institutions and agencies (e.g. better coordination);
  ◆ untie aid (greater effectiveness and to stimulate local businesses in developing countries).
► For multilateral development institutions:
  ◆ apply the Monterrey recommendation of specialization and partnership to private sector development activities (e.g. reduce or eliminate overlap);
  ◆ address informality in developing countries (see above).

PUBLIC-PRIVATE SPHERE
► Facilitate access to broader financing actions;
► Assist skill and knowledge development;
► Make possible sustainable delivery of basic services, particularly energy and water.

PRIVATE SPHERE
► For the private sector:
  ◆ channel private initiative into development efforts;
  ◆ develop linkages with multinational and large domestic companies to nurture smaller companies;
  ◆ pursue business opportunities in bottom-of-pyramid markets (i.e. the 4 billion people earning less than $1,500 per year);
  ◆ set standards (especially in corporate governance and transparency).
► For civil society and labour organizations:
  ◆ increase accountability in the system;
  ◆ develop new partnerships and relationships to achieve common objectives.

The Commission's overall recommendations were forwarded for consideration to heads of the national and multilateral development agencies, as well as to leaders in the private sector.

The co-chairs of this commission were Rt. Hon. Paul Martin (Canada), member of parliament, former prime minister of Canada, former finance minister of Canada, former owner of Canada Steamship Lines; and Emesto Zedillo (Mexico), director of the Yale University Centre for the Study of Globalization, and former president of Mexico.

More recently, there has been more discussion about the importance of public-private partnerships in the context of international aid. There are a number of examples of successful public-private partnerships in the developing world. For example, the United Nations Development Program's (UNDP) Public-Private Partnerships for the Urban Environment (PPPUE) financial facility supports the development of innovative partnerships at the local level. These projects bring together financial resources and know-how into a risk-sharing arrangement that allows projects to proceed, that perhaps otherwise wouldn't have. One needs to be careful, however, about overstating the scope of Public-Private Partnerships (PPPs) and the role that they can play in developing countries. To engage the private sector, present and future earnings streams must, of necessity, be part of the equation. We tend to think of PPPs in the context of toll roads, for example, where there is a strong benefit/cost for users and the toll is affordable. They are particularly viable where no-cost alternatives exist in high-density traffic lanes.

But PPPs in the developing world have potential application in urban transit projects, and the development of an array of infrastructure. We should not believe, however, that the private sector would participate unless the financial returns are attractive and the risk levels acceptable.

While such evolution in thinking is positive, in my view we need a more fundamental re-think of international aid—one that is premised on the paramount importance of the development of financial markets in developing countries, and a greater amount of risk-taking and investment by local investors and entrepreneurs.

Pass effective laws that sanction individuals and corporations that pay bribes to public officials. In some countries bribes can be deducted by corporations for income tax purposes as a legitimate business expense. Imagine what message this delivers to society. In some countries the sanctions for bribery and corruption by public officials are very light. One of the challenges is enacting legislation that introduces tougher sanctions for this type of behaviour when some or many of the legislators are corrupt themselves. This is what organizations like the Global Organization of Parliamentarians Against Corruption is attempting to address by reaching parliamentarians around the world and building a critical mass of like-minded elected representatives who can force this type of legislation through their respective legislatures.

Reform the civil service in developing countries and reduce the culture of corruption by paying public servants a fair wage and penalizing those who accept bribes. If a bribe is required for service in a government department or agency, it is akin to a tax or user fee—with one big difference: the fee does not accrue to the general taxpayers; it goes directly into the pocket of the government employee. People are paying for the service either way, but a culture of bribery and corruption is being perpetuated. It would be better to pay the public servants a decent wage and then credit any fees collected to the public purse. The economic cost is about the same, but one avoids perpetuating the notion that bribes are an acceptable societal norm if they are eliminated.

Reduce unnecessary red tape in governments to encourage entrepreneurship and reduce the temptation to expedite decisions through bribes. One might intuitively think that large doses of government regulation are the perfect antidote for corruption. In fact, the evidence suggests that the exact opposite may be true. More red tape can have the effect of creating a larger number of opportunities for would-be bribe-givers to try and expedite the process with some cash. The World Bank's Cost of Doing Business survey estimates that starting a business requires US $5,531 in Angola (more than eight times the per capita income) and about $28 in New Zealand (far less than one per cent of the per capita income). This added red tape increases the likelihood of corruption.

By the same token, too much discretion on the part of government bureaucrats can be viewed as a standing invitation for bribes to avoid unwanted obstacles being put in one's way. As Paul Salembier notes, "Even the best regulatory system cannot eliminate corruption. What it can do is avoid institutionalizing it. By maximizing predictability and minimizing the potential for corruption, a properly functioning regulatory system can be a key factor in maintaining investor confidence and ensuring economic vitality."[146]

Reduce the debt loads of poor countries that are committed to good governance and fighting corruption. Countries like Nigeria are so mired in debt that it is next to impossible for them to make the necessary changes to the way they operate because of the resources required just to service their national debt. The Heavily Indebted Poor Countries Initiative (HIPC) attempts to confront this problem by providing relief to those countries who are committed to good governance. The Government of Canada had played a leading role in this program and it should produce results. Good governance is the key, otherwise 20 years hence the global community will be faced again with the same problem as national assets and resources are siphoned off for the few.

Remove trade barriers so that developing economies can more fully participate in the global economy. Allowing developing countries the ability to grow their own economies is probably the factor most critical for success in the fight against corruption. A growing economy will help alleviate poverty and this, together with the right public institutions and public policies, should help battle corruption.

Some of this is happening naturally, as Thomas Friedman points out in his book *The World is Flat: A Brief History of the 21st Century*, with developments like out-sourcing and off-shoring which are serving as a great boon to the economies of countries like India and China. We can do much more, however, so that countries like this and many others can market and sell their agricultural products and textiles into the developed world without running up against unfair tariff and non-tariff barriers. The WTO is addressing these matters but progress is painfully slow. As a show of good faith Canada will need to relax and eventually eliminate its own supply management regimes that artificially protect poultry and dairy farmers in Quebec and Ontario.

Better educate the public worldwide of the costs and negative impacts of bribery and corruption. Too often bribery and corruption are seen as culturally acceptable norms that are engrained into society and difficult if not impossible to eliminate. It is true that eliminating bribery and corruption completely may be an impossible task, but we can surely do much better. The body politic needs to better understand the cost to society of bribery and corruption and also how it distorts the distribution of income and wealth. With the general public on side, politicians will be better armed for the fight.

CHAPTER 11

Conclusion

We know that poverty and corruption are linked. What we don't know for sure is which comes first—the poverty or the corruption. A reduction in the levels of bribery and corruption in any country will have a positive impact on the economy, which can reduce GDP anywhere from eight to 15 per cent—an enormous amount.

Some argue that corruption should not be a focal point in the fight against poverty in the less developed countries. Corruption, they point out, is endemic and woven into the socio-economic fabric of so many nations that we are wasting our time. This is a tempting notion that must be rejected for a number of reasons:

- ► Corruption is compounding the problem of poverty throughout the world because it inhibits public and private investment. Who wants to invest in countries where corruption creates additional uncertainty, as well as additional costs and the stigma of unethical conduct?
- ► Bribery and corruption lead to a sense of hopelessness amongst the citizenry and results in huge disparities in the distribution of national income and wealth. A few do well while many remain mired in poverty.

► Bribery and corruption provide fertile ground for international terrorists.
► It is ethically and morally wrong to condone corruption.

While one cannot be naïve about these matters, even incremental progress in the fight against corruption at some point may be enough to turn the tide—probably never to the point when bribery and corruption are eliminated—but it could result in significantly reduced corruption and a world where it is no longer the accepted norm.

Organizations like the Global Organization of Parliamentarians against Corruption, with which I have been associated for a number of years, is having a positive impact by reaching out to like-minded parliamentarians around the world—those who have had enough of bribery and corruption and are prepared to do something about it.

It is in everyone's interest to try to lessen the gap between the rich and poor countries. Not only is it the right thing to do but attacking this problem is a real way to assist in creating more international stability and fewer opportunities for would-be terrorists. But reducing poverty is currently constrained by a number of factors, not the least of which is the proliferation of bribery and corruption in the developing world. It needs to be said that no country is immune to corruption. Transparency International offers the most objective ranking of countries around the world. Some are ranked as very corrupt—such as Chad, Bangladesh, Turkmenistan, Myanmar (Burma), and Haiti—and others are considered quite immune to corruption —Iceland, Finland, New Zealand, Denmark, and Singapore. Canada was in the top five of the least-corrupt states until it encountered its own sponsorship scandal at which time it slid to twelfth place. The fact that bribery and corruption of some sort exist in almost every country is no excuse for not dealing with this terrible problem.

Money laundering goes hand-in-hand with corruption as well as with terrorism, drug crime, and tax evasion. People in corrupt countries become disheartened when they witness corrupt money being laundered with ease by their leaders to offshore banking centres like Luxembourg and the Bahamas. More needs to be done on this front to remove some of the incentive to engage in corrupt activities. The ability to "salt away" huge sums of money that rightly belongs to the average citizen is all too tempting for some.

We need to start thinking outside the box in our search for answers to the vexing challenges of bribery and corruption. The problem has too often been swept under the carpet in the past. Until James Wolfensohn took over the reins of the World Bank, it was politically incorrect to use terms like bribery and corruption. Terms like "implicit taxes" or "rent-seeking behaviour" were used. While this is no longer the case, terms like good governance are often used to avoid terms like corruption and bribery. Internationally, we have to accept that this is real problem and begin dealing with it more directly.

Paul Wolfowitz, James Wolfensohn's successor at the World Bank, was committed to the fight against corruption. Regrettably, he got caught up in an internal World Bank scandal and left the bank before he could make a major impact on the organization's attack on corruption.

Continents like Africa, despite all the attention and promises, do not seem to be making much headway in the fight against poverty. When trapped in endless circles of poverty, citizens seek their opportunities abroad—forcing unnatural migration patterns in these efforts to improve their standard of living. Most would rather stay at home, but they cannot if they want to improve their condition.

A crisis of confidence exists for both public and private investors who might otherwise be interested in supporting development projects, but who are also very concerned about the quality of governance in many of the less developed jurisdictions. Until such time as confidence is regained, the developing world will have to focus on ways to generate more capital domestically, whether through public policies that encourage more savings and more employee share ownership and micro credit, through more developed local capital markets, or by freeing up "locked capital" in real estate. Foreign investors, both public and private, will want to see the citizens of less-developed countries invest in themselves. This will reduce risk, and over time reduce the extent of bribery and corruption.

At the same time, developing countries will need to more fully develop their institutions to support better governance. Institutions like a strong parliament, which can better hold their executive branch to account, together with a free press, a corrupt-free judiciary, and auditor-general-like agencies. Better and more transparent reporting of natural resource revenues and the income and assets of public officials would be good steps forward as well. Reducing unneeded red tape would help to reduce the opportunities for bribery, as would paying bureaucrats a fair wage.

Internationally, the world community and organizations like the United Nations should consider naming corruption a crime against humanity. Its impact on citizens can be almost as pernicious as genocide or ethnic cleansing. International conventions or treaties to stem the flow of laundered money would be another positive step recognizing that "a chain is only as good as its weakest link." We should also be removing artificial trade barriers which are preventing the less-developed countries from reaching their full potential, which in turn would alleviate poverty in those countries. Again, on the international stage, more could be done to educate the citizens of the world about the cost and injustice of poverty and corruption.

Developed countries should have mechanisms by which to reward countries that enjoin the fight against corruption, with tangible support, so that the word starts to spread that if you reduce or eliminate corruption, the developed world will recognize this in a tangible way.

The task is a big one. Why would we avoid doing the right thing because the job is not easy? The costs, not just economic, of inaction are huge. We need to question how this problem has been addressed up until now and find new ways to attack it. We owe it to ourselves and to the generations that will follow us.

The Index of Public Governance

By Tony Hahn / June 2005

Introduction

The year 2005 has seen a number of significant developments around the issue of governance both in the developed and undeveloped world. Across the Atlantic, the recent rejection of the draft European Union constitution by the French and the Dutch were seen by many commentators as a rejection of economic integration and institutional overstretch in favour of the ethic of identity and national sovereignty. At home, there is much anxiety over the health of our democratic institutions, with political participation declining and public cynicism at an all-time high. Many activists are taking their causes outside of the political arena to raise awareness. Actor Liam Neeson tells us that in Africa, children are needlessly dying in the time it takes for Cameron Diaz and Justin Timberlake to snap their fingers, and furthermore, that "all these deaths are avoidable." For his part, Sir Bob Geldof is renewing his Live Aid project of 20 years ago to bring the issue of Third World poverty back to the public consciousness.

What is the informed observer to make of these issues of identity, sovereignty, and prosperity, and the role of government in reconciling all of the competing interests to create an environment where people are governed well? What is good governance, and how can it be measured?

This survey tries to answer that question. By taking four indices and combining them to make an overall ranking for 114 countries, policy analysts can gain a better understanding of how countries around the world are governing their citizens, and if those approaches are effective in creating opportunity, reducing poverty, and giving individuals around the globe a reason to believe in political engagement through liberal, democratic, free-market government as a worthwhile pursuit once again to improve quality of life for the human race.

Methodology

The Index of Public Governance combines four indices to come up with a composite ranking of 114 countries for which data exists.

The first two indices used are from the well-respected and non-partisan organization Freedom House and their indices of political rights and civil liberties as contained in the Freedom in the World 2004[147] report. Both of these indices rank countries from 1 (free) to 7 (not free) on both of these measures. Those scales have been changed to a scale of 2.5 (free) down to 0 (not free) by multiplying the original ranking by a factor of 1.666 for a score out of 10, and then dividing that figure by 4 to achieve a score out of 2.5.

The second index comes from Transparency International's Corruptions Perceptions Index 2004,[148] which aims to measure public-sector corruption. Rankings were originally out of 10, with a higher ranking indicating less corruption. These were then proportionally brought down to a rating out of 2.5 as well, in this case by dividing the original rating by a factor of 4, with a score of 2.5 being the highest possible score and 0 being the lowest.

Finally, the last index comes from the Economic Freedom of the World *2004 Annual Report*.[149] This index measures 38 variables across five themes: the size of government, legal structure and protection of property rights, access to sound money, international trade, and regulation. Once again, countries were ranked out of 10, with a higher ranking indicating more economic freedom. For the Index of Public Governance, these rankings were brought down to a score ranging from 0 to 2.5 by dividing the original ranking by 4, with 2.5 once again representing a perfect score.

The rankings out of 2.5 for each of the measures of political rights, civil liberties, corruption and economic freedom were then added up for each country for a composite ranking out of 10.

This survey comes from a liberal, democratic, capitalist perspective. Rather than rehash the debate over the merits of big versus small government, participatory democracy versus rule by elites, it is recognized from the outset that ethical governments, voted in by their citizens while encouraging free enterprise and the exercise of civil liberties, are governments who provide the optimal conditions for the alleviation of poverty, the improvement of quality of life, and the creation and perpetuation of a robust, vibrant civic culture.

So how do the countries in the survey measure up?

TABLE 4: The Index of Public Governance (IPG)

	Overall Rankings Place	IPG	Political Rights	Civil Liberties	Corruption	Economic Freedom
1.	New Zealand	9.45	1/7=2.5	1/7=2.5	9.6/10=2.4	8.2/10=2.05
2.	Finland	9.35	1/7=2.5	1/7=2.5	9.7/10=2.425	7.7/10=1.925
3.	Switzerland	9.325	1/7=2.5	1/7=2.5	9.1/10=2.275	8.2/10=2.05
4.	Iceland	9.275	1/7=2.5	1/7=2.5	9.5/10=2.375	7.6/10=1.9
	Denmark	9.275	1/7=2.5	1/7=2.5	9.5/10=2.375	7.6/10=1.9
5.	United Kingdom	9.2	1/7=2.5	1/7=2.5	8.6/10=2.15	8.2/10=1.875
6.	Australia	9.175	1/7=2.5	1/7=2.5	8.8/10=2.2	7.9/10=1.975
7	Sweden	9.125	1/7=2.5	1/7=2.5	9.2/10=2.3	7.3/10=1.825
8.	The Netherlands	9.1	1/7=2.5	1/7=2.5	8.7/10=2.175	7.7/10=1.925
	Canada	9.1	1/7=2.5	1/7=2.5	8.5/10=2.125	7.9/10=1.975

Overall Rankings Place		IPG	Political Rights	Civil Liberties	Corruption	Economic Freedom
9.	Luxembourg	9.05	1/7=2.5	1/7=2.5	8.4/10=2.1	7.8/10=1.95
10.	Norway	8.975	1/7=2.5	1/7=2.5	8.9/10=2.225	7.0/10=1.75
	Austria	8.975	1/7=2.5	1/7=2.5	8.4/10=2.1	7.5/10=1.875
11.	U.S.A.	8.925	1/7=2.5	1/7=2.5	7.5/10=1.875	8.2/10=1.875
12.	Germany	8.875	1/7=2.5	1/7=2.5	8.2/10=2.05	7.3/10=1.825
13.	Ireland	8.825	1/7=2.5	1/7=2.5	7.5/10=1.875	7.8/10=1.95
14.	Belgium	8.725	1/7=2.5	1/7=2.5	7.5/10=1.875	7.4/10=1.85
15.	Chile	8.675	1/7=2.5	1/7=2.5	7.4/10=1.85	7.3/10=1.825
16.	France	8.475	1/7=2.5	1/7=2.5	7.1/10=1.775	6.8/10=1.7
17.	Malta	8.4	1/7=2.5	1/7=2.5	6.8/10=1.7	6.8/10=1.7
18.	Portugal	8.375	1/7=2.5	1/7=2.5	6.3/10=1.575	7.2/10=1.8
19.	Uruguay	8.25	1/7=2.5	1/7=2.5	6.8/10=1.7	6.2/10=1.55
20.	Barbados	8.225	1/7=2.5	1/7=2.5	7.3/10=1.825	5.6/10=1.4
21.	Spain	8.135	2/7=2.085	1/7=2.5	7.1/10=1.775	7.1/10=1.775
22.	Japan	8.06	1/7=2.5	2/7=2.085	6.5/10=1.725	7.0/10=1.75
23.	Slovenia	8.05	1/7=2.5	1/7=2.5	6.0/10=1.5	6.2/10=1.55
24.	Estonia	8.01	1/7=2.5	2/7=2.085	6.0/10=1.5	7.7/10=1.925
25.	Cyprus	8.0	1/7=2.5	1/7=2.5	5.4/10=1.35	6.6/10=1.65
26.	Italy	7.95	1/7=2.5	1/7=2.5	4.8/10=1.2	7.0/10=1.75
27.	Hungary	7.61	1/7=2.5	2/7=2.085	4.8/10=1.2	7.3/10=1.825
28.	Costa Rica	7.585	1/7=2.5	2/7=2.085	4.9/10=1.225	7.1/10=1.775
29.	Botswana	7.52	2/7=2.085	2/7=2.085	6.0/10=1.5	7.4/10=1.85
30.	Lithuania	7.435	1/7=2.5	2/7=2.085	4.6/10=1.15	6.8/10=1.7
31.	Israel	7.418	1/7=2.5	3/7=1.668	6.4/10=1.6	6.6/10=1.65
32.	Mauritius	7.41	1/7=2.5	2/7=2.085	4.1/10=1.025	7.2/10=1.8
	South Africa	7.41	1/7=2.5	2/7=2.085	4.5/10=1.125	6.8/10=1.7
33.	Taiwan	7.395	2/7=2.085	2/7=2.085	5.6/10=1.4	7.3/10=1.825
34.	Greece	7.385	1/7=2.5	2/7=2.085	4.3/10=1.075	6.9/10=1.725
35.	Czech Rep.	7.36	1/7=2.5	2/7=2.085	4.2/10=1.05	6.9/10=1.725
36.	Latvia	7.335	1/7=2.5	2/7=2.085	4.0/10=1.0	7.0/10=1.75
37.	Panama	7.31	1/7=2.5	2/7=2.085	3.7/10=0.925	7.2/10=1.8
38.	Slovakia	7.235	1/7=2.5	2/7=2.085	4.0/10=1.0	6.6/10=1.65
39.	Belize	7.11	1/7=2.5	2/7=2.085	3.8/10=0.95	6.3/10=1.575
	Bulgaria	7.11	1/7=2.5	2/7=2.085	4.1/10=1.025	6.0/10=1.5
40.	South Korea	7.07	2/7=2.085	2/7=2.085	4.5/10=1.125	7.1/10=1.775

	Overall Rankings Place	IPG	Political Rights	Civil Liberties	Corruption	Economic Freedom
41.	Poland	7.06	1/7=2.5	2/7=2.085	3.5/10=0.875	6.4/10=1.6
42.	Mexico	6.695	2/7=2.085	2/7=2.085	3.6/10=0.9	6.5/10=1.625
43.	Ghana	6.645	2/7=2.085	2/7=2.085	3.6/10=0.9	6.3/10=1.575
44.	El Salvador	6.603	2/7=2.085	3/7=1.668	4.2/10=1.05	7.2/10=1.8
45.	Singapore	6.56	5/7=0.834	4/7=1.251	9.3/10=2.325	8.6/10=2.15
46.	Croatia	6.495	2/7=2.085	2/7=2.085	3.4/10=0.85	5.9/10=1.475
47.	Namibia	6.378	2/7=2.085	3/7=1.668	4.1/10=1.025	6.4/10=1.6
48.	Mali	6.37	2/7=2.085	2/7=2.085	3.2/10=0.8	5.6/10=1.4
49.	Peru	6.328	2/7=2.085	3/7=1.668	3.5/10=0.875	6.8/10=1.7
	Thailand	6.328	2/7=2.085	3/7=1.668	3.6/10=0.9	6.7/10=1.675
50.	Benin	6.32	2/7=2.085	2/7=2.085	3.2/10=0.8	5.4/10=1.35
51.	Jamaica	6.303	2/7=2.085	3/7=1.668	3.3/10=0.825	6.9/10=1.725
52.	Argentina	6.245	2/7=2.085	2/7=2.085	2.5/10=0.625	5.8/10=1.45
	Romania	6.245	2/7=2.085	2/7=2.085	2.9/10=0.725	5.4/10=1.35
53.	Trinidad and Tobago	6.161	3/7=1.668	3/7=1.668	4.2/10=1.05	7.1/10=1.775
54.	Brazil	6.153	2/7=2.085	3/7=1.668	3.4/10=0.85	6.2/10=1.55
55.	Dominican Rep.	6.128	3/7=1.668	2/7=2.085	2.9/10=0.725	6.6/10=1.65
56.	Philippines	6.053	2/7=2.085	3/7=1.668	2.6/10=0.65	6.6/10=1.65
57.	India	6.028	2/7=2.085	3/7=1.668	2.8/10=0.7	6.3/10=1.575
58.	Senegal	5.953	2/7=2.085	3/7=1.668	3.0/10=0.75	5.8/10=1.45
59.	Sri Lanka	5.711	3/7=1.668	3/7=1.668	3.5/10=0.875	6.0/10=1.5
60.	Nicaragua	5.611	3/7=1.668	3/7=1.668	2.7/10=0.675	6.4/10=1.6
61.	Honduras	5.511	3/7=1.668	3/7=1.668	2.3/10=0.575	6.4/10=1.6
	Bolivia	5.511	3/7=1.668	3/7=1.668	2.2/10=0.55	6.5/10=1.625
62.	Madagascar	5.486	3/7=1.668	3/7=1.668	3.1/10=0.775	5.5/10=1.375
63.	Kenya	5.461	3/7=1.668	3/7=1.668	2.1/10=0.525	6.4/10=1.6
64.	Papua New Guinea	5.386	3/7=1.668	3/7=1.668	2.6/10=0.65	5.6/10=1.4
	Albania	5.386	3/7=1.668	3/7=1.668	2.5/10=0.625	5.7/10=1.425
65.	Paraguay	5.361	3/7=1.668	3/7=1.668	1.9/10=0.475	6.2/10=1.55
66.	Ecuador	5.336	3/7=1.668	3/7=1.668	2.4/10=0.6	5.6/10=1.4
67.	Tanzania	5.194	4/7=1.251	3/7=1.668	2.8/10=0.7	6.3/10=1.575
68.	Turkey	5.094	3/7=1.668	4/7=1.251	3.2/10=0.8	5.5/10=1.375
69.	Kuwait	5.085	4/7=1.251	5/7=0.834	4.6/10=1.15	7.4/10=1.85
70.	Malawi	4.994	3/7=1.668	4/7=1.251	2.8/10=0.7	5.5/10=1.375
71.	Malaysia	4.96	5/7=0.834	4/7=1.251	5.0/10=1.25	6.5/10=1.625

Overall Rankings Place	IPG	Political Rights	Civil Liberties	Corruption	Economic Freedom
72. Bahrain	4.893	5/7=0.834	5/7=0.834	5.8/10=1.45	7.1/10=1.775
73. Indonesia	4.869	3/7=1.668	4/7=1.251	2.0/10=0.5	5.8/10=1.45
74. Sierra Leone	4.844	4/7=1.251	3/7=1.668	2.3/10=0.575	5.2/10=1.35
75. Zambia	4.802	4/7=1.251	4/7=1.251	6.6/10=1.65	2.6/10=0.65
76. Colombia	4.777	4/7=1.251	4/7=1.251	3.8/10=0.95	5.3/10=1.325
77. Jordan	4.743	5/7=0.834	5/7=0.834	5.3/10=1.325	7.0/10=1.75
78. Guatemala	4.652	4/7=1.251	4/7=1.251	2.2/10=0.55	6.4/10=1.6
79. Venezuela	4.644	3/7=1.668	4/7=1.251	4.6/10=1.15	2.3/10=0.575
80. Oman	4.626	6/7=0.417	5/7=0.834	6.1/10=1.525	7.4/10=1.85
81. Uganda	4.385	5/7=0.834	4/7=1.251	6.6/10=1.65	2.6/10=0.65
82. Niger	4.377	4/7=1.251	4/7=1.251	2.2/10=0.55	5.3/10=1.325
Ukraine	4.377	4/7=1.251	4/7=1.251	5.3/10=1.325	2.2/10=0.55
83. Bangladesh	4.352	4/7=1.251	4/7=1.251	1.5/10=0.375	5.9/10=1.475
84. Nigeria	4.327	4/7=1.251	4/7=1.251	1.6/10=0.4	5.7/10=1.425
85. United Arab Emirates	4.234	6/7=0.417	6/7=0.417	7.5/10=1.875	6.1/10=1.525
86. Gabon	4.185	5/7=0.834	4/7=1.251	3.3/10=0.825	5.1/10=1.275
87. Nepal	4.11	5/7=0.834	4/7=1.251	2.8/10=0.625	5.6/10=1.4
88. Tunisia	4.076	6/7=0.417	5/7=0.834	5.0/10=1.25	63/10=1.575
89. Morocco	3.943	5/7=0.834	5/7=0.834	3.2/10=0.8	5.9/10=1.475
90. Congo (Rep.)	3.885	5/7=0.834	4/7=1.251	2.3/10=0.575	4.9/10=1.225
91. Russia	3.618	5/7=0.834	5/7=0.834	2.8/10=0.7	5.0/10=1.25
92. Cote d'Ivoire	3.201	6/7=0.417	5/7=0.834	2.0/10=0.5	5.8/10=1.45
92. Pakistan	3.201	6/7=0.417	5/7=0.834	2.1/10=0.525	5.7/10=1.425
93. Egypt	3.184	6/7=0.417	6/7=0.417	3.2/10=0.8	6.2/10=1.55
94. Algeria	3.076	6/7=0.417	5/7=0.834	2.7/10=0.675	4.6/10=1.15
95. Iran	3.059	6/7=0.417	6/7=0.417	2.9/10=0.725	6.0/10=1.5
96. Chad	3.026	6/7=0.417	5/7=0.834	1.7/10=0.425	5.4/10=1.35
97. Cameroon	2.759	6/7=0.417	6/7=0.417	2.1/10=0.525	5.6/10=1.4
98. Haiti	2.709	6/7=0.417	6/7=0.417	1.5/10=0.375	6.0/10=1.5
99. China	2.692	7/7=0	6/7=0.417	3.4/10=0.85	5.7/10=1.425
100. Congo (Dem.)	2.434	6/7=0.417	6/7=0.417	2.0/10=0.5	4.4/10=1.1
101 Zimbabwe	2.259	6/7=0.417	6/7=0.417	3.4/10=0.85	2.3/10=0.575
102. Syria	2.2	7/7=0.00	7/7=0.00	3.4/10=0.85	5.4/10=1.35
103. Myanmar (Burma)	1.05	7/7=0.00	7/7=0.00	1.7/10=.425	2.5/10=0.625

Rankings

Corruption and Economic Freedom: the Difference in the Liberal Democracies New Zealand has the strongest model of public governance of all of the 110 countries surveyed. With a ranking of 9.45, it scores very well on all four measures.

Next in line are the four countries of Finland, Switzerland, Iceland and Denmark, with rankings of 9.35, 9.325, 9.275, and 9.275, respectively. In the case of Finland, Iceland and Denmark, their strengths were in the areas of corruption while Switzerland was one of only five countries to score over 8.0 on the Economic Freedom index, the others being front-runner New Zealand, the UK, the US and Singapore.

Rounding out the top 10 are the United Kingdom (9.2), Australia (9.175), Sweden (9.125), Canada and the Netherlands (9.1), Luxembourg (9.05), and Austria and Norway (8.975). Each of these countries had a perfect score in the areas of political rights and civil liberties.

Interestingly, spots 11 and 12 belong to the United States and Germany, two countries who seem to be of increasingly divergent opinions on numerous issues. Their scores on economic freedom and corruption seem to mirror each other, with Germany getting 8.2 on corruption to the United States' 7.5, and the US getting 8.2 on economic freedom compared to Germany's 7.3. Celtic tiger Ireland is close behind at 13th, with room for improvement on corruption (7.5) and economic freedom (7.8). It will be interesting to see if further liberalization in Ireland has a positive effect on their Index rating in future years.

Japan and Italy: More Work to Do One of the more surprising findings of the Index of Public Governance is that Japan (ranked 22nd with 8.075) and Italy (ranked 26th at 7.95) are outranked by Chile (15th at 8.675) and Uruguay (19th at 8.25). While Italy scored perfectly on the political rights and civil liberties scales and received a 7.0 rating for economic freedom, it scored a dismal 4.8 on the corruption scale. Japan scored the same as Italy did (7.0) for economic freedom and had a 6.5 corruption rating, but lost points for civil liberties (2.1—this is the only G-7 country with less than perfect ratings in both of the Freedom House rankings.)

Italy finds itself behind other rapidly transitioning Eastern European nations Slovenia (23rd, 8.05) and Estonia (24th, 8.01) as well. If these trends continue, Italy is in danger of remaining the sick man of Europe for some time to come, especially in the face of European enlargement.

Botswana Leads the Way—Or Does It? In 29th place is the former British protectorate of Botswana, with a composite score of 7.52. Botswana is the leading African country, with Mauritius and South Africa close behind in 32nd place at 7.41.

However, it is estimated that over a third of Botswanans are living with HIV/AIDS, and unemployment is over 20 per cent.

The fact that a country like Botswana, which is facing considerable public health and public finance challenges, can finish on top of all African nations in the Index of Public Governance is reason to compare Index rankings with common indicators of development such as life expectancy, literacy and GDP per capita to see if the governance model is having a positive effect in the developing world.[150]

Comparing the life expectancies of Botswana, South Africa and Mauritius shows wide disparity. In Botswana, life expectancy is a measly 33.87, and in South Africa, figures are slightly better at 43.27. Mauritians can expect to live to 72.38 years of age.

Figures for GDP per capita and literacy, two common indicators of development, are comparable, but Botswana once again finishes at the bottom of all three measures. Botswana has GDP per capita of $9,200, South Africa $11,100, and Mauritius $12,800. Mauritius also leads the way in literacy rates—85.6 per cent compared to S. Africa's 86.4 per cent and Botswana's 79.8 per cent.

Moving on down the list, the African country of Ghana places 43rd, at 6.675, ahead of transitioning, democratizing nations such as Romania and Argentina (tied for 52nd at 6.245). Ghana's life expectancy is 56 years of age, while Romanians can expect to live to 71.35 and Argentinians 75.91. Moreover, Ghana's literacy rate is at 74.8 per cent, while 98.4 per cent of Romanians and 97.1 per cent of Argentinians can read—a difference of well over 20 per cent.

Even on the measure of GDP per capita, Argentinians ($12,400) score much higher than both Romanians ($7,700) and Ghanaians ($2,300).

Let's compare two other countries, India and Turkey. On the Index of Public Governance, India scored 6.028 (57th place) and Turkey 5.094 (68th place).

Life expectancy in the two countries is significantly different, with Turkey at 72.36 years and India at 64.35 years. A total of 86.5 per cent of Turks are literate, compared to a dismal 59.5 per cent of East Indians. And in terms of GDP per capita, Turkey once again leads— $7,400, compared to India's $3,100.

Tied for 82nd place are two countries that could not be more different—Ukraine and Niger, with a rating of 4.377. Indicators show, however, that despite their identical ranking, life expectancy in the Ukraine is higher at 66.85 versus Niger's 42.13 years, with similar disparities in GDP per capita (Ukraine's $6,300 versus Niger's $900) and literacy (Ukraine's 99.7 per cent versus Niger's 17.6 per cent).

Finally, one other comparison is worth noting. War-torn Sierra Leone scores 4.844 (74th place) on the Index of Public Governance, ahead of both Russia (3.618, 91st place) and China (2.692, 99th place).

However, on all three indicators of development, there is no comparison.

Russia has a GDP per capita of $9,800, with China at $5,600 and Sierra Leone at $600. On literacy, 99.6 per cent of Russians are literate, 90.9 per cent of Chinese citizens are literate, but less than a third (31.4 per cent) of those in Sierra Leone are literate. And finally, in terms of life expectancy, the Chinese live until 72.27 years of age on average, Russians 67.1 years of age, and those from Sierra Leone only 42.52 years of age.

These figures should give the reader pause, and they raise two important questions. First, what are the possible explanations for a generally positive ranking in the Index of Public Governance yet poor outcomes in key indicator areas such as life expectancy, literacy and GDP per capita? Secondly, how can two nations with identical rankings in the Index of Public Governance have wide disparities in terms of development indicators? Thirdly, and most importantly, are democratic institutions, free markets, and relatively uncorrupted governments enough to ensure quality of life?

Conclusions

Not only do we see differences at the middle and bottom of the Index of Public Governance in key indicator areas, but there are also significant differences at the top, too. For instance, top-ranked New Zealand (9.45) has a GDP per capita of $23,200, while 16th-ranked France (8.475) has a GDP per capita of $28,700. These differences, and those in the other key indicator areas as demonstrated above, indicate that there needs to be further research done over time to investigate what the effects of liberal, democratic, market-based reforms are. If the premise of this study is correct, countries like New Zealand will eventually eclipse France, but this of course depends on the political will to maintain good governance regimes.

Another conclusion can be drawn in terms of culture. For instance, what are the factors that have given rise to low life expectancy rates in Botswana, despite its structure of good governance? The rate of AIDS in Botswana has a very pronounced downward effect on the key indicator of life expectancy there. Over time, we will see if a country like Ghana, with much lower levels of infection, becomes more developed by comparison if it maintains and improves its governance model while resisting the conditions that lead to widespread sexually transmitted diseases. Conversely, a country like Botswana may decline in terms of life expectancy despite having all the right conditions for good governance. If that were to be the case, cultural differences could explain the variance.

One must also assign a role for history in the development of nations. Ukraine was part of the Soviet Empire for almost 80 years, which, despite all of its shortcomings, did lead to at least some industrialization as well as natural resource development. Niger, on the other hand, has had to deal with numerous coups since establishing free elections in 1995, and has never really had an adequate state apparatus to help promote economic development, or education and good health practices, for that matter. With the recent election of Viktor Yushchenko in the Ukraine and the continuing movement towards real democracy in Ukraine, these disparities will most likely increase.

Finally, another hard question must be asked; that is, what is the response of capital to governance regimes? In other words, do capital flows really respond to considerations of public sector corruption, political rights and civil liberties in addition to deregulation, ease of trade and the size of government overall? All indications from this snapshot are that capital goes where it can most easily make a return without regard for liberal, democratic norms.

However, it is important to look at this over time.[151]

Looking at an earlier example, although Russia has much higher GDP per capita than does Sierra Leone right now, if Sierra Leone sticks to its path of (comparatively) good governance, and Russia does not, then in proportional terms, that indicator of development should rise quite considerably in Sierra Leone proportionately in comparison with Russia—if there is truth in the argument that free markets, democratic institutions and uncorrupted governments lead to prosperity.

In another example, although India is well behind Turkey on the development indicators, India leads Turkey in the Index of Public

Governance. Economically and politically, India continues to make great strides. If these reforms continue, there is no reason to believe that they will not narrow the gap between themselves and countries such as Turkey because of they are improving on their governance model.

On the other hand, if the standard of living, literacy and health outcomes improve in countries with weak models of governance, especially in comparison with countries with strong models of governance, further investigation will be required. It could very well be that the existence of one or more of the factors of either political rights, civil liberties, lack of corruption, and/or economic freedom do not have a positive effect one way or the other on the prosperity of a nation and its citizens.

It will be revealing to see how the countries in the Index fare five to ten years into the future.

My expectation and my hope is that despite the barriers posed by cultural and historical factors, as well as the seemingly lukewarm response of capital to political reforms, that countries such as Botswana, India and Sierra Leone will be examples for countries all across the developed and developing world—that liberal, capitalist democracy is indeed a force for good.

Notes

1. Gross national product (GNP) measures the total amount of goods and services that a country's citizens produce regardless of where they produce them. By contrast, gross domestic product (GDP) measures the total amount of goods and services that are produced within a country's geographic borders.
2. World Bank Survey, World Bank, Washington, D.C.
3. Madelaine Drohan, "How we can help Africa (without spending a cent)," *Globe & Mail,* 17 August 2004.
4. Geoffrey York, "China's frantic crackdown on corruption," *Globe and Mail,* 28 May 2005.
5. David Landes, *The Wealth and Poverty of Nations* (New York: Norton, 1998).
6. Ibid.
7. Mike Apsey, *What's All This Got to Do with the Price of 2 × 4's?,* (Calgary: University of Calgary Press, 2006).
8. Peta Thornycroft (*Daily Telegraph*), *Globe & Mail,* 29 September 2004, A-13.
9. Thomas Homer-Dixon, *The Ingenuity Gap* (New York: Knopf, 2000).
10. United Nations Economic Commission for Africa, *Transform-*

ing Africa's Economy: Economic Report on Africa 2000, 2001 (New York: United Nations).

11. Department of Foreign Affairs, Current Issues and Events, "The New Partnership for Africa's Development (NEPAD), October 2001," Republic of South Africa, last update 29 October 2001.

12. Lt.-Gen. Roméo Dallaire, *Shake Hands with the Devil* (Toronto: Random House Canada, 2003).

13. Homer-Dixon, *The Ingenuity Gap*.

14. John C. Polanyi, *Toronto Star*, 16 June 2003.

15. M.G. Vassanji, *The In-Between World of Vikram Lall* (Toronto: Doubleday Canada, 2003), 291.

16. Ibid., 333.

17. Simon Roughneen, "Corruption trumps tribalism," *International Herald Tribune*, 10 January 2008.

18. Ibid.

19. William H. Overholt, *The Rise of China* (New York: Norton, 1993).

20. Peter Eigen, chairman, Transparency International, statement at the Foreign Press Association, London, 7 October 2003.

21. "Tropics, Germs and Crops: How endowments influence economic development," NBER Working paper 9106 (Cambridge, Mass.: National Bureau of Economic Research).

22. *The Economist*, 2 March 2002, 12.

23. Refer to Appendix: The Index of Public Governance.

24. Purchasing Power Parity or PPP is a method of measuring the relative purchasing power of different countries' currencies over the same types of goods and services. Because goods and services may cost more in one country than in another, PPP permits more accurate comparisons of standards of living across countries. PPP estimates use price comparisons of comparable items, but since not all items can be matched exactly across countries and times, the estimates are not always "robust."

25. George T. Abed and Sanjeev Gupta, eds., *Governance, Corrup-*

tion, and Economic Performance (Washington, D.C.: International Monetary Fund, 2002).

26. Transparency International, *Global Corruption Report 2001* (Berlin, Germany: Transparency International), Table 1, 256.

27. Johann G. Lambsdorff, "Corruption in Empirical Research: A Review," Transparency International working paper, 1999.

28. Ibid.

29. The technique isolates the pure impact of corruption on a variable by using instruments (i.e., another variable) which are correlated with corruption and which have no impact on the studied variable.

30. Paolo Mauro, *Corruption: Causes, Consequence, and Agenda for Further Research* (Washington, D.C.: IMF, 1998).

31. Lambsdorff, "Corruption in Empirical Research."

32. Transparency International, *The Global Corruption Report 2004.*

33. Peter Goodspeed, *National Post*, 18 December 2003, A-1.

34. Transparency International, 1999 Corruption Perceptions Index.

35. Peter Eigen, chairman, Transparency International, *National Post.*

36. Goodspeed, ibid.

37. *National Post* (Agence France-Press), 15 July 2004.

38. Taiwo Akinola, "Awolowo/Akintola: The Tango Between Vision and Compromise, DAWODU.COM: Dedicated to Nigeria's Socio-Political Issues," 28 April 2004. http://www.dawodu.com/awolowo3.htm.

39. Ryszard Kapuściński, *The Shadow of the Sun* (Toronto: Knopf Canada, 2001), 106.

40. *Toronto Star*, 19 January 2003, B5 (excerpted from *Newsweek Magazine*).

41. *National Post*, 9 November 2004, 1.

42. Ibid, A12.

43. "The State and Civil Society in the Fight Against Corruption: Defining the Challenge," 8th International Anti-Corruption Conference, New York, 2006.

44. Shang-Jin Wei, *How Taxing is Corruption on International Investors?* (Cambridge, Mass.: Harvard University, February 1997), mimeograph.

45. J. Paul Salembier, "Designing Regulatory Systems: A Template for Regulatory Rule-Making—Part I," *Statute Law Review*, Vol. 23, Number 3, 168.

46. V. Tanzi and H. Davoodi, "Roads to Nowhere: How Corruption in Public Investment Hurts Growth," *Economic Issues*, 1988/12, IMF.

47. "Tropics, Germs and Crops: How endowments influence economic development," NBER Working Paper 9106.

48. *The Economist*, 5 October 2002, 74.

49. Vito Tanzi, "Corruption Around the World: Causes, Consequence, Scope and Cures," IMF Staff Papers, Vol. 45, No. 4, (Washington, D.C.: IMF, December 1998), 586.

50. Paolo Mauro, "The Effects of Corruption on Growth, Investment, and Government Expenditure," IMF Working Paper 96/98 (Washington, D.C.: IMF, 1996), 86.

51. Tanzi, "Corruption Around the World," 584.

52. Paolo Mauro, "The Effects of Corruption," 87.

53. Ibid.

54. Susan Rose-Ackerman, *Corruption: A Study of Political Economy* (New York: New York Academic Press, 1978), 32, chapter preview, Institute of International Economics, http://www.iie.com/publications/chapters_preview/12/2iie2334.pdf.

55. Tanzi, "Corruption Around the World," 581.

56. Susan Rose-Ackerman, "Corruption: A Study of Political Economy," *Journal of Economic Literature*, Vol. 17, No. 2, June 1979.

57. Susan F. Martin, "New Issues in Refugee Research," Working Paper No. 41, prepared for UNHCR, Global Migration Trends and Asylum, April 2001, 2.

58. Ibid., 3.

59. UNHCR web site.

60. Chris Mathers, *Crime School: Money Laundering* (Toronto: Key

Porter Books, 2004), 165.

61. Ibid., 166.

62. Margaret E. Beare and Stephen Schneider, *Money Laundering in Canada: Chasing Dirty and Dangerous Dollars* (Toronto: University of Toronto Press, 2007), 279.

63. Yossef Bodansky, *Bin Laden: The Man Who Declared War on America* (New York: Prima Publishing, 1999), xiii–xiv.

64. Stewart Bell, *Cold Terror* (Toronto: John Wiley & Sons Canada, 2004).

65. *The Economist*, 19 February 2005, 11.

66. Bill Clinton, *My Life (The Presidential Years)* (New York: Vintage Books, 2005).

67. Transparency International, 1999 Bribe Payers Index.

68. Beare and Schneider, *Money Laundering in Canada.*

69. *Profiling Money Laundering in Eastern and Southern Africa,* edited by Charles Goredema, monograph, executive summary.

70. Beare and Schneider, *Money Laundering in Canada.*

71. A nominee director is someone who rents his or her name. The basic function of the nominee director is to shield working executives of limited and other companies from the public disclosure requirements that exist in other jurisdictions.

72. Bakerplatt: A Specialist Professional Group, "Money Laundering and the Misuse of Trusts," 18 August 2005, http://www.bakerplatt.com/upload/public/Files/1/Money%20Laundering%20and%20the%20Misuse%20of%20Trusts.pdf.

73. Ibid.

74. Bakerplatt, "Understanding Money Laundering," 18 Aug. 2005, http://www.bakerplatt.com/upload/public/Files/1/Understanding%20AML.pdf.

75. Ibid.

76. Ibid.

77. Ibid.

78. Ibid.

79. Ibid.

80. Ibid.
81. Bakerplatt: A Specialist Professional Group, "Riggs Bank the Fall of an Institution—A Salutary Lesson for us All?" 18 August 2005.
82. Ibid.
83. Kelly McParland, *National Post,* 10 April 2004.
84. Beare and Schneider, *Money Laundering in Canada,* 86.
85. Dual criminality requires that an accused be extradited only if the alleged criminal conduct is considered criminal under the laws of both the surrendering and requesting nations.
86. Double jeopardy is a procedural defence that forbids that a defendant be tried twice for the same crime.
87. Paul Knox, *Globe & Mail,* 13 January 2004, A5.
88. United Nations, *Millennium Development Goals Report 2005* (New York: United Nations, 2005).
89. Gary Duncan, *The Times,* 10 July 2004.
90. Canadian International Development Agency, *Statistical Report of Official Development Assistance Fiscal Year 2002–2003* (Ottawa: Government of Canada, 1 May 2004), http://www.acdi-cida.gc.ca/INET/IMAGES.NSF/vLUImages/stats/$file/StatRep_02_03.pdf.
91. The G8 is an informal group of eight countries: Canada, France, Germany, Italy, Japan, Russia, the United Kingdom and the United States. The European Union also participates and is represented by the president of the European Commission and by the leader of the country that holds the presidency of the European Council at the time of the G8 Summit. The first summit, with six countries participating, took place because of concerns over the economic problems that faced the world in the 1970s. It was held in 1975 in Rambouillet, France. Since then, the group has grown to eight countries, and the process has evolved from a forum dealing essentially with macroeconomic issues to an annual meeting with a broad-based agenda that addresses a wide range of international economic, political, and social issues.

92. IMF, *Heavily Indebted Poor Countries (HIPC) Initiative Statistical Update March 31 2004* (Washington, D.C.: International Monetary Fund, 5 May 2004), http://www.imf.org/external/np/hipc/2004/033104.pdf.

93. Graham Searjeant, *The Times*, 10 July 2004.

94. Kapuściński, *The Shadow of the Sun*.

95. Phil Hirschkorn and Liz Neisloss, "Oil for food probe names two suspects." CNN.com 17 August 2004, http://www.cnn.com/2005/WORLD/meast/08/08/oil.food/.

96. Ibid.

97. Ibid.

98. "Independent Inquiry Committee in to the UN Oil for Food Programme 17 August 2004," press release, 8 August 2005, http://www.iic-offp.org/.

99. Ibid.

100. Ibid.

101. Hirschkorn and Neisloss, "Oil for food probe names two suspects."

102. Kwame Holman, "The Oil for Food Scandal," PBS Online News Hour 17 August 2004, http://www.pbs.org/newshour/bb/middle_east/july-dec04/oil-for-food_12-3.html.

103. Juan Marsiaj, "Local Empowerment in Civic Society," lecture for POL210Y1, Politics of Development: Issues and Challenges, Isabelle Bader Theatre, University of Toronto, Toronto, 23 March 2004.

104. Inter-American Development Bank, 20 April 2004, http://www.iadb.org/.

105. "Secretaries of Defense Histories," United States Department of Defense, 23 April 2004, http://www.defenselink.mil/specials/secdef_histories/bios/mcnamara.htm.

106. Denise Dresser, "Mexico: From PRI Predominance to Divided Democracy," in Jorge I. Dominguez and Michael Shifter, eds., *Constructing Democratic Governance in Latin America*, second ed. (Baltimore: John Hopkins University Press, 2003).

107. Chris Mathers, *Crime School*, 98.

108. Anita Chan and Robert J.S. Ross, "Racing to the bottom: International Trade without a Social Clause," *Third World Quarterly* 24 (6) 1011–1028 (2003), 1011.

109. Robert Z. Lawrence, "Trade Multinationals and Labor," Working Paper 4836 (Cambridge, Mass.: National Bureau of Economic Research, August 1994).

110. Janine Jackson, "Broken Promises," *FAIR* [Fairness and Accuracy in Reporting], September/October 1997.

111. André Raynauld, *Labour Standards and International Competitiveness: A Comparative Analysis of Developing and Industrialized Countries* (Cheltenham, UK: Edward Elgar Publishing, 1998).

112. Organization for Economic Co-operation and Development, "OECD Employment Outlook, July 1994," Paris, Chapter 4, Labour Standards and Economic Integration.

113. Jeffrey D. Sachs, *The End of Poverty* (New York: Penguin, 2005).

114. Ibid.

115. Ibid.

116 James Tobin, *The Tobin Tax on International Monetary Transactions* (Ottawa: Canadian Centre for Policy Alternatives, 1995).

117. Joy Kennedy, "Currency Transaction Tax: Curbing Speculation, Funding Social Development," in Richard Sandbrook, ed., *Civilizing Globalization: A Survival Guide* (Albany, NY: State University of New York Press, 2003).

118. Heikki Patomaki, *Democratizing Globalization: The Leverage of the Tobin Tax* (London: Zed Books, 2001).

119. *The Economist*, 4–10 March 2005.

120. Sachs, *The End of Poverty*.

121. Ibid.

122. John Kenneth Galbraith, *The Economics of Innocent Fraud* (Boston: Houghton Mifflin, 2004), 27.

123. Governor General of Canada, Speech on the Occasion of the Arrival to Canada of His Excellency John Agyekum Kufuor,

President of the Republic of Ghana, and Her Excellency Theresa Kufuor, Government of Canada, 21 April 2004, http://www.gg.ca/media/doc.asp?lang=e&DocID=1340.

124. Unpublished letter dated 30 August 2002, from Roy Cullen, MP, to Prime Minister Jean Chrétien.

125. Ibid.

126. Ibid.

127. Report on Somali Peace and Reconciliation Conference, 26 April 2003, Etobicoke North, Toronto, Canada.

128. Millennium Challenge Corporation, web page, 7 Dec. 2004, http://www.mca.gov/index.shtml.

129. Ibid., http://www.mca.gov/about_us/overview/index.shtml.

130. United Nations Economic Commission for Africa, *Transforming Africa's Economy: Economic Report on Africa 2000* (New York: United Nations), 7.

131. Canadian International Development Agency (CIDA), "Expanding Opportunities: Framework for Private Sector Development," consultation document (Ottawa: February 2003).

132. United Nations Development Program, *Unleashing Entrepreneurship: Making Business Work for the Poor* (New York: United Nations, 1 March 2004).

133. Sikander Hashmi, *Toronto Star*, 3 June 2005, A-17.

134. C.K. Prahalad, *The Fortune at the Bottom of the Pyramid* (Philadelphia: Wharton School Publishing, 2005), 81.

135. Ibid.

136. Irshad Manji, *The Trouble with Islam* (Toronto: Random House Canada, 2003), 177.

137. Tim Allen and Alan Thomas, eds., *Poverty and Development into the 21st Century* (Oxford: Oxford University Press, 2000), 388.

138. Ibid.

139. Hernando de Soto, *The Mystery of Capital* (New York: Basic Books, 2000), 32.

140. Ibid., 30.

141. Irshad, *The Trouble with Islam*, 179.

142. Prahalad, *The Fortune at the Bottom of the Pyramid*, 79.

143. Jeff Gates, *The Ownership Solution: Toward a Shared Capitalism for the 21st Century* (Reading, Mass.: Addison-Wesley, 1998).

144. Ibid., 231.

145. Ibid., 33.

146. J. Paul Salembier, "Designing Regulatory Systems: A Template for Regulatory Rule-Making—Part 1," *Statute Law Review*, Vol. 23, No. 3, 168.

147. Freedom House, *Freedom in the World 2004* (Washington, D.C.: Freedom House), http://www.freedomhouse.org/research/freeworld/2004/table2004.pdf.

148. Transparency International, 2004 Corruption Perceptions Index, http://www.transparency.org/cpi/2004/cpi2004.en.html #cpi2004.

149. Economic Freedom Network, *2004 Annual Report* (Vancouver, B.C.: The Fraser Institute), http://www.freetheworld.com/2004/efw2004complete.pdf.

150. All figures for life expectancy, literacy and GDP per capita from: Central Intelligence Agency, *World Factbook*, 2005 edition (Washington, D.C.: Central Intelligence Agency), http://www.odci.gov/cia/publications/factbook.

151. Due to incomplete data for one or more of the sub-indices in the Index of Public Governance, it is not possible to create an Index for previous years and compare it with outcomes now.

Sources

Abed, George T., and Sanjeev Gupta, eds.. *Governance, Corruption, and Economic Performance*. Washington, D.C.: International Monetary Fund, 2002.

Akinola, Taiwo. "Awolowo/Akintola: The Tango Between Vision and Compromise." DAWODU.COM: Dedicated to Nigeria's Socio-Political Issues. 28 April 2004.

Allen, Tim, and Alan Thomas, eds. *Poverty and Development into the 21st Century*. Oxford: Oxford University Press, 2000.

Apsey, Mike. *What's All This Got To Do With The Price of 2 × 4's?* Calgary: University of Calgary Press, 2006.

Bakerplatt: A Specialist Professional Group. *Money Laundering and the Misuse of Trusts*. 18 August 2005.

———. *Understanding Money Laundering*. 18 August 2005.

———. *Riggs Bank the Fall of an Institution: A Salutary Lesson for Us All?* 18 August 2005.

Beare, Margaret, and Stephen Schneider. *Money Laundering in Canada: Chasing Dirty and Dangerous Dollars*. Toronto: University of Toronto Press, 2007.

Bell, Stewart. *Cold Terror*. Toronto: John Wiley & Sons Canada, 2004.

Bodansky, Yossef. *Bin Laden: The Man Who Declared War on America*. New York: Prima Publishing, 1999.

Bremmer, Ian. *The J Curve: A New Way to Understand Why Nations Rise and Fall*. New York: Simon & Shuster, 2006.

Canadian International Development Agency. "Expanding Opportunities: Framework for Private Sector Development." Consultation document. February 2003.

Chan, Anita, and Robert J. S. Ross. "Racing to the bottom: International Trade without a Social Clause." *Third World Quarterly* 24 (6) 2003.

Clinton, Bill. *My Life (The Presidential Years)*. New York: Vintage Books, 2005.

Cullen, Roy (caucus committee chair). "Corporate Governance in Canada: The Role of the Federal Government." Unpublished report. September 2003.

Dallaire, Lt.-Gen. Roméo. *Shake Hands with the Devil*. Toronto: Random House Canada, 2003.

de Soto, Hernando. *The Mystery of Capital*. New York: Black Swan Books, 2000.

Dresser, Denise. "Mexico: From PRI Predominance to Divided Democracy." Jorge I. Dominguez and Michael Shifter, eds. *Constructing Democratic Governance in Latin America*, second edition. Baltimore: John Hopkins University Press, 2003.

Galbraith, John Kenneth. *The Economics of Innocent Fraud*. Boston: Houghton Mifflin, 2004.

Gates, Jeff. *The Ownership Solution: Toward a Shared Capitalism for the 21st Century*. Reading, Mass.: Addison-Wesley, 1998.

Goredema, Charles, ed. *Profiling Money Laundering in Eastern and Southern Africa*. Monograph.

Governor General of Canada. Speech on the Occasion of the Arrival to Canada of His Excellency John Agyekum Kufuor, President of the Republic of Ghana, and Her Excellency Theresa Kufuor. Government of Canada. 21 April 2004.

Hahn, Tony. "The Index of Public Governance." Unpublished monograph. 2005.

Heikki, Patomaki. *Democratizing Globalization: The Leverage of the Tobin Tax*. London: Zed Books, 2001.

Homer-Dixon, Thomas. *The Ingenuity Gap*. New York: Knopf, 2000.

Irshad, Manji. *The Trouble with Islam*. Toronto: Random House Canada, 2003.

Jackson, Janine. "Broken Promises." *FAIR* [Fairness and Accuracy in Reporting] September/October 1997.

Kapuściński, Ryszard. *The Shadow of the Sun*. Toronto: Knopf Canada, 2001.

Kennedy, Joy. "Currency Transaction Tax: Curbing Speculation, Funding Social Development." *Civilizing Globalization: A Survival Guide*, ed. Richard Sandbrook. Albany: State University of New York Press, 2003.

Lambsdorff, Johann G. "Corruption in Empirical Research: A Review." International Anti-Corruption Conference, 2004.

Landes, David. *The Wealth and Poverty of Nations*. New York: Norton, 1998.

Lawrence, Robert Z. "Trade Multinationals and Labor." Working Paper 4836. National Bureau of Economic Research, August 1994.

Mandel-Campbell, Andrea. *Why Mexicans Don't Drink Molson: Rescuing Canadian Business from the Suds of Global Obscurity*. Vancouver: Douglas & McIntyre, 2007.

Marsiaj, Juan. "Local Empowerment in Civic Society." Lecture for POL210Y1, Politics of Development: Issues and Challenges. Isabelle Bader Theatre, University of Toronto, Toronto, 23 March 2004.

Martin, Susan F. "New Issues in Refugee Research." Working Paper No. 41. Prepared for UNHCR, Global Migration Trends and Asylum, April 2001.

Mathers, Chris. *Crime School: Money Laundering: True Crime Meets the World of Business and Finance*. Toronto: Key Porter, 2004.

Mauro, Paolo. "The Effects of Corruption on Growth, Investment, and Government Expenditure." IMF Working Paper 96/98. Washington: International Monetary Fund, 1996.

———. "Corruption: Causes, Consequence, and Agenda for Further Research." IMF, 1998.

Naylor, R.T. *Satanic Purses: Money, Myth, and Misinformation in the War on Terror.* Montreal/Kingston: McGill-Queen's University Press, 2006.

Organization for Economic Co-operation and Development. OECD Employment Outlook, July 1994. Paris, Chapter 4, Labour Standards and Economic Integration.

Overholt, William H., *The Rise of China.* New York: Norton, 1995.

Prahalad, C.K. *The Fortune at the Bottom of the Pyramid.* Philadelphia: Wharton School Publishing, 2005.

Raynauld, André. *Labour Standards and International Competitiveness: A Comparative Analysis of Developing and Industrialized Countries.* Cheltenham, UK: Edward Elgar Publishing, 1998.

Rose-Ackerman, Susan. *Corruption: A Study of Political Economy.* New York: New York Academic Press, 1978. Chapter Preview, Institute of International Economics.

Sachs, Jeffrey D. *The End of Poverty.* New York: Penguin, 2005.

Salembier, J. Paul. "Designing Regulatory Systems: A Template for Regulatory Rule-Making, Part I." *Stature Law Review*, Volume 23.

Statistics Canada reports.

Tanzi, V. and Davoodi, H. "Roads to Nowhere: How Corruption in Public Investment Hurts Growth." *Economic Issues*, 1988/12. IMF.

Tanzi, Vito. "Corruption Around the World: Causes, Consequence, Scope and Cures.: IMF Staff Papers, Vol. 45, No. 4, December 1998.

Tobin, James. *The Tobin Tax on International Monetary Transactions.* Ottawa: Canadian Centre for Policy Alternatives, 1995.

Transparency International, Global Corruption Reports.

"Tropics, Germs and Crops: How endowments influence economic development." NBER Working Paper 9106.

UNDP. "Unleashing Entrepreneurship: Making Business Work for the Poor." 1 March 2004

United Nations Economic Commission for Africa. *Transforming Africa's Economy: Economic Report on Africa 2000.*

Vassanji, M.G. *The In-Between World of Vikram Lall.* Toronto: Doubleday Canada, 2003.

Wei, Shang-Jin. *How Taxing is Corruption on International Investors?* Mimeograph. Harvard University, February 1997.

World Bank. *2003 World Bank Atlas.*

Index

2nd Global Conference of the Global Organization of Parliamentarians Against Corruption, 104–6

Abacha, Sani, 3, 37, 40
Acres International, 75, 76, 77
Action Plan on Terrorist Financing, 99, 100
Act Respecting User Fees (Canada), 83, 84
Afghanistan, 120
African Development Bank, 114
African National Congress, 83
African Parliamentarians Network Against Corruption, 95
African Union, 2
Aidid, Mohamed Farrah, 119
Aid Effectiveness Discussion Forum, 114
Akintola, Samuel Ladoke, 43
Albania, 24, 190
Aleman, Arnoldo, 37
Algeria, 24, 191
All China Federation of Trade Unions, 134
Anaraki, Majid, 72
Angola, 25, 26, 30, 40, 120, 180

Annan, Kofi, 121, 142, 153
Antigua, 121
Apsey, Mike, author of *What's All This Got to do with the Price of 2 x 4's?*, 6
Aquino, Corazon, 70
Arab Region Parliamentarians Against Corruption, 95
Arafat, Yasser, 44
Argentina, 10, 24, 26, 143, 190, 194
Armenia, 24
Asia-Pacific Economic Cooperation (APEC), 47
Australia, 22, 27, 66, 78, 143, 188, 192
Austria, 22, 26, 114, 189, 192
Azerbaijan, 25, 26, 30

Babangida, Ibrahim, 128
Bahamas, 40, 88, 92, 172, 184
Bahrain, 22, 191
Bangladesh, 16, 21, 25, 26, 30, 78, 135, 168, 169, 183, 191
Barbados, 189
Barings Bank, 54
Beare, Margaret E., and Stephen Schneider, authors of *Money Laundering in Canada*, 40
Belarus, 23, 26

Belgium, 22, 26, 114, 189
Belize, 23, 189
Bell, Stewart, author of *Cold Terror*, 73
Benin, 190
Bermuda, 141
Bodansky, Yossef, 72
Bolivia, 24, 190
Bosnia and Herzegovina, 23
Botswana, 22, 27, 189, 193, 195–7
Brazil, 10, 23, 57, 122, 142, 143, 190
Bre-X Minerals, 54
Bribe Payers Index, 78
Bulgaria, 23, 189
Bush, George, 73, 162
Business International Corporation, 46

Cameroon, 25, 26, 30, 191
Canada
    anti-money-laundering bill, 98–9
    anti-terrorism bill, 98
    auditor general, 7, 96, 149
    bribery laws, 75, 77
    Bribe Payers Index, 78
    Charter of Rights and Freedoms,
        175
    companies operating overseas, 42,
        77
    corruption in corporations, 54,
        75–7
    corruption in government, 6, 7, 26
    Corruption of Foreign Public Of-
        ficials Act, 77, 79
    Corruption Perceptions Index, 2, 5,
        22, 26
    counterfeit goods, action on, 62–3
    ethics commissioner, 158–9
    index of public governance, 27, 188,
        192
    international migration to, 66–7
    international security, role in, 153
    member of G-20, 143
    money laundering in, 68, 88, 90
    North American Free Trade Agree-
        ment, 133
    parliamentary governance model,

        83, 149
    oil sands development, 42
    overseas development assistance, 3,
        4, 113–15, 118, 123
    refugees, abuse of system, 68–70
    Somalia assistance, 161–2
    Tobin Tax, 142
    trade linked to labour standards,
        133
    UN Convention Against Corrup-
        tion, 79
    user fees, legislation on, 83–4
Canadian International Development
    Agency (CIDA), 96, 114, 123, 161,
    165, 166
Canadian Standards Association, 64
Cardin, Benjamin L., 85
Caribbean Parliamentarians Against
    Corruption, 95, 102, 103
Castor Holdings, 54
Cayman Islands, 141
Central Bank of Russia, 68
Centre for Global Development, 26, 47
Chad, 120, 183, 191
Chile, 22, 26, 44, 92, 140, 142, 189, 192
China, 4, 5, 11, 12, 16, 18, 23, 28, 44,
    49–51, 62, 64, 78, 131, 134, 143, 181,
    191, 194
Chrétien, Jean, 73, 160
Cinar, 54
Citibank, 40
Clay, Edward, 39
Clinton, Bill, 44, 73
Coalition to End Global Poverty, 114
Cohon, George, 57
Collier, Paul, 80
Colombia, 23, 26, 71, 129, 191
Commission on the Private Sector and
    Development, 154, 175–8
Congo, Republic of the, 25, 191
Convention on Combating Bribery of
    Foreign Officials in International
    Business Transactions, 77
corruption
    causes of, 16, 17, 19, 32, 40, 41, 51,
        52

corporate corruption, 54–6, 61–4, 146, 147
corruption and money laundering. *See* money laundering.
impacts of corruption, 9, 10, 19, 27, 29, 30, 32, 33, 35, 36, 38, 42, 45–7, 53, 57–61, 64–68, 70, 71, 73, 115, 125, 127–131, 182, 183
measures to control corruption, 4, 20, 77–86, 144, 148–152, 154, 155, 157–159, 161–5, 167, 172–5, 179,–81, 185
relationship to good governance, 26, 28, 148, 149, 159, 161, 162, 167, 173, 174, 179, 180
relationship to poverty, 2, 3, 5, 16, 28–30, 35, 163
types and examples, 3, 9, 16, 18, 36–45, 51, 53, 54, 75, 76, 119–121, 130, 131, 139
world-wide extent, 2–5, 26
Corruption of Foreign Public Officials Act (Canada), 77, 79
Corruption Perceptions Index, 1, 21–6, 30, 38, 187
Costa Rica, 23, 189
Cote d'Ivoire, 25, 191
counterfeit products, 62, 63, 64, 71
Croatia, 23, 190
Cuba, 23
Cullen, Roy
An Act Respecting User Fees, 83, 84
anti-money-laundering workshops, 101, 105
Chinese MDF mill project, 50
comments on African aid, 160
Etobicoke North riding, 67
Proceeds of Crime (Money Laundering) and Terrorist Financing Act, 98
Russian pulp mill project, 47–50
speech on counterfeit goods, 63
speech on economic crimes, 19
speech on role of IMF and World Bank, 117–18
speech on role of United Nations, 153
vice-chair, Standing Committee on Public Safety and National Security, 63
Currency Transaction Tax(CTT). *See* Tobin Tax.
Cyprus, 22, 189
Czech Republic, 23, 189

Dallaire, Lt.-Gen. Roméo, author of *Shake Hands with the Devil*, 11, 153
Denmark, 22, 26, 27, 113, 114, 183, 188, 192
de Soto, Hernando, author of *The Mystery of Capital*, 169–71, 176
Dominican Republic, 10, 23, 190
Duvalier, J.-C., 37

Easterly, William, 47
Economic Freedom of the World, 27, 187
Ecuador, 25, 190
Egypt, 24, 170, 191
El Salvador, 23, 190
Employee share ownership, 171, 172
Enron, 54
environment, 47, 55, 77, 127–30, 142, 158, 176, 186
impact of corruption on, 127–31
impact of standards on economic growth, 127
Environmental Sustainability Index, 130
Equatorial Guinea, 92, 93
Estonia, 22, 189, 193
Estrada, Joseph, 37
Ethiopia, 24, 69, 70
European Bank for Reconstruction and Development, 46, 167, 168
European Central Bank, 143
European Commission, 63
European Parliamentarians Against Corruption, 95
European Union, 63, 67, 143

Extractive Industries Transparency
Initiative, 41, 80
Ezekwesili, Oby, 1, 2

Financial Action Task Force on Money
Laundereing (FATF), 94, 95, 97, 98,
100, 101, 104, 106, 107, 150, 155,
173
Financial Transactions and Reports
Analysis Centre (FINTRAC), 98, 99
Finland, 22, 26, 27, 183, 188, 192
foreign aid, 110–18, 120, 122–4
affected by corruption, 110, 111,
117, 120
debt-relief programs, 115, 116, 118
UN Millenium Development Goals,
111, 112
Foreign Corrupt Practices Act (USA),
79
Fox, Vincente, 130
France, 22, 26, 54, 66, 139, 142, 143,
189, 195
Frank, Barney, 71
Freedom House, 27, 187, 193
freedom of the press, 149, 174, 175
Friedman, Milton, 55, 181
Fujimori, Alberto, 37

G-20 (Group of Twenty), 99, 100, 143
Gabon, 191
Galbraith, John Kenneth, 6, 146
Gambia, 24
Gandhi, Mahatma, 72
Gates, Jeff, author of *The Ownership
Solution*, 171, 172, 209
Geldof, Bob, 186
General Committee on Economic
Affairs, Science, Technology, and
Environment, 86, 100
Georgia, 25, 26, 30
Germany, 22, 26, 44, 66, 141, 143, 189,
192
Ghana, 24, 112, 159, 160, 161, 165,
190, 194, 195

Gini coefficients, 10
Global Organization of Parliamentar-
ians Against Corruption (GOPAC),
82, 84, 86, 95–8, 101–9, 147, 150,
155
Global Witness, 80
GOAL, 17
Gomery, Mr. Justice John, 6
Gorbachev, Mikhail, 18, 48
Grameen Bank, 168, 169
Greece, 23, 113, 114, 189
Guatemala, 24, 191

Habr Gidr, 119
Hahn, Tony, 27, 28, 186
Haiti, 25, 26, 30, 37, 170, 183, 191
Haween Enterprises, 168
Heavily Indebted Poor Countries
(HIPC) debt relief program, 115,
116, 119, 180, 181
HIV/AIDS, 16, 27, 112, 139, 193, 195
Homer-Dixon, Thomas, author of *The
Ingenuity Gap*, 10, 13
Honduras, 24, 190
Hong Kong, 22
Hungary, 23, 189
Hussein, Saddam, 43, 120

Ibrahim, Mo, 128, 161
Iceland, 22, 26, 27, 188, 192
Immigration and Refugee Board
(Canada), 68, 69
INDEM Foundation, 75
Index of Public Governance, 27–9,
186–8, 192–6
correlation with GDP, 28
India, 11, 12, 16, 24, 45, 67, 143, 166,
181, 190, 194, 196, 197
Indonesia, 16, 25, 26, 37, 40, 41, 43, 57,
58, 129, 139, 143, 191
Inter-American Convention Against
Corruption, 102, 103
Inter-American Development Bank,
123, 150

International Compliance Association, 103, 106
international financial markets, 70, 126, 138–43
International Monetary Fund (IMF), 29, 38, 58, 95, 108, 115, 117, 119, 138–41, 147, 150, 155
International Organisation for Migration, 65
International Public Sector Accounting Standards Board, 84
International Risk Guide, 46
Interpol, 71
Iran, 24, 72, 191
Iraq, 25, 113, 120, 121, 153
Ireland, 22, 26, 89, 189, 192
Islamists, 72, 73
Israel, 22, 26, 189
Italy, 23, 78, 79, 113, 114, 143, 189, 192, 193

Jamaica, 10, 23, 166, 190
Japan, 22, 44, 57, 79, 139, 141, 143, 189, 192, 193
Jauregui, César, 101, 103
Jong-il, Kim, 44
Jordan, 23, 191

Kapuściński, Ryszard, author of *The Shadow of the Sun*, 43, 119
Kazakhstan, 24
Kennedy School of Government (Harvard University), 46
Kenya, 14, 16, 17, 21, 25, 26, 30, 38, 39, 70, 162, 174, 190
Kenyatta, Jomo, 14
Kerviel, Jerome, 54
Khomeini, Ayatollah, 72
Ki-moon, Ban, 135, 142
Kibaki, Mwai, 17, 38, 39, 70
Korean Confederation of Trade Unions, 134
Kufuor, John, 159, 161, 209
Kuruneri, Christopher, 93

Kuwait, 23, 44, 120, 190
Kyoto agreement, 127
Kyrgyzstan, 25

labour standards, 126, 127, 131–5
impact on poverty, 131–6
Laidlaw, 54
Lambsdorff, Johann G., 31–3
Landes, David, author of *The Wealth and Poverty of Nations*, 4
Latin American Parliamentarians Against Corruption, 95, 102, 103
Latvia, 23, 189
Lazarenko, Pavlo, 37
Lebanon, 24, 44, 71
Leeson, Nick, 54
Lesotho, 75, 76
Lesotho Highlands Water Authority, 76
Levine, Ross, 47
Libya, 25
Lithuania, 23, 189
Livent Inc., 54
LTTE (Tamil Tigers), 71
Luxembourg, 22, 26, 40, 79, 89, 113, 114, 172, 184, 189, 192

Macedonia, 24
Machel, Samora, 56
Madagascar, 24, 164, 190
Malawi, 24, 116, 190
Malaysia, 23, 26, 78, 190
Malaysian Trade Union Congress, 134
Mali, 24, 190
Malta, 189
Manji, Irshad, author of *The Trouble with Islam*, 170, 210
Marcos, 37, 40, 44, 70
Martin, Paul, 116, 118, 142, 143, 167, 178
Mauritius, 23, 27, 189, 193
Mauro, Paolo, 31, 33, 58
Mbeki, President (South Africa), 83
McDonald's Restaurants, 57

McNamara, Robert, 123, 124
Mengistu, President, 69
Mexico, 10, 23, 40, 52, 53, 60, 66, 101, 103, 104, 109, 111, 126, 130, 131, 133, 138–40, 143, 153, 166, 178, 190
Millennium Challenge Account, 162, 163, 164
Millennium Challenge Corporation, 162, 163, 164
Millennium Development Goals, 111, 112, 113, 115, 135
Millennium Summit, 111
Milosevic, Slobodan, 37
Moi, Daniel arap, 14, 16, 38, 39
Moldova, 24
money laundering, 7, 36, 70–2, 79, 81–3, 85, 87–109, 120, 121, 141, 147, 150, 152, 155–8, 172, 173, 183, 226
    anti-money-laundering measures, 88, 91, 94–102, 104, 107, 108
    definition, 87
    linked to corruption, 87, 88
    role of offshore banking centres, 88–92, 107–9
    techniques, 88, 91–3, 104
    worldwide extent, 87
Morocco, 24, 191
Mozambique, 4, 24, 55, 56, 116
Mozambique Liberation Front, 56
Mugabe, Robert, 9, 82, 93, 160
Myanmar (Burma), 25, 26, 30, 191

Namibia, 23, 190
National Accord for Transparency and Combating Corruption, 130
National Post, 44, 93
natural resources development corruption problems, 125, 129–31
Nauru, 68
Nepal, 191
Netherlands, 22, 113, 188, 192
Newly Independent States Parliamentarians Against Corruption, 95
New Zealand, 22, 26, 27, 180, 183, 188,

192, 195
Nicaragua, 24, 37, 190
Niger, 191, 196
Nigeria, 1–3, 16, 25, 26, 30, 37, 40, 43, 128, 129, 180, 191
North Atlantic Treaty Organization (NATO), 70
North-South Institute, 116
North/South issues, 126
Northern Ireland, 71
Northwest Territories Housing Corporation, 122, 164
North American Agreements on Labour and Environmental Cooperation, 133
North American Free Trade Agreement (NAFTA), 133
North American Parliamentarians Against Corruption, 95, 96
North East Asian Parliamentarians Against Corruption, 95
North Korea, 44
Norway, 22, 26, 113, 189, 192
Nystrom, Lorne, 142

Offshore Group of Banking Supervisors (OGBS), 107, 108
Ogoni people (Nigeria), 128
Oil for Food Program, 120, 121
Oman, 22, 191
Open Society Institute, 80
Organization for Security and Cooperaton in Europe (OSCE), 85, 86, 100
Organization of American States, 150 (OECD), 61, 63, 77, 79, 88, 89, 94, 97, 135, 157, 211
Organization of Economic Development and Co-operation Convention on Bribery, 79, 157
Oxfam, 8, 80, 168

Pakistan, 24, 67, 191
Palestine, 24, 44, 73
Palestine Liberation Organization, 44

Panama, 23, 189
Papua New Guinea, 25, 190
Paraguay, 25, 26, 30, 190
parliamentarians, role in fighting corruption, 81, 82, 84, 86, 87, 95, 96, 98, 100–2, 104, 105, 148, 149, 150, 151, 155, 158, 172, 179, 183, 226, 227. *See also* Global Organization of Parliamentarians Against Corruption.
Parliamentarians for Parliamentary Control, 95
Parliamentary Assembly of the Council of Europe, 19, 63, 117, 152, 154
Parliamentary Network of the World Bank (PNoWB), 71, 150–2
Peru, 23, 37, 171, 190
Philippines, 16, 24, 37, 40, 44, 70, 190
Phillip Services, 54
Pinochet, Augusto, 44, 92
piracy (copyright infringement), 61–3
Poland, 23, 26, 190
Porte Allegri, 122, 123
Portugal, 22, 189
poverty
    benefits of poverty reduction, 12
    cause of, 2, 6, 8, 9, 115
    disparity between rich and poor nations, 4, 5, 10, 11
    effects of corruption on poverty, 2, 3, 9, 16, 18, 28–31, 35, 111, 120, 182, 183
    impacts of, 11, 12, 67, 72, 73, 127–9
    impact of conflict on poverty, 8
    income disparity within nations, 9, 10
    international aid, 111–120, 123, 124, 162
    poverty reduction measures, 125, 126, 128, 131, 135–7, 139–42, 163,–72, 175–7, 179, 180
Powell, Colin, 13, 107, 108
Prahalad, C.K., author of *The Fortune at the Bottom of the Pyramid*, 167, 171, 211
Primorskiy Krai, 131

Proceeds of Crime (Money Laundering) and Terrorist Financing Act (Canada), 98
Publish What You Pay, 4, 41, 79, 80

Qatar, 22, 137

Raynauld, André, 134, 135
Red Cross, 114
refugees, 5, 12, 65, 67, 68
Revenue Watch Institute, 41, 80
Riggs Bank, 92, 93
Romania, 24, 190, 194
Roughneen, Simon, 17
Royal Canadian Mounted Police (RCMP), 88, 93
Russia, 5, 10, 18–20, 24, 28, 40, 41, 44, 47–50, 57, 68, 70, 75, 90, 95, 96, 126, 130, 131, 138, 143, 148, 174, 175, 191, 194, 196. *See also* Union of Soviet Socialist Republics (USSR).
Russian Forest Program, 131
Russian mafia, 10, 68, 69

Sachs, Jeffrey, 135, 136, 145
Salembier, J. Paul, 46, 180
Salinas, Raul, 40
São Tome, 116
Sarbanes-Oxley Act (2002), 54
Saro-Wiwa, Ken, 128
Saudi Arabia, 23, 143
Save the Children UK, 80
Scorpions, 83
Securities and Exchange Commission, 54
Seko, Mobutu Sese, 3, 37
Selassie, Halie, 69, 70
Senegal, 24, 190
Serbia and Montenegro, 25
Sevan, Benon, 121
Sierra Leone, 25, 28, 129, 191, 194, 195, 196, 197
Singapore, 11, 22, 26, 183, 190, 192

Sithole, Majozi, 88
Slovakia, 23, 189
Slovenia, 22, 189, 193
Smith, Ian, 9
Société Générale, 54
Sole, Mr. (Lesotho Highlands Water
    Authority), 76
Somalia, 78, 115, 119, 120, 160, 161,
    162
Soros, George, 80
Southeast Asian Parliamentarians
    Against Corruption, 95
South Africa, 23, 27, 56, 76, 82, 83,
    132, 143, 189, 193
South Korea, 23, 58, 78, 143, 189
Spain, 22, 189
Sri Lanka, 23, 67, 71, 72, 190
Standing Committee on Industry, 63
Standing Committee on Public Safety
    and National Security, 62
State Food and Drug Administration
    (China), 64
Sudan, 25, 120
Suharto (president, Indonesia), 37, 43
Swaziland, 88
Sweden, 22, 26, 78, 113, 114, 188, 192
Swiss banks, role in money launder-
    ing, 40, 43, 44
Switzerland, 4, 22, 27, 44, 88, 89, 114,
    141, 172, 188, 192
Syria, 23, 191

Taiwan, 22, 78, 189
Tajikistan, 25, 26, 30
Tamils, 67, 72
Tanzania, 24, 104, 105, 190
tariffs. See trade barriers
taxes, global, to fight poverty, 139, 140,
    141, 142
tax havens, 89, 90, 141, 158. See also
    money laundering.
terrorism, 11, 12, 60, 71–3, 79, 81, 87,
    88, 90, 98, 99, 101, 106, 183
Thailand, 24, 41, 51–3, 56, 58, 126,
    139, 190

Tobin, James, 140, 141
Tobin Tax, 139–42
Toronto Stock Exchange, 55, 172
trade agreements, 133, 134
trade barriers, 125, 137, 138, 180, 185
Transparency International, 1, 3, 21,
    22, 25, 27, 29, 30, 37, 38, 78, 80, 129,
    155, 183, 187
Trinidad and Tobago, 23, 190
Tunisia, 23, 26, 191
Turkey, 24, 143, 190, 194, 196, 197
Turkmenistan, 183

Uganda, 25, 26, 191
Ukraine, 25, 37, 70, 191, 194, 196
UK Banking Act, 141
UNICEF, 114, 117
Union of Soviet Socialist Republics
    (USSR), 10, 18, 20, 48, 49, 70, 90.
    See also Russia.
United Arab Emirates, 23, 191
United Kingdom, 21, 22, 27, 54, 66,
    141, 143, 188, 192
United Nations Commission on the
    Private Sector and Development, 154
United Nations Convention Against
    Corruption (UNCAC), 79, 85, 106,
    152, 154, 157
United Nations Development Program
    (UNDP), 129, 141, 166, 175, 178
United Nations Economic and Social
    Council (ECOSOC), 154, 165
United Nations High Commissiner for
    Refugees UNHCR, 65, 67
United Nations International Conven-
    tion for the Suppression of the
    Financing of Terrorism, 98
United Nations Office of Drugs and
    Crime (UNODC), 18, 150
United Nations Security Council, 99,
    154
United States of America (USA), 22,
    26, 27, 54, 66, 71–3, 79, 92, 113,
    114, 128, 133, 128, 141, 143, 162–4,
    189, 192

Uruguay, 22, 189, 192
US Aid, 10, 150
Uzbekistan, 24

Vassanji, M.G., author of The In-Be-
    tween World of Vikram Lall, 14
Venezuela, 24, 40, 191
Vietnam, 24
Volcker, Paul, 121, 147

Wei, Shang-Jin, 46
Williams, John, 96
Wolfensohn, James D., 46, 123, 145,
    184
Wolfowitz, Paul, 110, 184
women, initiatives for, 169
WorldCom, 54
World Bank, 1, 3, 21, 29, 30, 38, 46,
    71, 106, 110, 114, 115, 117–19, 123,
    124, 138, 145, 147, 150–2, 155, 169,
    180, 184

World Economic Forum, 33, 77
World Trade Organization (WTO),
    125, 137, 181
World Wildlife Fund (WWF), 130, 131

Yakovlev, Alexander, 121
YBM Magnex, 54
Yeltsin, Boris, 48
Yemen, 24
Yugoslavia, 37
Yunus, Muhammad, 168
Yushchenko, Viktor, 196

Zaire (Democratic Republic of the
    Congo), 16, 37
Zambia, 24, 42, 116, 191
Zedillo, Emesto, 178
Zheng, Mr., 64
Zimbabwe, 9, 25, 26, 82, 93, 160, 175,
    191
Zuma, Jacob, 83

Credits

Writing a book is challenging and daunting task—not made any easier when one is a sitting Member of Parliament. Without the support and encouragement of a number of people, this project would not have been possible.

I am indebted to Patrick Boyer, founder and president of Blue Butterfly Books, for having faith and confidence that my book was important and would make a difference. Dominic Farrell painstakingly reviewed the manuscript and made a number of important suggestions which I have incorporated in the book. I thank him for that.

I would like to thank my wife, Ethne, for her encouragement and support throughout the development of this book, and for her thoughtful advice and time-consuming review of the manuscript. Candice Debi assisted with some very useful research and analysis, and I am indebted to her for this. Len Pizzi was very helpful with data entry and information processing. Tony Hahn was very cooperative by allowing me to access his work—The Index of Public Governance—which helped me examine factors other than corruption and their impact on governance. Meaghan Campbell has been very helpful to me in my continuing work on the fight against money laundering. David Cuddemi, Ryan Murphy, and Fran Watt have provided me with needed assistance in the form of advice and logistics—both essential requirements for bringing this project to fruition.

Many thanks to Gary Long for his work on the book design, and to Bill Belfontaine and Bill Hushion of White Knight Book Distribution Services Ltd. for the marketing and distribution of *The Poverty of Corrupt Nations.*

My Conservative colleague in the House of Commons, John Williams, was a founding member of the Global Organization of Parliamentarians Against Corruption (GOPAC) and he has been its guiding force ever since. I thank him for the inspiration that led me to conclude that even though the fight against corruption is a formidable challenge, it is well worth the effort. We are beginning to see some positive results, but much more needs to be done. I would like to thank Martin Ulrich for his very capable support of the work of GOPAC.

Finally, I thank the constituents of Etobicoke North in Toronto for the confidence they have placed in me over the years, and for the opportunity to engage in the fight against corruption and money laundering—an important initiative I believe, and one that I am deeply committed to.

Born in 1944 in Montreal, Roy Cullen earned his B.A. in Business Administration and a Master of Public Administration. He qualified as a Canadian Chartered Accountant in 1972. During his career, Mr. Cullen served as an assistant deputy minister in the British Columbia Ministry of Forests and as a vice-president in the Noranda Forest Group (now Norbord). Initially elected to the House of Commons in Ottawa in a by-election in 1996, he was re-elected in the 1997, 2000, 2004, and 2006 general elections, and remains a member of Parliament today.

As a member of the Chrétien and Martin governments, Mr. Cullen served as chair of the House of Commons Standing Committee on Finance, as parliamentary secretary to the minister of finance and to the deputy prime minister and the minister for public safety and emergency preparedness, and as chair of the Ontario Liberal caucus. He has also served as Official Opposition critic for natural resources. He was sworn in as a member of the Privy Council of Canada in 2004.

During his tenure as parliamentary secretary to the minister of finance, Mr. Cullen was actively involved in designing and implementing Canada's anti-money-laundering regime. Since being elected Mr. Cullen has been very active with the Global Organization of Parliamentarians Against Corruption (GOPAC) in the international fight against corruption and money laundering. He has spoken out on these scourges and has played a leadership role at several anti-corruption and anti-money-laundering workshops and conferences.

Mr. Cullen lives with in Toronto his wife, Ethne. They have one son, Peter.

PHOTO: *Roy Cullen speaks at a Commonwealth Parliamentary Association Workshop, "Ensuring Accountability," in Nairobi, Kenya, December 2001.*

Interview with the Author

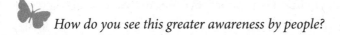 *Your book seems to express an optimistic realism. Is this a correct take on how you see things?*

ROY CULLEN: In addition to being an optimist by nature, I have seen first hand how world leaders who are committed to contain corruption can curtail it in their home countries. I am also encouraged by the fact that citizens of the world are becoming more aware of the incidence and cost of corruption, and the need to do something about it.

I don't think we want the kind of unhinged optimism that lets people be naïve about the enormous challenges involved in eliminating or significantly reducing the incidence of global corruption. The pessimist's alternative, however, of just turning a blind eye to the problem or shrugging it off, is not a course of action I can accept. We have moral responsibilities.

How do you see this greater awareness by people?

CULLEN: I think the Convention Against Corruption, which was adopted by the United Nations General Assembly in 2003, is a good example of the world coming together to tackle this huge problem. That is realism, but you don't act that way unless you have hope that something can be done.

Resolutions are important, and show awareness, but action by corrupt countries will be the real test.

 What are the chances of that?

CULLEN: Through my work with the Global Organization of Parliamentarians Against Corruption, or "GOPAC" for short, I have seen how courageous parliamentarians have taken on the challenge of fighting corruption. Sometimes, in fact quite often, they are doing this at great personal risk to themselves. I am now more aware of the crucial role that legislators can play in holding their governments to account for their corrupt activities through effective oversight.

A free and independent media, an honest judiciary, institutions like the office of auditor-general and a public accounts committee or their equivalents, are all tools that parliamentarians can use to fight corruption and money laundering in their own jurisdictions, and achieve results.

You are very passionate about the scourge of poverty and the problem of corruption. How did you get involved with this issue?

CULLEN: Back in 2000 the chair of GOPAC, John Williams, who is a colleague of mine in the House of Commons in Ottawa, invited me to join the fight against global corruption. I guess he recognized that because I have worked and lived abroad, and also participated in meetings with parliamentarians from many other countries, I had been exposed to the huge economic and social costs of corruption. So I readily accepted his invitation and I have been closely involved with GOPAC ever since.

In 2002, for instance, I participated in theGlobal Conference of Parliamentarians Against Corruption in Ottawa which brought together over 150 parliamentarians to officially launch GOPAC as an institution. GOPAC has now grown to over 700 parliamentarians in all regions of the world.

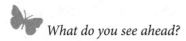 *What do you see ahead?*

CULLEN: Fighting and eliminating corruption will involve a massive concerted effort involving organizations, institutions, governments and parliaments around the world. These efforts, however, will be orchestrated by individuals, like myself and many others, whose work and dedication will have an impact and result in collective action.

GOPAC is now an excellent vehicle to engage parliamentarians in this fight, frankly, and individual parliamentarians are making a difference. I am hoping that *The Poverty of Corrupt Nations* will cause citizens of the world and policy makers to take up the challenge to accelerate the fight against corruption and money laundering.

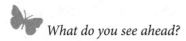 *What do you see as the challenges in overcoming corruption, considering the role of more developed and democratic countries?*

CULLEN: In a perfect world corrupt regimes would not receive the support of democratically elected and ethical governments. One should recognize, however, that no country in the world is completely free of corruption. It is a matter of degree, and equally misleading to equate the level of corruption in a country like Bangladesh with that in, say, the United Kingdom. We can compare the incidence of corruption in different jurisdictions in relative terms only.

In addition, sometimes national security interests trump our distaste for corruption. This was true during the Cold War when the West was prepared to look the other way if a regime was opposed to communism, for example, and it is still a factor more recently in the new world context. Afghanistan is a good example. Corruption is rife in that country but the United Nations and NATO countries have been strongly committed to supporting the Afghan government of President Hamid Karzai because of a view that stability in that country is an important piece in the fight against international terrorism.

 What motivated you to write this book?

CULLEN: *The Poverty of Corrupt Nations* draws on my international experience in both the private and public sectors. It is the work of a general practitioner, not an academic expert in the field of corruption and money laundering.

Not every proposition, theory or hypotheses presented in this book is accompanied by tomes of research data. Some are, but other ideas are drawn from my own personal experience and my devotion to this topic over many years.

In that context, I wrote this book in the hope readers will consider my comments and proposals and draw their own conclusions. I am confident that ideas and suggestions in this book, some of my own and others that I report, can help us collectively to move the yardsticks, to advance the fight against corruption.

ORDERING INFORMATION
for Blue Butterfly Books

TRADE DISTRIBUTION (CANADA)

White Knight Book Distribution
Warehouse/fulfilment by Georgetown Terminal Warehouse
34 Armstrong Avenue, Georgetown, Ontario L7G 4R9
Tel 1-800-485-5556   Fax 1-800-485-6665

TRADE DISTRIBUTION (U.S.A.)

Hushion House Publishing Inc.
Warehouse/fulfilment by APG Books
7344 Cockrill Bond Boulevard, Nashville, Tennessee 37209
Tel 1-800-275-2606   Fax 1-800-510-3650

ON-LINE PURCHASE (WORLD WIDE)

www.bluebutterflybooks.ca

About this book

Many of the world's most impoverished nations are also among the world's most corrupt. Zaire's Mobutu Sese Seko, the Philippines' Ferdinand Marcos, and Indonesia's Suharto all skimmed billions from their countries' treasuries while their people starved. In Africa today, some $150 billion is lost every year to corruption; in China, corruption diminishes the annual gross domestic product by 15 per cent. The pattern repeats itself around the world.

This bleak situation compounds the poverty problem because wealthier nations are understandably reluctant to provide assistance to countries where leaders steal and launder public funds for their own use. Private investment in developing economies is similarly stunted when corruption and poor governance increase the cost and risk of doing business. Corrupt officials are responsible for natural resource development that is not environmentally sustainable, and for compromised product standards that endanger health and safety. Great disparities in income and the hopelessness felt by the impoverished—all consequences of corruption—lead to crime, social unrest, and international terrorism that affect every nation.

The Poverty of Corrupt Nations is a straightforward, easy-to-read exposition of the nature and scope of global corruption. Roy Cullen examines the links between world poverty, corruption, terrorism, global migration patterns, and money laundering. He then outlines a practical 20-point program to increase transparency and accountability in governments around the world and remove the shackles that constrain the economic opportunities of developing nations and their poorest citizens. By breaking the cycle of corruption and poverty that brings misery to millions, these measures can help build a safer, freer, and more prosperous world for all people.